GARDE TA FOY

THE RICHE HERITAGE OF FELSTED SCHOOL 1564–2014

GARDE TA FOY

THE RICHE HERITAGE OF FELSTED SCHOOL 1564–2014

Alastair Grierson Rickford

THIRD MILLENNIUM
PUBLISHING, LONDON

GARDE TA FOY: THE RICHE HERITAGE OF FELSTED SCHOOL, 1564–2014

© Felsted School, A.N. Grierson Rickford and
Third Millennium Publishing Limited 2013

First published in 2013 by Third Millennium Publishing Limited,
a subsidiary of Third Millennium Information Limited.

2–5 Benjamin Street
London
United Kingdom
EC1M 5QL
www.tmiltd.com

ISBN: 978 1 906507 86 2

British Library Cataloguing in Publication Data
A CIP catalogue record for this book is available from the British Library.

Project Manager	Susan Millership
Photo Researcher	Robert Leadbetter
Design	Susan Pugsley
Production	Bonnie Murray
Reprographics	Studio Fasoli, Verona, Italy
Printing	Gorenjski Tisk, Slovenia

PICTURE ACKNOWLEDGEMENTS

The majority of the images in this book come from the School Archive. The School
and TMI Publishers would like to thank all those who have contributed modern
images, particularly Charles Best, Dr Charles Lee and Joe Pearce along with the
following individuals and agencies who have granted permission for copyright
material to be reproduced:

Bridgeman Art Library: pp26–7 (Sudeley Castle, Winchcombe, Gloucestershire,
UK), p29 (Lambeth Palace, London, UK), 30 (top left), 35 (Corcoran Gallery
of Art, Washington D.C., USA), 40 (with kind permission of the University of
Edinburgh), 49 (Marylebone Cricket Club); Revd David Chesney/Church of the
Ascension, Victoria Dock: p97 (top); Essex Records Office: pp12, 14, 18, 21 (bottom
left and right), 38; Sir Robert Finch: p176 (bottom); Fraser's Autographs: p24;
Jonathan Godwin: p173 (bottom); Peter L. Herring: p28, 46; Simon Knott: p15, 31,
46 (right), 51 (top); Robert Leadbetter: pp7, 19, 72, 78 (top right), 79, 98, 110, 117,
120 (bottom), 123, 126, 131(right); Dr Charles Lee: pp4, 76 (bottom right), 104, 111
(top right), 120 (left), 127, 133 (bottom), 134–5, 136, 138 (top), 139, 140 (right),
151 (top), 153, 154, 157 (right top and bottom), 160–1, 164 (right), 165 (right),
166 (bottom), 168 (left and top), 170 (bottom), 171 (bottom), 176 (top); little_
miss_sunnydale: p25; Lydiard House and Park: p51; Mary Evans Picture Library: p23;
Maureen Long: p17; National Archives, Kew: p26; National Portrait Gallery: pp36
(bottom), 43, 45 (bottom right), 51 (bottom), 55, 94; Sergio Álvarez de Neira: p89
(top); David Plested: cover painting, pp80–1, 84; Prof. Lucilla Poston: p175; Sheila
Robinson/The Fry Art Gallery: pp 32–3; The Master and Fellows of Trinity College,
Cambridge: p39; The Virginia Historical Society: p41; Whipper_Snapper: p20.
While every effort has been made to contact copyright holders, if you have been
inadvertently overlooked please contact TMI Publishers.

CONTENTS

Headmaster's Foreword

It is a privilege to introduce this major new History of Felsted, beautifully written by Alastair Grierson Rickford to celebrate the 450th Anniversary of its foundation in 1564. The year 2014 marks a milestone in our school's great history, as we confirm our place in a very select club of the most historic independent schools. Alastair has a profound knowledge and experience of Felsted, as a Housemaster, a Head of Department, and a long-serving and deeply committed member of the Common Room. His is a labour of love, accessible, intelligent, informative, and a balanced tribute to a unique community.

Lord Riche's vision is encapsulated in his Collate, read every year by the Headmaster at the Founder's and Benefactors' Service; '… as also by hys example to styrr up many others to the like liberalitie to the mayntenaunce of good lernyng, releving of the poore and setting forthe of thy glory…' It remains true today, and is the heart of a school which is itself a jewel at the centre of so many people's lives.

The extended Felsted community is everyone at the school, everyone who has gone through the school in previous years, and everyone who is yet to come, as well as everyone living and working here, or associated with this lovely place. Felstedians are very special people: passionate, engaged, determined to make a difference in whatever communities they also belong to later in life, whether local, regional or the global community itself. They are a dynamic living testament to the Founder's wishes.

I hope that, in reading and enjoying this volume, you also celebrate the school and all it stands for, as well as the first 450 years … Garde Ta Foy!

Dr M.J. Walker
Felsted
July 2013

Author's Preface

In taking up this project, entrusted to me by the present Headmaster, Dr Mike Walker, and the Chairman of the Governors, John Davies, I was initially somewhat flattered by their implied confidence in my literary and historiographical competence. As the research period drew on my trepidation grew; could I possibly ever reach a happy conclusion to the complex task of narrating the full 450 years of the School's varied and kaleidoscopic existence? Whether their confidence or my trepidation be proven the more percipient others must judge.

The aim of this volume is to trace the broad sweep of Felsted's progress down the ages, and in piecing together a good part of the story I am indebted to the School's two previous chroniclers, John Sargeaunt (Master in the 1880s) and M.R. Craze (Master 1936–69). To Michael Craze's detailed and wide-ranging publication of 1955 I must pay especial tribute. I am grateful, too, to the many Old Felstedians who have taken the trouble to offer me their personal reminiscences and comments; I hope they will forgive the absence of formal acknowledgement of their helpful communications, many of which have been sewn into the weft of this book. My thanks are also due to the three living past Headmasters, Tony Eggleston, Edward Gould and Stephen Roberts, and to a goodly number of Common Room colleagues past and present: their contributions have been of invaluable assistance as I have woven together what I hope will prove to be a comprehensive and accurate portrait of the more recent decades of Felsted's history.

In offering thanks to those whose help and support has been instrumental in aiding my endeavours, I should include in particular the School Archivist, Christopher Dawkins (Master 1976–2007) and Mrs Jules Wallis. Their extensive labours have ensured that avenues of archival searches have been opened up and suitable illustrations located and digitised ready for the attentions of the editorial team. At Third Millennium, I have relied particularly upon the expertise and patience of Susan Millership, Robert Leadbetter and Susan Pugsley, without whom the project could not have been realised. I very much hope that the resulting volume will be favourably received by Felstedians and friends of the School alike.

Alastair Grierson Rickford
July 2013

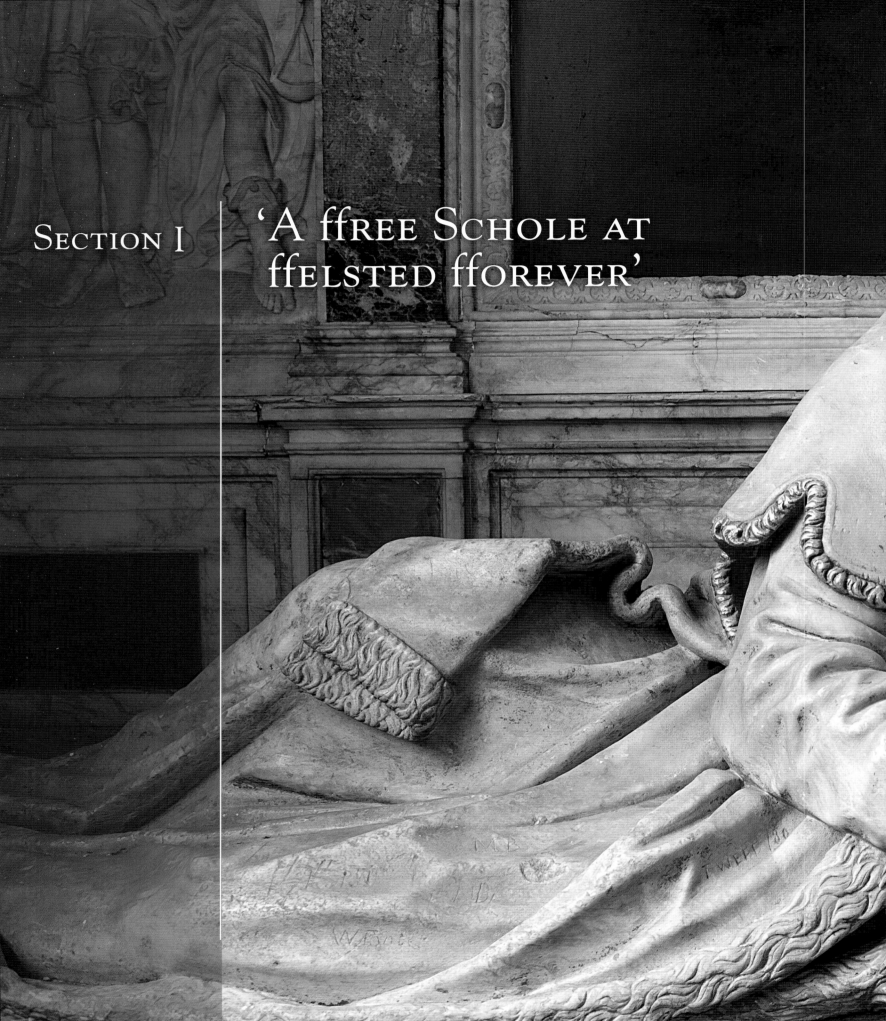

SECTION I | 'A ffree Schole at ffelsted fforever'

At the Going Down of the Sun: Felsted 1567

The long march draws towards its end.
In the distance, a low cluster of plastered dwellings begins to materialise before the outriders' view, funnelling the way towards the village centre. A larger timbered structure, with prominent window openings at first-floor level, stands squarely across the roadway, blocking further progress to the north; in solitary eminence the church's Saxon tower protrudes above the thatched and red-tiled rooftops, the main south entrance just discernible in shadow, beyond an open arch of shop fronts. Journey's end in more ways than one.

As the straggling, sable-suited cortege draws closer to the Trinity Guildhall and Holy Cross Church, a few curious villagers begin to gather at the roadside, drawn forth by the promise of some unprecedented excitement in the life of their community. Despite a history dating back to Domesday times and beyond, nothing to match this momentous occasion has ever been witnessed in these isolated and inward-looking rural purlieus: the funeral rites of a national colossus, no less, orchestrated by the College of Arms and marshalled in person by three of its leading officials, the Heralds Windsor, Lancaster and Somerset. Close by the great west door at the tower's foot, discreetly restrained by the black-gowned figure of their Master, a small group of local lads, no more than a dozen strong perhaps, awaits the great spectacle with scarcely contained glee. After all, they could hardly have hoped that a Tuesday in early July, the 8th to be precise, would be furnishing them with a whole holiday away from their books. The earthly remains of Richard, Baron Riche of Leez, are nearing their preordained final resting place in the chancel of the church of his most favoured of all Essex villages, Felsted.

The lengthy and difficult funerary procession had begun some days previously, at Lord Riche's residence at Rochford Hall, where a month before, on 11 June 1567, Riche had died aged 71. After three weeks lying in state at Rochford, the body had been made ready for the stately march to Leez Priory, Lord Riche's greatest house, in the northern part of the county. According to long-standing custom, the corpse was washed, dressed in state robes and sealed into a lead-lined casket. The coffin had been loaded onto a great funeral carriage, festooned in black silk draperies and adorned with beautifully worked tapestry replicas of the deceased nobleman's coat of arms. His armour, sword of state and armorial bearings had all been polished to perfection and entrusted to the care of the College Heralds, to be carried at the forefront of the procession. Costumes of black velvet and silks had been distributed to the entire company of mourners, numbering some 500 persons of varying rank and degree. Several hundred horses had been requisitioned for use by the knights and yeomen-at-arms who would attend the cortege along its slow march across the Essex countryside. In truth, all casual observers would have recognised in this sumptuous and expensive send-off the funeral obsequies for a personage of the highest national esteem: the late Lord Chancellor of England no less.

Rochford Hall (above) and detail from Lord Riche's tomb in Holy Cross Church, Felsted (opposite page).

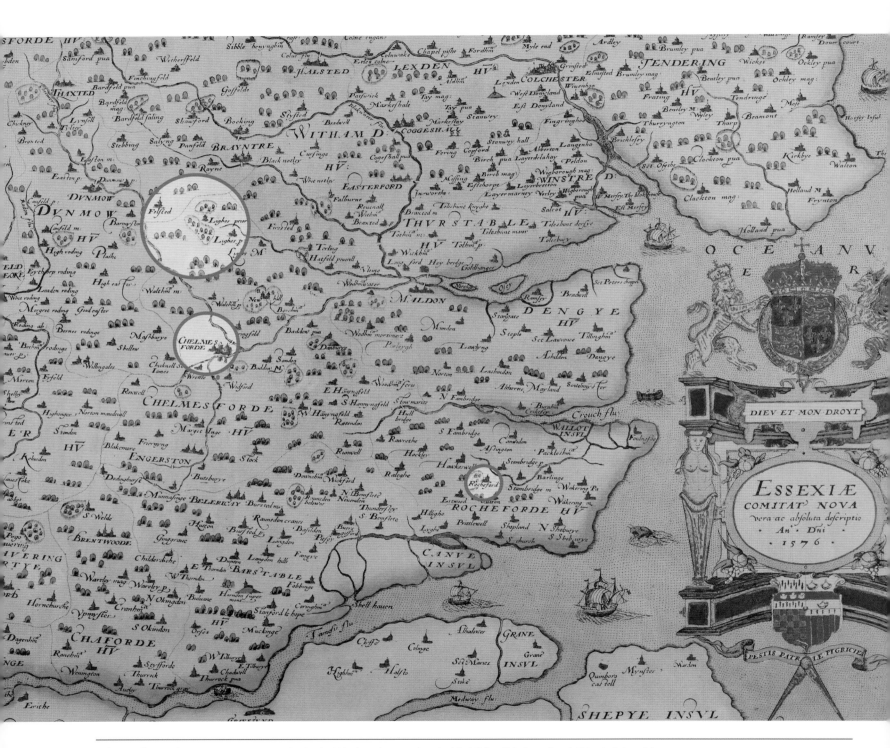

Early map of Essex, showing approximate route taken by the Riche funeral cortege from Rochford Hall to Holy Cross Church, Felsted, via Leez Priory.

The road system in Tudor times being anything but well-defined and certainly for the most part uncharted, the precise route to be taken might well have proved problematical. Felsted and Leez Priory, situated then as now within a triangle of ancient tracks dating back to Roman times, and used by succeeding generations for passage between the main centres of civic commerce, were nevertheless a mile or more off the beaten track at the end of the trek. Rochford, on the other hand, was well connected to London and the seat of government by river and road, but was cut off from the rest of Essex by the considerable natural barriers presented by the rivers Crouch and Blackwater. The going would not be easy for the heavy black-draped hearse, the 500-strong mounted company and the many dozens of outriders, foot-slogging retainers and attendants detailed by the King of Arms to accompany the coffin to its burial place, laden down with hatchments, banners and standards, escutcheons of arms and all the panoply of a great lord's funeral cortege.

Rochford to Chelmsford necessitated threading a path along a tedious zigzagging course through the low-lying near-swampland of south Essex. The twisting streets of the county town, Chelmsford, would be difficult to negotiate, especially since it happened to be the time of the great Assizes, always an opportunity for the outlying farming folks to head for the hustle and bustle of the markets, perhaps harbouring a frisson of hope that there might be a hanging or two to liven the holiday, should the judges be so minded! The arrival of the Riche cavalcade would no doubt add scope for country-dwelling folk to gawp in awe at the pomp and ceremony unfolding before them. After Chelmsford the route might be expected to prove more straightforward, although the villages of Broomfield and Great Waltham, linked only by threadlike walkways and long greens, are hardly passable by agricultural horse and cart, let alone by lordly hearse and its attendant hordes. Thence to Leez Priory, and an overnight pause: there accommodation and food must be provided for several hundred travel-weary members of his late lordship's entourage. The funeral baked meats must be prepared, and the pomp and pageantry of the morrow's ceremonies rehearsed to perfection.

And so it has come to pass: all is ready for the magnificent state funeral, to be enacted in a small country church in the Essex back-of-beyond.

Dare one conjecture that the ancient stones of the desecrated priory might evince on this occasion some quiet rejoicing at the knowledge that death had laid low their nemesis, the late Lord Chancellor of England and former Chancellor of the Court of Augmentations? For he it was who sent the monks packing, back in 1536, pillaged their coffers for the King's Treasury, then built a mighty private mansion for himself amid the ruin he had wrought. One thing is certain: the enduring legacy, bequeathed by Richard, Lord Riche, to the little village of Felsted a couple of miles distant where his tomb still stands, has done a great deal to restore the good name of that truly influential Tudor grandee.

Journey's end: the Old Schoolroom of Felsted School, seen from the porch of Holy Cross Church.

2 | LORD RICHE'S FOUNDATIONS AT FELSTED 1555–64

Throughout a long and often necessarily contorted political career, spanning as it did four different reigns, Richard, Lord Riche, sustained a personal religious conviction of the most conservative nature. To conclude that he was always a good practising Roman Catholic might be to go too far; it would certainly have brought him to the Tower and the block had this been demonstrably the case. Nevertheless, what does emerge is a readiness on Riche's part to sail as close as he safely could to the prevailing winds of religious orthodoxy, tacking and veering whenever political expediency, not to mention personal security, required it.

It is not unreasonable to surmise that what weighed most heavily upon Riche's conscience, as the years passed and the prospect of his approaching demise loomed ever larger, was his executive role in the abolition of so many centuries-old Roman

Catholic religious foundations, often ones with parent houses on the Continent, still substantially a bastion of the Roman faith. Particularly close to home, apart from the Priory of Leez, which he had annexed as his home, was the matter of the Trinity Guild of Felsted, which had been abolished in 1547, along with all the other guilds and chantries in the land. With staunchly Catholic Mary now on the throne, the way was open for Riche to make due provision for such a foundation, in a location best suited to his penitential purposes.

THE CHANTRY DEED OF 1555

On 10 April 1555, with that consummate political craftsmanship honed to perfection over many years of courtly service, Riche had letters patent drawn up under the Great Seal of England and issued at Hampton Court, establishing at Felsted in the County of Essex, a 'corporation' for the

Lord Riche's residence at Leez Priory (above) and Leez Priory gatehouse today (opposite page).

A CHANTRY FOR THE RICHES AND A HERRING DOLE FOR THE POOR

On 26 April 1555, Lord Riche signed the official foundation charter, which detailed in closely defined legalistic detail his wishes concerning the new charity. The significant nub of the small print lies in Riche's requirement that the Chaplain should say Mass three times every week of the year, taking special care to pray fervently for the soul of Henry VIII, and for 'our most virtuous Quene Mary ... her heyres while they shalbe lyving and for theyr sowles after they shalbe departed oute of thys worlde ... and for me, Richard, lord Riche, my wyff and mine heyres whyl we be lyving and for owre sowles when we shal depart thys world'. Essentially, individual chantries were set up to fund the professional services of priests, who would conduct intercessions for the souls of their departed sponsors. Riche's cleverly camouflaged foundation, under guise of making provision for the alleviation of poverty in the parishes of Felsted and the Walthams, is a revivalist chantry in all but name. But we must think no less of him for this, since it would seem to reveal in Riche a sincerity of faith, despite the twists and turns of his public facades. Perhaps, too, the pivotal part he had played in Henry's constitutional 'fight to the death' with Sir Thomas More, some 20 years before, and the rapid rise to power and eminence he had enjoyed as a direct result of the services rendered on that occasion, were a heavy burden in his last years. The eleven barrels each of white and red herrings to be doled out to the paupers of the locality during Lent were an annual manifestation of Riche's penitential state of mind as he contemplated his approaching death.

The Felsted Chantry Deed of 1555.

sustentation of the poor folks of the parish. The governance of the Foundation would be vested in a Chaplain, to be appointed by the Founder, and his heirs after him, and in the two Churchwardens of Holy Cross Church, Felsted. Riche tied up the legalities with characteristic exactitude: the endowment in land worth £50 per annum would be specifically and in perpetuity exempt from the various petty taxes (levied at that time with equal avarice by both Church and State) likely to vitiate its financial viability over time.

The dissolution of the monasteries after 1536 and the abolition of all chantries and choir schools by the Edwardian Act of 1547 led to a disastrous reduction in the provision of academic education in Tudor England. Whereas before these measures considerable numbers of young boys of 'towardly partes' had been able to gain first-rate training in literacy, Latin language and grammar, and the skills of debating and disputation in schools linked to the great cathedrals and religious houses of the land, no more than a handful of such establishments had managed to escape the vandalism of the sectarian cull. Colleges whose foundations were independent of 'parent' religious institutions or whose statutes designated them as royal foundations tended to avoid the predatory gaze of the commissioners; thus Winchester (1384) and Eton (1440), among a very few, felt less directly the disturbing winds of change, where the ancient cathedral schools at Westminster, Canterbury and York were caught up in the turbulence of the times, their future survival by no means assured.

It is greatly to his credit that Edward VI saw the damage caused by sweeping away the teachers along with the foundations that funded them in their vocation, and determined to do something positive to redress this potential national catastrophe. A goodly number of the ancient grammar schools associated with the great city churches and cathedrals were re-founded as King's Schools, many surviving to this day as independent or maintained schools of good standing. Thus was initiated a positive torrent of educational fervour, which endured well into the next century. Many of these Tudor and Elizabethan foundations, established in this rush of optimism and philanthropy, would wither and ultimately disappear over the course of the next four centuries. Village foundations, not unexpectedly, were to prove the least durable, as we shall see.

In 1550, during the first flush of enthusiasm for the educational renaissance, Lord Riche had himself been officially involved in the re-founding of the choir and chantry school at Bury St Edmunds; as Lord Chancellor, he assented to the deed which gave new birth to the defunct abbey seminary as the King Edward VI School. More than a dozen years were to pass before this occasion would resurface in Riche's mind, turning his attention towards a venture of this nature in his own name. In the meantime, he focused on weightier state affairs, and to the contemplation of his own conscience. Edward's untimely demise, aged just 16 years, brought his eldest sister, Mary, to the throne; with her accession came a reactionary lurch in religious policy. The English Reformation was to be 'reformed', and who best to orchestrate this process? Lord Chancellor Riche, of course.

Riche's Felsted chantry had no sooner initiated the philanthropic operation of its Founder's decrees when the violent political and religious pendulum began to swing: Mary's death in November 1558 brought Elizabeth to the throne. Riche may well have had in mind the part he had played more than 20 years before: the promulgation into parliamentary Act of Henry's wish, when he contracted his third marriage to Jane Seymour in 1537, that the daughter of Anne Boleyn

be repudiated as 'illegitimate' issue and specifically debarred from the succession. For elder statesman Riche, now aged over 60, it was time for another *volte face* revision of his political and personal strategy. He had navigated the dangerous and unpredictable waters of three reigns, but the tipping scales of fortune might need some highly sensitive counterbalancing if he was to thrive under a fourth monarch.

THE FREE SCHOOL AND ALMSHOUSES

The new administration set about reasserting the Protestant ethos; the chantries were again to be dissolved. Riche found himself faced with a challenging legal conundrum: how to preserve his Foundation, along with its beneficial effects on his reputation. With characteristic percipience, Riche saw the solution: he could sustain his original purposes in a translation of his redundant chantry into a fully fledged almshouse foundation, at the same time instituting a free grammar school, such as were springing into existence in extraordinary profusion the length and breadth of England. Indeed, in Essex alone several dozen new foundations had begun life in the Edwardian and Elizabethan educational frenzy, most of them endowed by local citizens or corporations of the larger towns. Often the founders were members of

Tudor shop windows in the Old Schoolroom archway with graffiti probably added by Felsted shoolboys over the centuries.

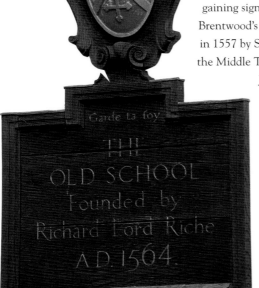

the Liveried Companies of London, who had made fortunes in their professional lives and were minded, like Riche, to leave a tangible legacy in their wake. Riche would have been aware that schools at Chelmsford, Saffron Walden and Colchester were gaining significant reputations in his county, and Brentwood's opulent establishment had been set up in 1557 by Sir Anthony Browne, a fellow lawyer of the Middle Temple and successor to Riche as Chief Justice of Common Pleas. Lord Riche had the perfect site for his schoolroom, and accommodation for a master and usher could easily be found. Riche signed his Foundation Deed on 21 May 1564 at Leez, and so was born the free grammar school of Richard, Lord Riche, at Felsted in the County of Essex.

On 22 May 1564, which was Whit Sunday, Riche signed a further codicil to the Foundation Deed, requiring the farmer at the Felsted Bury to pay annually the sum of £20 towards the salaries of the chaplain/master and usher. All the

Old School plaque (above); the Old School today (right) and the interior of the Old School, c.1910 (inset).

necessary legalities had been punctiliously laid down, but like all new ventures, the planning is the easiest part of the undertaking, and Riche was destined to survive his founding of the School by barely three years. On 8 July 1567, the first dozen Felsted free grammar school boys would witness their illustrious benefactor's funeral obsequies.

Atonement even at the last gasp of life remains a prime tenet of Christian doctrine. It would appear that in his failing health, towards the end, Richard Riche had been determined to ensure that his good works should carry his name and legacy forward in a more positive light.

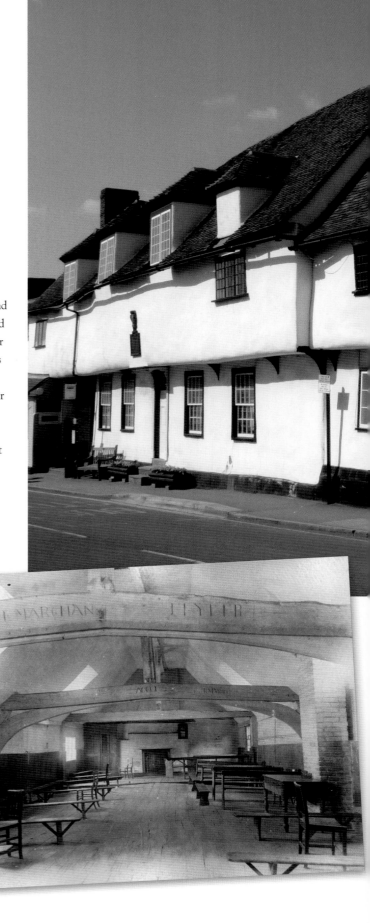

A FREE GRAMMAR SCHOOL AT FELSTED FOR EVER

The Foundation Deed explains in diplomatic terms the reasons why the original chantry 'corporation' was to be changed. In effect, the new Foundation would transfer the role of 'sustentation of the poor' to the newly established almshouse institution, and the newly constituted chaplain would have dual oversight of the new school and almshouse alike. The deed puts it thus: 'I the said Lord Riche do ordeyne and constitute that the Chapleyne of the saide ffoundacion and hys successours shalbe an able person and sufficient in lernyng and qualities to teache and instruct such male childerne borne or hereafter shalbe borne in Essex to the nombre of foure score in the lernyng of Grammer and other Vertues and godly lernyng according to Christes religion.' The Chantry Foundation Deed of 1555 had been amended, not supplanted, and the Lenten herring doles were to continue, at least until such time as the almshouse construction should be completed.

The vacant Trinity Guildhall would serve as a commodious schoolroom; there was living space available 'in a chamber at thende of the said schole' for the usher's lodging; while the chantry chaplain's house, Ingram's Close, would now house the new schoolmaster. In addition to the educational provisions of the deed, Lord Riche decreed that the foundation date of Whit Sunday should be commemorated annually by a sermon preached by the vicar in Holy Cross Church, to be attended by the master, the usher and all the scholars of the Foundation. Further, Riche laid down his wish that a 'collate' (collect) be said in thanksgiving for the Founder's generosity:

Allmyghtie and most mercifull ffather among thy manifolde and greate benefitts whiche thou haste bestowed uppon us we yelde the humble thankes for thys also that yt hathe pleased the to styrr upp the goode mynd and liberalitie of our founder Richard lorde Riche whereby the youthe here is relieved and broughte upp in the knowledge of goode lernyng and of thy holy worde and sundry poore folks mercifully comforted to the glory of thy holy name.

The Riche seal and a section of the Felsted Charities Deed of 1564.

3 | Richard Riche, Politician for All Seasons

Shakespeare speaks of a man's reputation as the 'bubble' to be sought 'e'en in the cannon's mouth'; to be sure, Richard Riche may be said to have faced most courageously the slings and arrows of that outrageous fortune that was the lot of all high-flying servants of the Tudor court. To conclude that Riche was a clever but unprincipled survivor is to judge him cruelly by the public morality of more recent times; in the cut and thrust of Tudor courtly affairs, self-preservation and self-interest were positive virtues: when all about him were losing their Sovereign's favour, and often their heads too, Riche steered a path of relative safety through uncharted courtly seas of unimaginably tempestuous vicissitude. To serve four autocratic and erratic monarchs

of widely divergent temperaments and political will, all the while maintaining his personal security and accruing matchless prosperity, speaks of a consummate intelligence and political dexterity seldom seen in any age, let alone one where your friends could become your mortal foes in a matter of hours, if and when the winds of royal favour veered against you.

Of Riche's early life and education little is known; his birth was variously cited as having been in London or at Basingstoke, Hampshire, from whence had originally emerged the Riches prominent in the Mercers' Company in the City. The first hard evidence we have is of a young man embarking

Lord and Lady Riche by Hans Holbein the Younger.

upon a career in the law, as he entered the Middle Temple
in February 1516. At this time the law could provide a rapid
rise to prosperity and wealth, especially for the truly gifted
mind. It was a sphere of activity open to all ranks of men,
and even the most humble of origins would prove no bar to
the highest achievement, as was borne out by the careers
of his near contemporaries, Thomas Wolsey and Thomas
Cromwell, both of whom rose from humble beginnings to
positions where they were empowered to wield the greatest
influence under their King. Unlike Riche, however, neither
was destined to avoid Henry's fatal 'non placet' frown; both
died disgraced, overwhelmed by the complex twists and turns
of royal favour and courtly factions. Riche made the most of
early opportunities to shine, establishing his credentials as an
able debater and innovative analyst of legal conundrums. He
soon came to the notice of those with influence in the highest
ranks of the legal world, through his precocious ambition,
allied to insouciant self-belief.

At the beginning of his career, Riche concentrated his
attentions on academic and practical legal work, rising rapidly
through the ranks at the Inns of Court. He was named Reader
of New Inn after only six years of service; then, in 1526,
he made his first major bid for advancement in public life:
he put his name forward as a candidate for the position of
Common Serjeant of the City of London, an important post

in the executive judiciary and a stepping stone towards his
recognition as a lawyer of stellar ability. The importance of
this potential promotion may be seen in the fact that Riche's
application failed; the King's preference had fallen upon his
rival, William Walsingham. Despite this setback, Riche's
name had come to the attention of two powerful future allies,
John de Vere, Earl of Oxford, and Sir Thomas Audley (later
Lord Chancellor), whose friendship and patronage he sought
assiduously throughout the late 1520s.

Thereafter, Riche's fortunes rose with dizzying speed.
In 1528, he was nominated to the House of Commons as
Member for Colchester, having already secured a number
of legal appointments in Essex, including that of Recorder
of Colchester, through the strong local support of his two
sponsors, both of whom held extensive estates and influence
in Essex and in the East Anglian hinterlands beyond.
Doubtless, Riche's attachment to the county dates from this
period; less than a dozen years later, he had begun to amass a
substantial portfolio of property in Essex. By the time of his
demise, three decades later, Riche had gained title to nearly a
quarter of the privately owned lands in the county.

Richard Riche's major break came with his appointment as
Attorney General for Wales in May of 1532. Barely 18 months
later he had risen to the position of Solicitor General, whence
he could bring his influence to bear on matters of national

Cardinal Wolsey, Lord
Chancellor at Westminster;
an early role model for a
young, aspirant lawyer,
Richard Riche.

23

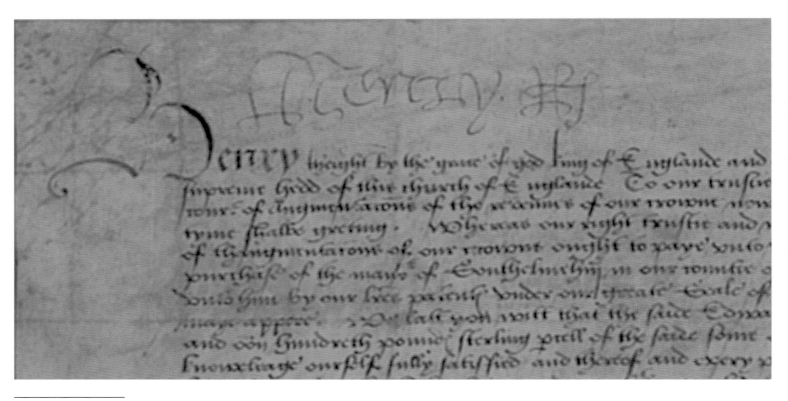

Henry VIII's signature on a letter to Sir Richard Riche.

significance. With this promotion came the knighthood he had long anticipated, the *sine qua non* for recognition as a gentleman at Court.

As the foremost lawyer of the realm, the newly dubbed Sir Richard Riche found himself for the first time seriously embroiled in the King's sinuous political manoeuvrings. Sir Thomas More, the Lord Chancellor, was frustrating Henry's intentions to legitimise his renunciation of his first Queen, Catherine of Aragon, and counselling against his intended marriage to Anne Boleyn; above all, More was implacably opposed to Henry's claim to supremacy over the Roman Catholic Church in England. By fair means or foul, More had to be discredited; in Riche, Henry had found a lawyer apt to his purposes: if a chink in More's armour of principle were to be searched out, the new Solicitor General was the man for the season. Detractors have alleged that Riche's brief hearsay testimony that brought More to the block was a fabricated perjury, and the circumstantial evidence is hard to refute, though the cowardice of those best placed to defend him against the calumnies of More's supporters is no less revealing. In hastening More's conviction for treason, Riche certainly

also learnt the fundamental lesson that royal favour more often than not will prove to be a distinctly mixed blessing.

In spite of having seen the rapid fall of several highly placed court officials, Riche rode his luck and his wits to good effect: his reward for facilitating one Henrician line in realpolitik was his appointment, in 1535, to the Chancellorship of the Court of Augmentations of the King's Revenue. In effect, Riche and his fellow commissioners were to scour the length and breadth of the kingdom, dissolving the smaller religious houses and transferring their portable wealth and the proceeds of the sale of their lands to the Treasury. Tudor morality seems not to have had scruples to any significant extent, if advancement in the King's service were to bring a measure of personal gain as a quid pro quo; in this sphere Riche proved to be an adept hand. Early on in his work at the Court of Augmentations, Riche secured the titles to the lands and buildings associated with the Priory at Leez and the Abbey of Syon. These territories, in the Hundred of Hinckford in Essex, were the first of a great many territorial acquisitions he made in the county and elsewhere over the ensuing two decades. This also marks the start of Riche's connections with Felsted: Leez Priory, a couple of miles to the south of the village, became his main seat away from Court, and the manor of Grauntcourts, previously a Syon holding, lay about the same distance away towards Braintree to the east. These two extensive demesnes were purchased from the King at advantageous rates, while the manor of the Felsted Bury, along with the advowson (the right to appoint the vicar), was granted as a personal gift by Henry in 1537. Grauntcourts Manor was destined to play a notable part in the School's story almost exactly a century later, having been leased from the Riche estates by the Bourchier family, wealthy London merchants whose fortune had been amassed over several generations at the forefront of the lucrative fur trade.

Riche's intuitive talent for avoiding the full glare of public opprobrium can be seen in his unabashed self-assurance in prosecuting the enemies of the state (that is, those who opposed Henry's policies) throughout the 1540s, right up until Henry's demise in January 1547. Many of Riche's patrons and supporters, notably Thomas Cromwell, were brought to book, yet it was the Solicitor General's task to ensure that the King's will be done, whether or not the course of true justice was served thereby. Henry VIII continued to rely greatly on Riche, though this royal confidence could bring its embarrassments, too. When appointed to be Treasurer of the French Wars, Riche was compelled to follow the Army into France, to act as campaign bursar, so to speak. Shortcomings in funding and provisioning led to probing questions from His Majesty's war council, alleging peculation against the officials concerned. Riche beat a somewhat hasty retreat, laid low by a timely illness that was to plague him for several years, but which saved him the awkwardness of impeachment on this occasion. Nowadays, we might diagnose a debilitating case of management stress, though in fact the illness may well have been of a 'diplomatic' nature: the King's beady eye would soon be focused elsewhere, and the great survivor would live to fight another day.

Riche continued to cultivate advantageous alliances with the powerful influences at Court, however, and skilful management of his friendships with the Seymour clan brought further advancement, once the youthful Edward VI had been crowned. Riche gave unequivocal support to the proposal that Edward Seymour, Duke of Somerset, should stand as Protector to the new King during the years of his minority.

This endorsement of Seymour reaped a significant reward in 1547, with Riche's nomination as Lord Chancellor of England (the highest-ranking lawyer of all, the senior judge and head of the judiciary). With this appointment came elevation to a peerage; Richard, Baron Riche, had scaled the heights of political and social success. Riche's intellectual talents and legal abilities were now put to best use. The verdict on his period in office speaks of Riche's diligence, skill and administrative mastery. He was, it would appear, supremely well-fitted for the role.

By 1551, however, Riche's star was in decline; Somerset was ousted as Protector and his successor, the Earl of Warwick, finally brought down the curtain on Riche's long-running legal career. Forced to resign the Great Seal of England, in December 1551, Riche retired from Court and set about restoring and extending his latest Essex acquisition of property at Rochford. There he established a comfortable and convenient residence, just far enough from London to avoid the limelight of Court intrigue, yet near enough for easy river access to the capital, should further opportunities for political rehabilitation ever present themselves.

Edward VI's brief life and reign came to an end in July 1553; this brought for Riche an opening he had been

The Great Seal of Henry VIII.

anticipating: there was dangerous uncertainty attendant upon the succession, and uncertainty was something Riche had always found to be grist to his political mill. Initially, he favoured the accession of Lady Jane Grey, but soon realised that popular opinion was flocking to the cause of Mary, who was poised to pounce from her Framlingham Castle fastness. Riche made known his support for Mary and offered his hospitality during her triumphal progress towards London. Immediately, he was back in royal favour and soon back in the corridors of power and influence, named to the Privy Council as Mary swept back to Court to claim the throne.

For the five years of Mary's reign, Riche wisely stayed aloof from Court political circles, preferring to render service to the returning conservative Catholic regime from his Essex estates, seeing to the coastal defences and overseeing the judicial prosecution of radical elements bent on disturbing the religious counter-revolution. By now, Riche was approaching his 60th year; a time of final reckoning before his Maker could not be forestalled indefinitely. He had, it should be said, shown a modicum of contrition for his active involvement in the dissolution of the monastic orders, by giving up his tenure to the lands of the Priory of St Bartholomew's in Smithfield, which Mary had voiced her intention of restoring to its former status. This gift was by no means a voluntary offering, however; when the Queen named a gift she had set her heart on, woe betide the naysayer.

All the time that he was engaged in prosecuting the Protestant heretics throughout the towns and countryside in Essex (several of whom had been consigned to the stake by his personal mandate), Riche's conscience was troubling him with increasing insistence. Mary's passing in November 1558, brought a termination to the resurgence of Catholic reactionary trends; as heir to the throne, Elizabeth's Protestant credentials were all too obvious, and her support rapidly coalesced into a formidable power base. Ever resourceful, Riche set sail upon the high tide in the affairs of men: he journeyed to Hatfield to present his loyal services to the new Queen, securing a knighthood for his last surviving son, Robert, in the process.

At first, it seemed likely that Baron Riche, despite advancing age, might again be found worthy of high office. However, his religious conservatism ultimately came to face its Rubicon: the Act of Uniformity. Riche had supported the reinstatement of the Royal Supremacy over the Church in England, but he could not and would not endorse an irrevocable break with the English Church's underpinning Roman traditions, which Henry had seen fit to retain. Further public service was out of the question; Riche retired from Court, and, as he had done once or twice before, put his mind to local affairs. To bring added strains and sorrows upon the elderly statesman, Lady Riche had died at Rochford in December 1558, only a few days after Elizabeth's accession.

An Allegory of the Tudor Succession by Lucas de Heere *c.*1570, depicting the four monarchs served by Richard, Lord Riche: Henry VIII enthroned (centre) with his children, Edward VI, Mary I and Elizabeth I in attendance.

Lord Riche's irrepressible nature could not lie low for long. In 1563, he gained audience with the Queen, and offered his advice on the matter of securing the succession, an issue that necessarily involved the broaching of the delicate subject of the Queen's marriage. He seems to have survived this tricky interview, and retained his fourth Sovereign's esteem and respect. Though perhaps more a sign of Elizabeth's rebarbative humour than of genuine friendship, she allowed Riche to offer her the hospitality of his house on at least three occasions, in 1561, 1565 and 1567, when her regular progresses took her along the Essex highways and into the vicinity of one or other of Lord Riche's many residences. The inordinate costs of accommodating the entire royal entourage was to be funded

entirely by the honoured host. Notwithstanding the strain on his finances occasioned by his Sovereign's near-ruinous generosity of favour, Riche continued to revel in his elder statesman role until the very end of his days.

By the prevailing morality of his age, it is hard to condemn Lord Riche: his longevity as a senior courtier, allied to the outstanding efficiency of his service to the Crown at the highest level of state affairs, is his testament. Perhaps it is a complex case of *autres temps, autres mœurs*: from the perspective of modern times, Sir Thomas More's withering assessment of the fledgling lawyer Riche as 'a man of no commendable fame' would find few today who know the full story endorsing More's stricture wholeheartedly.

27

4 | THE FIRST FOUR SCHOOLMASTERS 1564–1627

Felsted's first chaplain-cum-schoolmaster was Revd John Daubeney (sometimes Dabney), whose origins remain somewhat obscure. His tenure lasted barely two years, and we must conclude that his appointment did not fulfil the Founder's expectations, since the majority of schoolmasters in similarly well-endowed and secure employment were wont to linger on for decades, often well beyond their competent years! Certainly, Daubeney would have been the first Schoolmaster to occupy the substantial early Tudor dwelling at Ingram's Close, generously provided for the use of the chantry Chaplain in the Founder's original arrangements.

Lord Riche's choice now fell upon the Revd John Berryman, MA, graduate of St John's College, Cambridge, and a vigorous man not yet 30 years of age. He was assisted by the Usher,

John Bicker, BA, of Corpus Christi College, Cambridge. Together, these two set about establishing the reputation of the fledgling school. Records of the School roll at this time are sketchy and it is impossible to assess accurately how the numbers of scholars waxed and waned over the next ten years. What is certain, though, is that Berryman and his boys would have witnessed the sumptuous funeral proceedings in July 1567, when the Founder was laid to rest in the chancel of the neighbouring Holy Cross Church. Since it appears that Revd Berryman was allowed to hold a succession of clerical livings alongside his tenure at Felsted, it must be assumed that numbers in the school remained relatively small, permitting the Master to absent himself at will, while leaving the school in the Usher's care. Bicker no doubt relished his freedom of opportunity, though he may well have resented his superior's

The 1564 Schoolroom (formerly the Trinity Guildhall) by Holy Cross Church.

enhanced income from the arrangement. Such pluralism was not uncommon, and in many cases was to prove the undoing of establishments of a similar standing, in Essex and throughout the land. It was no doubt with the second Lord Riche's blessing that Berryman resigned his post in 1576, to devote himself to his parish work at Rochford, where his Patron had the advowson and had installed him as Rector a couple of years earlier.

Berryman's successor, Revd Henry Greenwood, also of St John's, Cambridge, would remain in post until 1597. It is a sure sign that the school at Felsted was beginning to flourish that seven of the next eight Masters stayed on for periods of 20 years or more. These were men of ample scholastic abilities who might well have sought preferment elsewhere had they felt the need to escape from uncongenial employment. It is from Greenwood's time, too, that the religious radicalism began to emerge that would lead in the first half of the next century to Felsted School's greatest early fame. The second patron, Robert, second Baron Riche, died in 1581, aged only 44. His heir, also Robert, had not yet reached the age of majority; thus he found himself thrust by circumstance into a position which, but for the recent death of his elder brother, would not have been his to embrace. Like so many young men in history who come into power and freedom too early, the third Baron Riche behaved with characteristic recklessness and indiscretion. An aggravating factor was that his father's illegitimate brother, Richard, remained very much in the family foreground, an unofficial warden to his nephew. This Richard Riche had been a toxic influence in his brother's household, with his unconventional opinions, especially his antagonistic attitudes towards the new Elizabethan religious observances; he was to play a part in Robert's youthful waywardness, too.

As with Shakespeare's Gertrude in *Hamlet*, Robert's father's funeral baked meats 'did coldly furnish forth the marriage tables'. Within weeks of his father's passing, he had concurred with the proposal of his influential friends, Sir Francis Walsingham and Lord Burghley, that the Queen be petitioned for permission for him to contract a marriage with the 18-year-old Penelope Devereux, ward of Lord Huntingdon and daughter of the deceased Walter Devereux, first Earl of Essex, with whom his father had quarrelled seriously as recently as 1573.

VILIFIED IN TIMELESS VERSE

The marriage between Robert Riche and Penelope Devereux (below) appears to have been undertaken in the accepted fashion of the day, that is, to cement alliances between the foremost landowning families in the region. The bride was certainly an unwilling party to the match, and the marriage elicited for Riche the rancid enmity of Sir Philip Sidney, the celebrated courtier, soldier and poet, whose sonnet sequence 'Astrophil and Stella' makes many disparaging plays upon the word 'rich', by way of public opprobrium for his rival in Stella/Penelope's affections.

In particular, Sonnet XXIV is strikingly forceful in its attack on the union between Riche and Devereux:

> *Rich fools there be whose base and filthy heart*
> *Lies hatching still the goods wherein they flow,*
> *And damning their own selves to Tantal's smart,*
> *Wealth breeding want, more blest, more wretched grow.*
> *Yet to those fools heaven such wit doth impart,*
> *As what their hands do hold, their heads do know;*
> *And knowing, love; and loving, lay apart*
> *As sacred things, far from all danger's show.*
> *But that rich fool, who by blind fortune's lot*
> *The richest gem of love and life enjoys,*
> *And can with foul abuse such beauties blot;*
> *Let him, deprived of sweet but unfelt joys,*
> *Exiled for aye from those high treasures which*
> *He knows not, grow in only folly rich!*

Lady Riche began a liaison with Charles Blount, 8th Lord Mountjoy, in 1595, and was formally separated from her husband with a decree in the London consistory court on 14 November 1605. Although it was not legal for her to remarry while her husband was still alive, William Laud married the lovers at Wanstead House, to general disapproval at Court. However, Mountjoy (by now elevated to the earldom of Devonshire) died just three months later, before there could be any serious reprisals.

John Aylmer, Bishop of London (1521–94).

At the time when Greenwood was establishing a sound and respectable local reputation for his School, the young Patron was bringing upon himself and his associates the wrath of the established Church of England, only recently secured in its reformed institutions and supported by draconian statutes enacted under Elizabeth's fiery ripostes to her sister Mary's Catholic reactionary ordinances of the mid-1550s. Robert Riche brought his Cambridge acquaintance, Robert Wright, a preacher of noted Calvinist views, to stay with him at Rochford Hall, where services of a distinctly Puritan temper were held, in direct contravention of the laws compelling all residents over the age of 16 years to attend their parish church when the incumbent so decreed. Riche's nonconformist behaviour brought him to the attention of the Queen, who ordered Bishop Aylmer to stamp out the perfidious practices in Essex. As a result of a violent altercation during an audience with the Bishop, Wright and Riche's uncle Richard (who had played his part in fomenting the proscribed activities) were arrested and imprisoned. Lord Riche himself seems to have escaped direct censure on this occasion, but it is clear that his irresponsible attitude to public life had brought him very near to catastrophe. In spite of this narrow escape, Riche pursued the dangerous course he had begun, and the quarrel with Aylmer was to persist for nearly a decade. In addition to the patronage of his grandfather's Felsted foundations, Riche had inherited the advowsons of some 18 livings in Essex; his manifest propensity in favouring candidates of markedly Calvinist credentials would prove a constant source of concern to the authorities, whose jurisdiction he was repeatedly undermining by his nonconformist nominations, when vacancies arose in rectories and vicarages throughout the county. Some 40 years later, the legacy of Puritanism would bring to Felsted its first great Schoolmaster and also a pupil whose destiny it was to rule the English Commonwealth.

Greenwood's tenure at Felsted saw the consolidation of the Foundation, but it fell to his successor, Revd George Manning, of Corpus Christi College, Cambridge, to ensure

GEORGE BOOTE THE BUILDER

That Manning was gaining for the School a widening arc of esteem is borne out by the expensive additions and alterations to the Schoolroom, carried out by the famous local builder, George Boote, whose work may be seen to this day in several timber-framed masterpieces in the heart of the village and elsewhere along the Chelmsford Road. Local legend has it that the hunched female figure supporting the jetty at the corner of the Boote House restaurant is an unflattering effigy in the likeness of the builder's own wife. By 1606, the schoolroom had been extended, panelling and fixed seating installed, and high dormer windows added to the austere edifice, evidence that Manning was a man of energy and foresight in his approach to his responsibilities. Further expenditure on the fabric was not to be required until some time after Manning's retirement in March 1627, aged nearly 70.

the survival and ultimate flourishing of the School. As his predecessors had done, Manning held sway in the Trinity Guildhall building, known to us today as the Old Schoolroom. He taught the older and more advanced pupils *ex cathedra* at the west end of the hall, perched imposingly on a chair of throne-like proportions. The Usher took his place at the opposite end, where the younger boys were put through the rudiments of Latin grammar and speech, seated on the long hard benches, known as forms, in strict order of their scholastic accomplishments. At the east end, then, began the slow graduation *ad parnassum*, from form to form; until the auspicious day when the burgeoning scholar could make the great leap forward, into the orbit of the great man on the dais at the senior end of School.

It is likely that Felsted's mode of instruction differed little from that employed in grammar schools throughout the land: the boys worked their way through various graded textbooks, often dictated by their teacher, and were in turn set on to recite from memory a previously construed passage. The teacher would then question his charges on the niceties of accidence and syntax, and require further evidence of thorough familiarity with the selected text. The boys were forbidden at all times outside the classroom from resorting to English in their interactions, and the penalties for transgression were usually corporal and severe. New entrants to similar schools at this time were expected to give their solemn oath to work diligently and to submit themselves to their master's corrections, whether verbally or physically administered; there seem to be no grounds for thinking that Felsted's practices were otherwise.

Two further events were to punctuate Manning's long and successful Mastership: the construction in 1607 of the Riche Chapel extension to the Holy Cross Church, and the subsequent elevation of Baron Riche to an earldom, in 1618. Robert Riche had survived his youthful indiscretions, and by dint of careful husbandry of his inherited landholdings had earned himself the soubriquet 'Cornucopia' Riche. He had caused to be built some 300 spacious residences on land he owned at Smithfield, which were let to well-to-do tenants desirous of accommodation near to the Court. With the proceeds of these and other leases, Riche added significantly to his disposable wealth. In return for the

Holy Cross Church, Felsted; with the Riche Chapel of 1617 (on left).

considerable subscription of £18,000 to King James's coffers came the increased kudos of the title Earl of Warwick. It is not inconceivable to infer that the School's growing reputation at this time was in some part due to its Patron's enhanced fame in national affairs. Ironically, he was not to enjoy the fruits of his labours for long; by the spring of 1619 he had died, and was buried in the vault of the newly fashioned Riche Chapel. His son, also Robert, would carry out the provisions of his father's will to have installed a worthy funerary memorial, commemorating in one substantial piece of sculpture the three deceased Barons Riche. The finished edifice may be seen to this day, somewhat altered and partly damaged, but nevertheless an impressive example of the accomplished skill and artistry of the sculptor, the renowned Epiphanius Gresham. Later renovations in Holy Cross Church led to the enclosure of the tomb within metal railings, which detract from the imposing aspect of the Riche memorial.

With the appointment of Manning's successor, the second Earl of Warwick set the seal on the School's consolidation as a centre of scholastic excellence of indisputable national renown.

31

SECTION II

'THE MERIDIAN OF SCHOLASTIC REPUTE'

5 A Puritan Hothouse of National Renown 1627–1725

Martin Holbeach, 1627–49

Revd Martin Holbeach must be acknowledged as Felsted's first great Master. During the 22 years of his tenure, the School produced a scintillating stream of scholars and statesmen to rival the alumni of the greatest of the established schools of the day. Among Holbeach's pupils were the four sons of Oliver Cromwell, one of whom, Richard, would succeed his father as Lord Protector of the Commonwealth of England, Scotland and Ireland. The future academic luminaries John Wallis and Isaac Barrow, as well as scores of future parliamentarians, explorers and divines are also numbered in the throng of successful Felstedians of Holbeach's time.

Taking up the reins in 1627, Holbeach came to join the newly appointed Usher, Lindsell, who had been locum tenens for a term since the departure of Manning. Holbeach was no stranger to the area, having served as schoolmaster in the rival grammar schools at Braintee and Halstead before accepting the Felsted post at the Earl of Warwick's behest. A graduate of Queens' College, Cambridge, Holbeach was the scion of an important Midlands dynasty, and was almost certainly a product of Rugby School, though evidence is hard to find to substantiate the supposition. Incontestable, however, is that Holbeach had carved for himself a secure reputation for his scholarship and pedagogical expertise, and he brought with him to Felsted a number of pupils from his previous incumbencies. In his memoirs published late in life, Dr Wallis recalls that when he came to Felsted in 1630 there were in the School 'above an hundred or six score Scholars, most of them Strangers, sent thither from other places upon reputation of the School; from whence many good Scholars were sent yearly to the University'. It is interesting to note that the tiny community within the village of Felsted was accommodating so many 'strangers', and that the School was gaining the sort of popularity thus far reserved only for the prominent urban establishments such as Shrewsbury, Rugby and Westminster.

Wallis goes on to give details of the rigorous and wide-ranging tuition he received at Holbeach's knee: 'I continued his Scholar for two years, and was by that time pretty well acquainted with the Latin and Greek tongues … and in such other Learning as is commonly taught in such schools … I learn'd there somewhat of Hebrew … and I was taught somewhat of Logick, as a preparation to a further study of it in the University … At this time I learned the rudiments of Musick and of the French tongue.' The breadth of Holbeach's scholarly range is considerable, and his devoted service to the needs of his pupils quite out of the ordinary for a country schoolmaster of the period. The school day was long in Elizabethan and Jacobean education, usually beginning at dawn, 5am in summer, and lasting until sunset, some 12 hours later, with a two-hour recess in the middle of the day. Pupils were forbidden the use of their mother tongue throughout those long hours of labour, a process which honed the communication and disputation skills of the students, such that they were able to profit from the narrowly classical university curriculum. Thence they could enter service in the state administration cadres, where the lingua franca was, of course, Latin.

But there was another powerful factor influencing the rising fame of the School and its Schoolmaster: Holbeach's Calvinist religious convictions, in which he was very much at one with his Patron, Warwick, whose political activities were gaining impetus as Charles I and the monarchy lurched towards disaster. It is not the purpose here to dilate upon the complexities of this definitive period in English history, except in so far as the School and its personnel are directly concerned. Suffice to say that Felstedians played their part in the developing civil catastrophe; some indeed were to be seen at the epicentre of the action. In pride of place among these must stand the three surviving Cromwell brothers, each of whom was to serve the Parliamentary cause to a significant extent.

It is necessary to relate how it was that Felsted came to be chosen for the education of Oliver Cromwell's four boys. As a rising parliamentary star during the early years of Charles I's reign, Cromwell's personal life was becoming ever more conflicted. He had begun life in comfortable circumstances, inheriting substantial property in and around Huntingdon, but a long-standing dispute with the dominant Montague family led Cromwell to dispose of this property and desert the town of his forbears, moving first to St Ives and then to Ely, where family lands were still available for occupation and use. During this period in the doldrums, Cromwell became radicalised in his religious views, and subsequently his vehement faith catapulted the yeoman farmer into radical politics and the military sphere that brought him to national notice. It was at just the time when their father was about to step into the public arena of the Short Parliament that the Cromwell boys found their way to Felsted.

Not far from the School lies the modest country estate of Grauntcourts, owned by the Riches of Leez since the Founder's time, and now leased to the boys' maternal grandparents, Sir James and Lady Bourchier of London and Stansfield Hall. Sir James had died in 1635, and his widow was compelled to relinquish her tenure of the family seat in favour of her son. She was therefore in convenient residence at Grauntcourts when her daughter Elizabeth's boys were approaching schooling age. It seems likely that Robert (at Felsted 1634–9), Oliver (1636–41), Richard (1639–44) and Henry (1636–40) were boarders at their grandmother's house, from whence the School was an easy daily horse-ride away. Sadly, Robert would die while still at school, aged 18; he was

Above: *Evening Party at Milton's* by Emanuel Gottlieb Leutze; showing the Lord Protector, Oliver Cromwell (seated centre, beside his wife) surrounded by his family, including his four Felstedian sons, being entertained by the poet John Milton and (below) Henry Cromwell.

35

Richard Cromwell.

buried in Holy Cross churchyard, and the Vicar wrote of him in the Burial Register that he was 'A young man of outstanding promise and exceptionally pious'.

In view of his brothers' subsequent high-flying careers in public life, there is no reason to take issue with this succinct eulogy. Oliver junior would prosper only briefly, at St Catharine's College, whence he followed his father and namesake into cavalry service and died of smallpox, having seen action with his father's regiment. Henry would rise to the position of Lord Lieutenant and Governor General of Ireland under the Protectorate; his brother, Richard, would rise still higher in rank, to succeed his father as Lord Protector and Head of State, though his star would burn but briefly in the political firmament.

Revd Holbeach's relatively comfortable early years in post were to bring him some disposable income, and he invested wisely in properties in the locality. Notably, he acquired the substantial messuage called Lawsells, directly opposite his tied residence at Ingram's Close. This and the other houses he came to own were let to tenants, and provided further accommodation for the steadily growing numbers of 'strangers' who were flocking to the School during the 1630s and early 1640s. To Felsted at this period came the sons of the East Anglian gentry, as well as some scions of the genuine nobility, these latter as casualties of the increasing hostilities of the English Civil War. Holbeach's name was well known in Parliamentary circles, through the powerful influences of the Earl of Warwick in the Lords and of Oliver Cromwell in the Commons; thus it was that the two sons of the Royalist Lord Arundell of Wardour, Thomas and Henry, captured by the Parliamentary army when Wardour Castle in Wiltshire

JOHN WALLIS (1616–1703), OXFORD UNIVERSITY SAVILIAN PROFESSOR OF GEOMETRY

John Wallis entered Felsted School in December 1630, and found the tutelage of Martin Holbeach to be entirely to his liking. His precocious intellect found in his Master the lodestone required to spur him on in his eager quest for knowledge. He proceeded to Emmanuel College, Cambridge, noted at this time for its Puritan ethos, where he was soon to immerse himself in a dizzying plethora of studies. A true Renaissance Man, the polymath Wallis regaled his mind with an astonishing range of subjects: Natural Philosophy, Anatomy, Medicine, Theology, Ethics and Metaphysics, along with the classical languages necessary to access the wider curriculum. His MA in 1640 was closely followed by ordination by the Bishop of Winchester.

By 1644, Wallis had established his burgeoning reputation for cutting-edge scholarship, especially in the new disciplines of the experimental physical sciences. The work he was engaged in and the collaborators with whom he worked would bear abundant fruit in due course with the foundation of the Royal Society, in 1660; in Wallis and Isaac Barrow, Felsted can boast of having two founder members of that august body among its former pupils. In 1649, Wallis was appointed Savilian Professor of Geometry in the University of Oxford, a post he held until his death in 1703.

In a long and distinguished career as a mathematician of rare genius, Wallis published many groundbreaking treatises on mathematical questions, entered into learned disputations with all the leading thinkers in Europe, including such luminaries in the field as Pierre de Fermat, Blaise Pascal and Thomas Hobbes. Most recognisable to modern minds is Wallis's invention of the universally employed symbol for infinity: ∞.

was taken, were put into Holbeach's care. A year later, they were removed from Felsted and exchanged for three Robartes brothers, sons of the second Baron Truro, who were hostages of the Royalist forces, who had captured them at the siege and taking of Llanhydrock House, in Cornwall. John, Hender and Robert Robartes were sent as boarders to the School, where all three prospered under Holbeach's steady influence. In time, each would make a significant contribution to public life in their native Cornwall, with service as Members of Parliament, and in Robert's case also as Ambassador to the Court of Denmark.

RICHARD CROMWELL (1626–1712), LORD PROTECTOR OF THE COMMONWEALTH

Richard Cromwell, third son of Oliver Cromwell, was schooled at Felsted between 1639 and 1644. His elder brothers, Robert and Oliver, both perished young, and by the time he left the School, Richard had become the heir to his father's modest estates in the Cambridgeshire Fenlands. If the English Civil War was to be the making of the father, it would in due course precipitate the son into a political role for which he had little preparation and perhaps less inclination. He had entered Lincoln's Inn in 1647, possibly with a view to pursuing a legal career, but little is known of his early adult life, except that he did not serve in the Parliamentary forces, where his younger brother Henry, also a Felsted alumnus, was prominent in the campaign in Ireland. His marriage to a wealthy heiress, Dorothy Major, in 1649, brought Richard the security and relative anonymity of a country squire's existence, at Hursley Park in Hampshire. It was not until 1654 that he was nominated as a Justice of the Peace and subsequently appointed MP for Hampshire in the New Parliament. It is clear that he took his duties seriously and proved himself an adept committee member.

It was Oliver Cromwell's failing health and the need to consolidate the country's governance that brought Richard somewhat unwillingly to the forefront of national and international affairs. He found himself being groomed to succeed his father, who appointed him Chancellor of Oxford University in July 1657, and to the Lord Protector's Council of State, and nominated him as a member of the second Chamber of Parliament. Upon Oliver Cromwell's demise in September 1658, Richard found himself proclaimed Head of State, aged 32. That he coped tolerably well with the debt crisis and the continuing war with Spain, in spite of his utter lack of experience in high-level politics, speaks volumes about his resilience of character. Richard Cromwell's speech at the Opening of Parliament in January 1659 reveals a determined and eloquent leader, who had found the confidence to rule, as his father had before him. There would be no happy outcome, however, as the Army, long unpaid and increasingly factious, mounted a coup against Richard's government, forcing him from power.

For over 50 years, from April 1659 until his death in July 1712, Richard Cromwell lived in self-imposed obscurity, intermittently hunted after the Restoration by his enemies, and haunted, no doubt, by his unwarranted reputation as a failure.

Handbill of 1658, publicising the appointment of Richard Cromwell as Lord Protector.

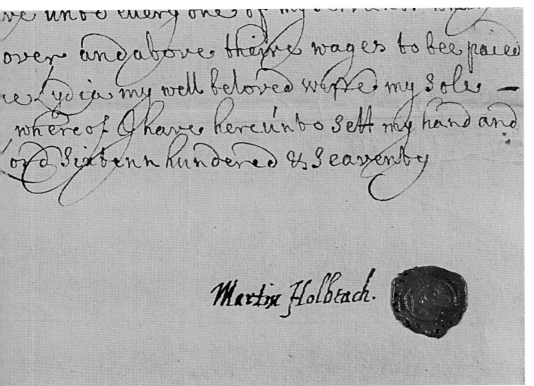

CHRISTOPHER GLASCOCK (1650–90)

With the departure of Holbeach, Warwick was left with a mighty pair of boots to fill: the School could truly count itself the equal of any institution of learning in the land, and this hard-won pre-eminence must be preserved and nurtured. Who better to continue the work of so prominent a Schoolmaster than one of his own former pupils? Thus it came about that the Patron's choice fell upon the Revd Christopher Glascock, whose parents were members of an important local family of sound yeoman credentials. A recent ancestor had held the tenancy of the Felsted Bury estate, and other relatives farmed the manors of Down Hall, Matching and Minchins at Great Dunmow.

Holbeach's signature and seal (above) and Schoolmaster Glascock's will (right).

Among a great many noteworthy pupils attending the School during this period, John Wallis and Isaac Barrow rank highest in academic achievement, while the Cromwell brothers take pride of place in the political sphere. For a rural Essex endowed school to number at one and the same time among its alumni the leading academics of Oxford and of Cambridge Universities, the Lord Lieutenant of Ireland and the ruling British Head of State must certainly constitute a unique distinction. It is a testament to the wide renown earned for Felsted School by its first truly important Schoolmaster, Martin Holbeach.

Holbeach resigned his Mastership at the School in 1649, to take up the post of Vicar at High Easter. His later years, it would appear, were not happy ones: he quarrelled with the Church authorities after the Restoration, was ejected from his living, and returned a disgruntled man to his Felsted home at Lawsells, where he died some ten years thereafter, aged 73. He is buried in Felsted churchyard, within yards of the Schoolroom where he held vigorous sway for so long and to such good effect.

ISAAC BARROW (1630–77), REGIUS PROFESSOR OF GREEK, LUCASIAN PROFESSOR OF MATHEMATICS AND MASTER OF TRINITY COLLEGE, UNIVERSITY OF CAMBRIDGE

Isaac Barrow came to Felsted at the tender age of eight. He had been sent to the newly founded Charterhouse School in London, but his education had been sorely neglected and the precociously talented child allowed to run wild. Felsted Schoolmaster Holbeach was immediately struck by the boy's potential, and took him under his aegis and into his personal household. Despite his extreme youth, Barrow was able to thrive in the more sheltered country environment, and his scholastic achievements were soon to match his extravagant intellectual gifts. Not yet a teenager, Barrow was engaged by Holbeach as 'little tutor' to the future Viscount Fairfax, a boarder in the Schoolmaster's own house — further proof of Barrow's academic promise. The Civil War was to play its part in Barrow's story, as it did with so many of his contemporaries: in December 1644, a promised scholarship at Peterhouse, Cambridge, was withdrawn when Barrow's family connections with the Royalist faction were discovered.

Barrow returned to Felsted, but soon departed in the company of Fairfax, who eloped with a local girl with whom he had fallen in love. In hopes of luring his star pupil back from his disastrous alliance with Fairfax, and as an inducement to make Felsted his permanent home, Holbeach offered to make Barrow his heir. Nonetheless, Barrow was determined to pursue his intention of entering the University. He was admitted to Trinity College, Cambridge, aged 16, in February 1646, and was soon rewarded with an academic scholarship, thus easing his precarious financial situation. He gained his BA in 1649 and was immediately elected to a fellowship. His Royalist political sentiments would from time to time lead to serious differences with the Parliament-minded University authorities, so his tenure at Trinity was often threatened.

Like Wallis, Barrow exhibited all the intellectual powers of the true polymath: in addition to his classical studies and his theological work (he would achieve the distinction of a Doctorate of Divinity in 1666), Barrow launched into the newly developing scientific and mathematical disciplines. He was appointed Regius Professor of Greek at Cambridge in 1660, resigning this post to become Cambridge's very first Lucasian Professor of Mathematics in 1663. He was also appointed Gresham College Professor of Geometry in London. At Trinity, Barrow was tutor to the young Isaac Newton, recognising his pupil's supreme mathematical acumen; with notable generosity, Barrow resigned the Lucasian post in Newton's favour. Barrow was appointed Master of Trinity by Charles II, and would serve as Vice Chancellor of the University of Cambridge shortly before his death in 1677. His marble statue graces the antechamber in Trinity College Chapel to this day. The Wren Library in Trinity is also a monument to Barrow's extraordinarily diverse academic and aesthetic contribution to College and University.

Statue of Isaac Barrow in Trinity College Chapel, Cambridge.

unpretentious Christian faith that numbers hardly fell at all in his first few years in charge, and the popularity of the School for the boarding 'strangers' was even enhanced. Glascock sent a very high percentage of his boys on to Cambridge University: between 1668 and 1672 upwards of 25 Felstedians went up, and that from an upper form of 20 boys or so. As it happened, Glascock's former employers at Ipswich School tried hard to lure him back when the headmastership there fell vacant in 1658. Warwick made sure that Glascock did not take the bait of the attractive salary and emoluments on offer by arranging for a long-standing Foundation lease, the manor of Moretons, to be signed over for his personal use.

Not long thereafter the male line of the Riche family of Leez was extinguished in a series of premature deaths: the elderly 2nd Earl's grandson passed away just months after solemnising his marriage to Frances Cromwell, daughter of Oliver senior; the second Earl of Warwick died just two months later, followed a year later by his son, the 3rd Earl, who left no male issue; so the title and the Patronage of Felsted School passed to his brother, Charles. By the time of Christopher Glascock's death in 1690, the 4th Earl too had died, leaving no direct male heir; by a complex series of legal contortions, the title and Patronage had passed to the Finch family, Earls of Winchilsea and Nottingham. The Finch seat was in distant Rutland, thus, from 1673 onwards, the School's affairs were directed very much at arm's length. Perhaps it is from this point that the imperceptible but steady decline in Felsted's fortunes may be traced; the process was by no means confined to Felsted, since there was a general falling-off in popularity of the endowed grammar schools throughout the country, as the fashion for 'utilitarian and modern' rather than 'classical and antiquated' gained widespread acceptance. The eighteenth century would see the demise of many scores of small (especially rural) establishments, or at least the translation of many into schools where the future tradesmen and merchants could be taught the mathematics and English language they would need in the world of business and commerce. The rising 'middling sort' would not fritter away their hard-earned cash on an outdated curriculum that appeared to have no direct application in the commercial world they were busy creating.

Illustrated letter signed by Charles Rich(e), 4th Earl of Warwick (Patron 1659–73).

Glascock had proceeded from Felsted to St Catharine's College, Cambridge, from whence he emerged with the degree of MA and a clear vocation for a teaching career. He held posts successively at Chipping Ongar and at Cardinal Wolsey's free grammar school at Ipswich, before accepting the Mastership at his alma mater in 1650. The School had endured a somewhat confused interregnum, presided over by three brothers named Skingle, all Cambridge graduates and all ultimately bound for careers in the clergy and grammar education; but changes of principal Master always send ripples of uncertainty through the fabric of a school, and in Glascock the Patron had made a wise choice.

As the Restoration steadily sought to eradicate the radicalism of the Commonwealth years, the Puritan ethos fostered under Holbeach would become less attractive to the present as well as to potential clientele; it says a great deal about Glascock's own sound scholarship and

Simon Lydiatt (1690–1712)

Glascock's demise, aged 77 and still actively engaged in his profession, left a pressing need for the new Patron, Daniel Finch, Earl of Nottingham, to turn his mind to the appointment of a new Schoolmaster for Felsted, his somewhat distant new fiefdom. Finch had himself attended Westminster School and Christ Church, Oxford, and had followed his father's lead into the political whirligig that was the English Court of that time. Finch had been intimately involved in the many twists and turns of James II's doomed reign, and despite his support for the fugitive king, he had been appointed Secretary of State under William and Mary. The exigencies of the succession at Felsted must have seemed particularly remote when viewed alongside the significant upheavals at the centres of national government with which Finch had become deeply embroiled, to say nothing of the Nine Years War (1688–97) waged against Louis XIV of France, which had broken out as a result of Catholic James's flight to France and the Protestant William and Mary's joint accession to the English throne. Nevertheless, a new Schoolmaster had to be found: Nottingham's choice fell upon Revd Simon Lydiatt, of Christ's Hospital and Christ Church,

Oxford. Like his two immediate predecessors, Lydiatt had already cut his pedagogical teeth before accepting the Felsted post, in his case a five-year stint as Undermaster at Merchant Taylors' School, in the City of London.

Lydiatt came to Felsted a newly married man and quickly made his mark as a sound scholar and inspirational teacher. By 1696 he had published a textbook of Latin and Greek epigrams for the specific use of his pupils in the upper forms, printed at London and dedicated to Finch in gratitude for his Patron's continuing favour. This was to prove sound good sense, as the financial wrangling that had beset him latterly would come to cloud the sunnier scenes of his early years of service. As was to happen again and again in the Felsted story, as in so many others, disputes over money could often bring catastrophe from relatively trivial antecedents.

In Lydiatt's case humiliating disaster did not eventuate, though the protracted conflict with his Usher, the Welshman David Price, a product of Westminster School (the Patron's alma mater, it should be noted) and Trinity College, Cambridge, was to blight in a most public way the necessary harmony of purpose between the teaching incumbents at the

WILLIAM BYRD II OF WESTOVER, VIRGINIA

William Byrd (right) came to Felsted in 1682, his education having been entrusted to his maternal grandfather, Wareham Horsmanden, and to his uncle, Daniel Horsmanden. We find boys with this surname in the School rolls of the early 1700s, so must assume that the family were perhaps local or at least familiar with Felsted's fine scholastic reputation. William's father, also William Byrd, was a founder of the colony of Virginia, and he imbued his son with the entrepreneurial spirit from an early age. After nine years at Felsted, followed by legal studies at the Middle Temple in London, Byrd junior returned to Virginia to forge a considerable career in the plantation business and in colonial politics. He is credited with the founding of several new communities, including Richmond (the Virginian State capital) and Petersburg, towns he established upon lands owned by the Byrd family alongside the James River. As a leading property owner and Member of the Council of State for Virginia, Byrd played his part in organising the defences of the colony against threats of French naval aggression in 1711. Byrd also mapped and fixed the boundary line between Virginia and North Carolina. Of special interest, too, was the suggestion in Byrd's own diaries that he played a leading role in establishing the game of cricket among the landed gentry in the American colonies, in the first instance as a *casus belli* for placing wagers, rather than for the pleasure of the contest of bat against ball.

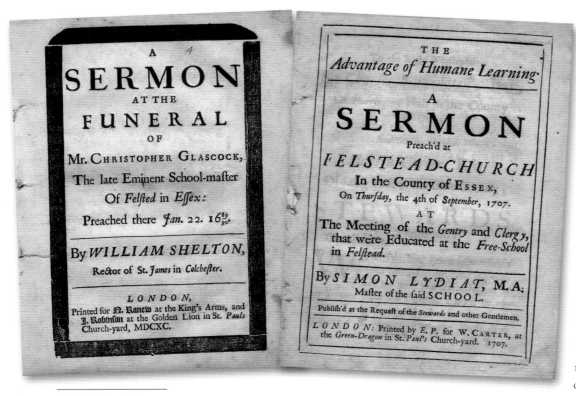

Front page of sermon at Glascock's funeral (left) and front page of sermon preached by Lydiatt.

School. The nub of the dispute lay in the practice of levying tuition fees from all pupils not admitted as free scholars on the Foundation, of whom there were fewer and fewer as time went on. Lydiatt believed himself entitled to all the emoluments thus collected, and thought Price well remunerated by his £25 per annum stipend alone. Price, who had begun his service under Glascock, had been allowed to retain all the fees paid by those in his charge in the lower forms, and resented Lydiatt's insistence that all such monies be forthwith forfeited. Letters flew back and forth between Master, Usher and Patron; the Vicar too, an Old Felstedian named Woodrooffe, was also brought into the fray. In the end, a compromise was negotiated: Price was compelled to recognise Lydiatt's nominal hegemony over all the pupils, and in turn Lydiatt allowed Price a one-third share of the fees paid by those in the Usher's care. The resolution in 1701 of the long-running legal case against Sir John Foch, who had acquired the lease of the Foundation's property at Broomfield, but withheld payments of rental due to the Chaplain of the Foundation (that is, Lydiatt) was also a timely boost to Lydiatt's financial situation: he received £175 in unpaid salary and nearly £40 in compensation and repayment of out-of-pocket expenses incurred over the seven years of the affair. David Price also gained the handsome sum of £94 and 10 shillings in back pay. Both parties seem to have been content to bury the hatchet at this juncture.

Lydiatt's legacy to the School includes his personal gift of a gallery at the west end of the Holy Cross Church nave, for the accommodation of the boys during Sunday services, and the institution in September 1707 of an 'Annual Meeting of the Gentlemen educated at this Schole', the very first instance of a reunion of Old Felstedians taking place. The gallery survived until the complete 'restoration' of the church in 1876, when Victorian 'improvements' swept away so much of the ancient character and charm of the building. The Annual Meetings continue, in altered but recognisable form to this day; until the latter part of the nineteenth century they were to constitute no more than a sporadic feature in the calendar, putting in an appearance very much at the Schoolmaster's whim. The inaugural occasion established a precedent for holding a service in the village church, speeches given by Old Felstedians of distinction, addresses in Latin and Greek (called School Exercises) by senior scholars, and a festive meal for the visitors and their guests.

That Lydiatt was recognised as having maintained and indeed perhaps enhanced the School's bright flame of academic reputation is given strong support in a speech delivered at the 1708 Annual Meeting by the Revd Bramston, DD, Master of Queens' College, Cambridge, who in addressing the assembled boys spoke from personal experience and with great authority of the School's 'Learned Master, to whose Conduct and great Abilities I owe the Education of two Sons.' He added, and surely not simply from a desire to please on this particular occasion, 'I cannot but Congratulate the Felicity of your Foundation, which has been blessed with a Succession of incomparable Masters; [Mr Lydiatt's] Predecessor raised the credit of it to a very considerable Reputation in our University, and the scholars sent by him do greatly increase the Opinion it hath had of the Happiness of an Education formed in Felsted School.'

Simon Lydiatt survived the serious outbreak of smallpox that struck the village and School in 1711, but, brought low by the 'great prejudice and loss of the Schole', he died the following year, aged 53. With his passing, Usher David Price was left in sole charge, and remunerated by payment of Lydiatt's salary in addition to his own. Hoping no doubt to profit further from the demise of his nemesis, Price made the journey to Burley-on-the-Hill to petition the Patron for the Mastership. The Earl of Nottingham proved disinclined to accede to his wishes, feeling no doubt that Price had already wreaked sufficient damage on the good name of the School; reports had also reached him from Vicar Woodrooffe that Price's attendance at Church had become desultory, to say the least. Price further blotted his copybook by laying claim to a sum of unpaid salary sent by the Patron to Lydiatt's widow. In short, Nottingham must briefly put aside affairs of state (he was currently Queen Anne's President of the Council) to deal with the Felsted succession.

HUGH HUTCHIN (1713–25)

Finch, for the second time, looked no further than Christ Church for a worthy schoolmaster. Revd Hugh Hutchin had an impeccable pedigree: educated first at Lincoln College and thereafter at Christ Church, Oxford, he had been appointed Master of the grammar school administered by his College, where he also appears to have acted as Junior Chaplain from time to time. With over ten years' schoolmastering service to his credit, Hutchin seemed the perfect choice. He found his new country posting most congenial, and fostered good relations with the residents, taking great pains to see to the needs of his pupils, including (and this was most unusual for the time) their domestic and physical well-being. He obtained funding from the Foundation to have constructed a house close to the Schoolroom to accommodate those of his scholars not boarded out elsewhere in the village. Hutchin managed to maintain the School's numbers at a time when country grammar schools were failing in ever greater numbers to survive; no less a commentator than Daniel Defoe passed favourable judgement on his tenure. In his *A Tour thro' the whole island of Great Britain* (confusingly placed in the section

entitled 'Norfolk and Cambridgeshire of 1722'), we read: 'Near [Braintree] is Felsted, a small place, but noted for a free school of an ancient foundation, for many years under the Mastership of the late Rev. Mr Lydiatt, and brought by him to the meridian of its reputation. It is now supplied, and that very worthily, by the Rev. Mr Hutchins [sic].'

Hutchin did not live long to enjoy his success as Master of Felsted School; his sudden death from a stroke, in April 1725, left the podium at the top of the Schoolroom vacant once more; again, Daniel Finch was called upon to nominate a new incumbent. From this time, too, dates the gradual decline in the School's fortunes, in common with so many ancient foundations. A new age of trade and commerce had dawned, which would shun its classical past and look to a future brimming over with bills of lading and written communications in plain vernacular English.

Daniel Finch, 2nd Earl of Nottingham and 7th Earl of Winchilsea (Patron 1686–1730). Attributed to Jonathan Richardson.

Daniel, Earl of Winchilsea & Nottingham. 1727.

6 | ENDOWED SCHOOLS ON THE WANE 1725–1835

It is quite conceivable that the rural backwater that was Felsted in the late seventeenth and early eighteenth century was cocooned from the wider realities of national and international affairs. Throughout its period of academic pre-eminence, the School and its denizens had ploughed the scholarly furrows with diligence and ambition. Masters of distinction had come and gone, and boys of all ranks and conditions had passed through the Schoolroom on their way to man's estate, untroubled, so it would appear, by the tribulations of the nation's political turmoil at home and intermittent serious military engagements abroad. Civil War, Commonwealth, Restoration, Glorious Revolution and the accession of the House of Hanover had left but small ripples in deepest Essex, though not a few Felstedians had made their mark in the pages of that history. With the 1700s well under way by the time of Hugh Hutchin's passing, a changing political and demographic landscape was beginning to emerge, even in the depths of the Hinckford Hundred of Essex.

The ancient endowed schools were finding their very existence threatened for the most fundamental of reasons: their *raison d'être* to provide classically trained minds for Court and University had become a creed outworn. The future would require accountants and commercially astute businessmen; and Latin and Greek epigrams no longer seemed to fit the requirements of a modern education. So very many of those grammar schools begun in a blaze of hope back in the Tudor and Elizabethan era withered and finally succumbed; adapt or die had become the watchword. Felsted School was perhaps among the most vulnerable; its isolation having been a positive asset in the previous century and a half was to prove a serious impediment to its survival over the next hundred years or so.

In hindsight, it may be some comfort to know that Felsted was not alone among Essex schools to feel the pinch; Chigwell, Chelmsford, Brentwood and Colchester were all entering a period of distinct peril, and several of the county's unsupported foundations would go to the wall before the eighteenth century was well advanced.

A Conversation Piece by James Russel (dated 1744), showing William Drake (Master 1750–78) seated left, with Thomas Townson (OF 1728–32) standing behind table (left); Sketch (below) of Bamber Gascoyne MP (OF 1738–42); John Constable's Dedham Vale: Morning (opposite page), an Essex landscape c.1810.

JOHN WYATT (1725–50)

For a third time, the Earl of Nottingham found it necessary to exercise his patronal right to select a successor as Schoolmaster for Lord Riche's grammar school at Felsted. Again, he sought a candidate from his own alma mater, finding another Christ Church man to fill the vacancy. Revd John Wyatt had very strong claims, both in his impeccable background and education and in his youthful and vigorous approach to his calling. He began very well, and appears to have been able to establish harmonious relations with Usher Price, who had by then been in post for well over 30 years. Together, Wyatt and Price maintained the steady stream of excellent scholars, and the colleges of Oxford and Cambridge continued to reap the harvest of their schoolroom labours. Of their pupils, Thomas Townson would go on to Christ Church, win a Fellowship at Magdalen, be offered and refuse the Regius Professorship of Divinity at Oxford and make his name as a pre-eminent theologian and preacher; John Duncombe was to gain a fellowship at Corpus Christi, Cambridge; and Bamber Gascoyne went on to The Queen's College, Oxford, was a Member of Parliament for 25 years and was latterly one of the Lords of the Admiralty. Price's death in 1731 brought a new Usher to Felsted: Hans de Veil served as Vicar of Saling and was later appointed Vicar of Felsted, but his sudden death in 1741 brought Mark Gretton, who had been a pupil under Wyatt, had migrated to Eton, graduated from Pembroke College, Cambridge and taken a Fellowship at Peterhouse. That the School could still attract academics of such distinction speaks most eloquently of Felsted's continuing renown, even as the decline in grammar school popularity was gathering pace elsewhere.

A major contributing factor to the atrophy being accelerated in the country establishments was the growing practice of pluralism. Clerics who could call upon powerful patrons were often nominated to a succession of lucrative livings, all of which they retained, despite not being able to fulfil the duties exigent upon them in those posts. Frequently, such pluralists would neglect their less attractive work in the schoolrooms to concentrate their efforts where the duties were more attractive and the emoluments more favourable. Usher Gretton had by 1749 acquired tenure of three local parishes: Good Easter, Margaret Roding and Little Dunmow; at the time he accepted the Rectorship at Woodham Mortimer in 1745, Wyatt was already Rector of both Little Waltham and Peldon. It is hard to imagine how the two Felsted Schoolmasters could have administered effectively all their clerical duties and also given due time and care to their academic responsibilities; the fact that Wyatt's successor inherited fewer than a dozen boys would seem to bear out the suspicion that neglect of the School had been the shaming compromise for both.

The School Deed of 1564 gives the Founder's clear direction that such behaviour should not be tolerated at Felsted School: 'yf the said scholemaster or ussher … shal be absent from the said schole by the space of eight dayes in one quarter of a yere or shal not travayl and teche the scholers of the said schole in such sorte and forme as ys aforesaide

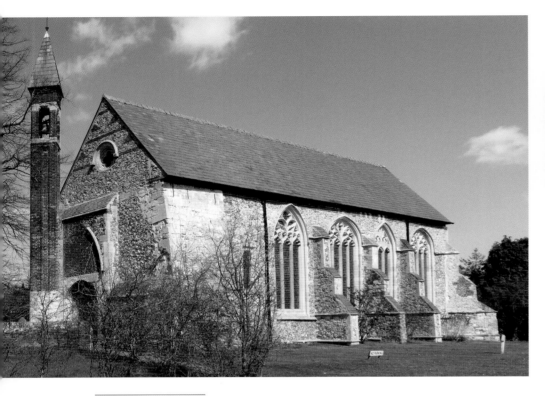

Little Dunmow (left) and Little Waltham churches; two of the six parochial livings held by Schoolmaster Wyatt and Usher Gretton while employed at the School.

(having no lawfull and true excuse by siknes or other greate and urgente debilitie and weaknes of body), then I and myne heires from tyme to tyme shal name prefer and collate to the saide office one other chapleyne and ussher.'

Wyatt's death in 1750, aged only 52, brought to an end a reign that had promised much at the outset, but had ended in culpable failure. The second Daniel Finch was no doubt relieved not to have to enforce the Founder's precept upon a disgraced Master, but in the event an outstandingly able and conscientious successor would have to be found to reverse the devastating decline that had set in.

WILLIAM DRAKE (1750–78)

Felsted School very probably owes its survival to the unusual talents of its next Master, Revd William Drake. Not only was he a fine scholar and teacher, but also a gifted publicist and adept at making the very best use of his wide range of contacts in the social and academic spheres of his day. By the time of his resignation, to take up the post of Vicar of Isleworth, Middlesex, the name of Felsted was again spoken of with confidence in the land.

Daniel Finch II, like his father before him, was educated at Westminster and Christ Church, and from those academic stables he sought a saviour for the School. Happily, he found there exactly the man he wanted: William Drake was a Yorkshireman by birth, but London and Oxford bred; indeed he had been Usher of the Third Form at Westminster School for a number of years prior to accepting the Felsted post, and he brought with him the 'best practice' in grammar school direction of his day.

Drake realised at once that his success or failure would rest upon raising again the numbers in the School; that would mean that scholastic standards would have be restored in a hurry and the wavering clientele wooed back. Drake made great play of reviving the Annual Feast, and publicised the event far and wide. He drew upon his Yorkshire and London antecedents, bringing to his new school the sons of his parents' North Country neighbours and the brothers of several former pupils at Westminster. Numbers rose steadily, and the University triumphs of the Felsted alumni again began to redound to the School's credit. That Drake's reputation was an instrumental factor in Felsted's revival may be seen in the quality of the two Ushers attracted to the post vacated when Gretton finally decided to concentrate his efforts on the parishes he had been collecting for so long. William Drake (no relation) of King's College, Cambridge, joined his namesake in 1752, and when he retired to his vicarage at Good Easter in 1773, a suitable replacement was found, albeit only for a brief interlude, in the person of Barlow Seale, a brilliant academic who had carried off

was a man who could take up the reins of command at Felsted without a hitch.

The first matter to be addressed was the wholesale refurbishment of the Schoolroom and its associated range of buildings, both outside and within. The crucial alteration included in Trivett's plans was the provision of the six large, high-level dormer windows in the Schoolroom itself. Henceforth, daylight could flood the working space, a considerable saving in candles could be made, and there would be no place to hide for the recalcitrant scholar who wished to evade his Master's beady eye. As it happened, the expensive new panelling, appended to conceal the existing much-defaced dado wainscoting, did not long survive in its pristine state – such is the desire in successive schoolboy generations to carve immortality into solid oak.

Trivett built successfully upon Drake's academic resurgence, sending some three dozen of his boys on to the Universities, and once or twice reversed the migration of younger boys from Felsted to Eton, thus giving an indication that the School under his influence was again recognised as having a national rather than merely a local reputation.

William Drake, 1790 (left) and Old Schoolroom staircase graffiti and carvings.

many University prizes at Cambridge, and was at the time of his appointment a Fellow of his college, Christ's.

By the summer of 1778, there were upwards of 60 boys in the School, and the crisis was, for the time being, averted. By this time, too, George III had embroiled Britain in a belligerent campaign against the colonists in North America; the Industrial Revolution had begun its root-and-branch reshaping of the nation's economy; and Walpole's Whig inheritors were bidding fair to abolish the Tory landed classes and dispossess them of all they stood for.

WILLIAM TRIVETT (1778–94)

The new Patron, George Finch, had succeeded his uncle Daniel two-thirds of the way through Wyatt's term of office, but did not reach his majority until 1773, so it is unsurprising that he was strongly influenced in his choice of a new Master by the views of the outgoing incumbent. To Westminster and Christ Church again, then, to secure the services of a worthy successor. Revd William Trivett, like Wyatt, had returned to Westminster to teach under his old Head Master and had been the Usher there for nearly a decade. Undoubtedly, this

WILLIAM CARLESS (1794–1813)

Trivett's decision to take on the Mastership at Colfe's Grammar School in Lewisham brought to Felsted Revd William Carless, a product of Eton and Merton Colleges. Unusually youthful at just 24 years of age, Carless had already held the Mastership at Chigwell School for no more than a year when he accepted George Finch's appointment.

From the outset, Carless was determined to raise yet further the tone of his new School. Trivett's renovations had refurbished the Schoolroom; now significant improvements must be put in train at Ingram's Close, the Schoolmaster's residence, where accommodation in the original Elizabethan house was woefully inadequate, not to say squalid. Carless prevailed upon a number of the Essex 'great and good', most of whom had attended the School, to subscribe to a fund for the purpose. The Patron gave his approval for the project and allowed some funding from Foundation reserves, too. Carless's ambitions were set upon a complete replacement of the decrepit old tenement, and an expanded provision to accommodate boarding 'strangers' under his own roof. With characteristic aplomb and using his growing array of well-to-do local contacts, he secured the services of architect John Johnson, County

Ingram's Close by Cyril B. Harcourt, *c*.1861.

Surveyor of Essex, whose style and vision had lately been realised in the newly completed Shire Hall at Chelmsford. The New School House was three years in construction and cost £1,708, a very considerable sum for the times.

After 1802, Carless was housed as befitted the Master of a re-emerging academic powerhouse, as he saw it, and he continued to labour hard to consolidate the recent advances. He further strove to raise the profile of the Annual Feast, which had proved so fruitful in fund-raising for the new building, and set his mind to improving the recreational facilities available to his pupils. Provision of playground areas was by no means universal in the endowed schools of his day; only the great collegiate establishments saw fit to allocate space and funding to non-academic pursuits, and even they tended to forbid the use of English speech in the hours of recess. A product himself of just such a collegiate school, Carless had no doubt embraced the notion of *mens sana in corpore sano* (a healthy mind in a healthy body), a precept only then beginning to permeate the thinking of radical reformers of the time-honoured, but increasingly redundant, grammar school curriculum. In furtherance of this avant-garde policy, Carless secured the tenancy of the farmer's field behind Ingram's (where the present Chapel, along with Gepp's and Deacon's Houses, now stand) for the use of his boys. They in turn helped him to fence off, level and turf the area, such that a workmanlike sports field was born. The turfing process brought the School into conflict with local landowners over the next decade or so, since the removal of suitable re-turfing materials from the pastures round and about was sometimes done without the express permission of the tenants. From this period we can date the emergence of cricket and some early forms of football as permitted and indeed encouraged activities at the School. Swimming in the Chelmer River and country pursuits such as bird-nesting and rabbit-snaring had certainly been indulged in since time immemorial, as in all rural establishments where boys were boys together; indeed, such unofficial pastimes are still spoken of in the reminiscences of Felstedians from periods as recent as the 1950s. One thing is certain, Lord Winchilsea would have approved of the Little Field innovation: he was himself a doughty cricketer, for the Hambledon Club in Hampshire, and in 1789 was a founder member of the Marylebone Cricket Club.

Despite his tireless efforts to combat the countrywide decline in endowed school popularity, Carless found that Felsted, too, was failing to buck that demoralising trend. His untimely death in 1813, aged only 43, saw the School's very existence again under threat, with only 20 boys on the roll. Britain, too, was reeling: the French revolutionary wars and the protracted Napoleonic campaigns had sapped the nation's spirit and its resolve; the Exchequer's cupboard was bare and political instability had become a reality in the land. The countryside had suffered particular hardship: the flight of the agricultural population in droves to the urban centres of manufacture had denuded the farms of their labour; crop failures had driven many landowners into insolvency; and food had become a costly luxury rather than a dependable staple of life. The Battle of Waterloo was still two years distant in an uncertain future.

EDMUND SQUIRE (1813–35)

Revd Edmund Squire, of Charterhouse and Christ's College, Cambridge, made a particularly impressive start to his time in charge. In modern terms, he proved himself to be a commendably astute accountant, as well as a canny marketing executive: by the time of the School Feast of 1818, he had more than doubled the number of boys in the School and inaugurated a school library of books in English, alongside the long-established collection of classical tomes housed in the Schoolroom since the Founder's time. However, he suffered from the old scourge of 'migration': once again, it appears that Felsted was perceived by some of its clientele as a preparatory establishment, and many high-fliers took their talents to the so-called 'great schools', after cutting their teeth under Squire. It must have been particularly galling to see so many of his most promising lads proceeding to his own alma mater, Charterhouse. By the early 1830s, Squire had but 20 boys to

Above: jug showing engraving by Thomas Fletcher of a match played at Lord's between Earls of Winchilsea and Darnley for 1,000 guineas; (left) portrait of George Finch, 9th Earl of Winchilsea in 1771 (Patron 1769–1826), by Nathaniel Dauce-Holland.

An early depiction of the Felsted Congregational Church and its adjacent manse.

teach: his early years of plenty had turned, yet again, to a time of dearth. To add to the School's sum of potential woes, the Government had, in 1816, instituted (and this would not be the last time such interference would be felt) an inquiry into the affairs of those 'Charities in England for the Education of the Poor'. Lord Brougham's Commission, while specifically required by an Amending Act passed in 1819 to ignore the six 'Great Schools', as well as foundations unconnected with the Church of England, began to peer disconcertingly closely into the conduct of the financial affairs of the ancient endowed schools and almshouses. An establishment such as Felsted School, of considerable prominence still, was certain to draw the Charity Commissioners' attentions, especially since the Patron, the Earl of Winchilsea, was a prominent Tory grandee and Lord Lieutenant of the County of Rutland; the Whig-led Commissioners had such individuals firmly in their reforming sights.

As matters turned out, Winchilsea was never troubled by the Commissioners, whose gaze did not fall directly on his patch. His death in 1826 released him from any culpability or risk of blame. His titles went to a cousin, George Finch-Hatton of Eastwell Park in Kent; the Patronage of Felsted School, for the first time in its history, passed to a commoner, Winchilsea's illegitimate son, also George. This George Finch took up residence in his father's former home, Burley-on-the-Hill, near Uppingham in Rutland, and proceeded to take in hand the School's affairs, showing flair and political acumen in his new responsibilities, in spite of his unprepossessing background and paucity of experience.

The greatest threat to Squire and to Felsted School lay much closer to home, however: there had for a number of years been direct competition for pupils in the village and environs from a strong constituency of Dissenters, whose Congregational Church and associated school had been set up in recent years and had grown significantly in popularity thereafter. The Eastern Counties were fertile tillage for the rising nonconformist sects, and the Church of England and Holy Cross Church in particular had been leaking support as a result. Riche's Foundation was withering, too; in truth, a goodly proportion of the local population would not have been loath to see both institutions go to the wall. The School's continuing reputation for fine scholarship and sound learning could not, in the eyes of its far-flung conservative clientele, outweigh the taint of religious dissent. How ironic that a Foundation whose finest hour had come as a bastion of Puritanism in the seventeenth century should find its nadir in the early nineteenth century by association with a radical movement.

Notwithstanding these local travails, there were other threats gathering their forces on the distant horizon: the mills of the Charity Commission were grinding exceedingly slowly, but the time of reckoning seemed inevitably to be moving closer. Finch decided to take the initiative. In 1834, perceiving attack to be the best form of defence, the new Patron invited the Commission to inspect the Felsted Charity's affairs. The denouement would not come until 1836, by which time Squire's reign had reached its end and a new Master had been appointed. At this point, Squire decided to jump ship: he had presided in the latter half of his term in office over a catastrophic fall in numbers, having failed to address any of the problems of competition posed by the Congregationalist cuckoo in the Felsted nest. The grammar school age was to all extents and purposes moribund; the future of the nation's education would have to be utilitarian and up-to-date.

THE PATRONS OF THE FREE GRAMMAR SCHOOL (1564–1851)

The Riche family patronage (1564–1686)

The Founder's will vested full responsibility for the governance of his school and almshouses in his heirs and successors. In effect, this required only occasional bouts of action on the nominated Patron's behalf, since day-to-day matters were dealt with by a committee made up of the Master, the Felsted Vicar and the churchwardens of the parish church, Holy Cross. The chief duty of concern to the Patron was to oversee the appointment of suitable Schoolmasters and Ushers when a vacancy should arise.

After his death, Lord Riche's family continued to direct the affairs of the Foundation for the next 120 years, a good deal longer than most personal patronage periods for similar Tudor establishments.

1564–7	Richard, 1st Baron Riche; the Founder
1567–81	Robert (I), 2nd Baron Riche (surviving son of Richard, Lord Riche)
1581–1619	Robert (II), 3rd Baron Riche and 1st Earl of Warwick (son of Robert I)
1619–58	Robert (III), 4th Baron Riche and 2nd Earl of Warwick (son of Robert II)
1658–9	Robert (IV), 5th Baron Riche and 3rd Earl of Warwick (son of Robert III)
1659–73	Charles, 6th Baron Riche and 4th Earl of Warwick (brother of Robert IV)
1673–86	After Charles's death, his widow, Mary, Countess of Warwick, assumed the role of Patron until her demise in 1678. Thereafter, the issue of the succession became a matter for the Court of Chancery.

The Earls of Nottingham and Winchilsea assume the patronage

After 1686, the responsibilities were transferred to the Earls of Nottingham and Winchilsea, as a consequence of the marriage of Lady Essex Riche to George Finch. The apportioning of the extensive and complex Warwick estates and holdings between the three surviving daughters of Robert Riche II and the three daughters of Robert Riche IV took the best part of another eight years to settle. Eventually, the house at Leez, along with the Felsted patronage and a good deal more besides, fell to the youngest of them all, Lady Essex Riche. She had married the second Earl of Nottingham in 1674, but her death in 1684 meant that after the settlement of the protracted case her properties passed to the Finch family of Burley-on-the-Hill in Rutland. Henceforth, the Patrons would be contemplating their responsibilities in rural Essex from a considerable geographical distance, not to say remoteness of personal engagement in the affairs of Felsted School and almshouses.

1686–1730	Daniel Finch (I), 2nd Earl of Nottingham (widower of Lady Essex Riche); later 7th Earl of Winchilsea
1730–69	Daniel Finch (II), 8th Earl of Winchilsea and 3rd Earl of Nottingham (son of Daniel I)
1769–1826	George Finch (I), 9th Earl of Winchilsea and 4th Earl of Nottingham (nephew of Daniel I) (a minor until 1773; Lady Charlotte Finch acted proxy)
1826–51	George Finch (II) (illegitimate son of George Finch I)
1851	'Felstead [sic] Charities Act' establishes Board of Trustees

Top: Statue of Robert, 3rd Baron Riche from the Riche monument in Holy Cross Church, Felsted; (middle) portrait of Robert, 5th Baron Riche, 3rd Earl of Warwick by John Greenhill; (bottom) portrait of Lady Charlotte Finch (née Fermor) by John Robinson.

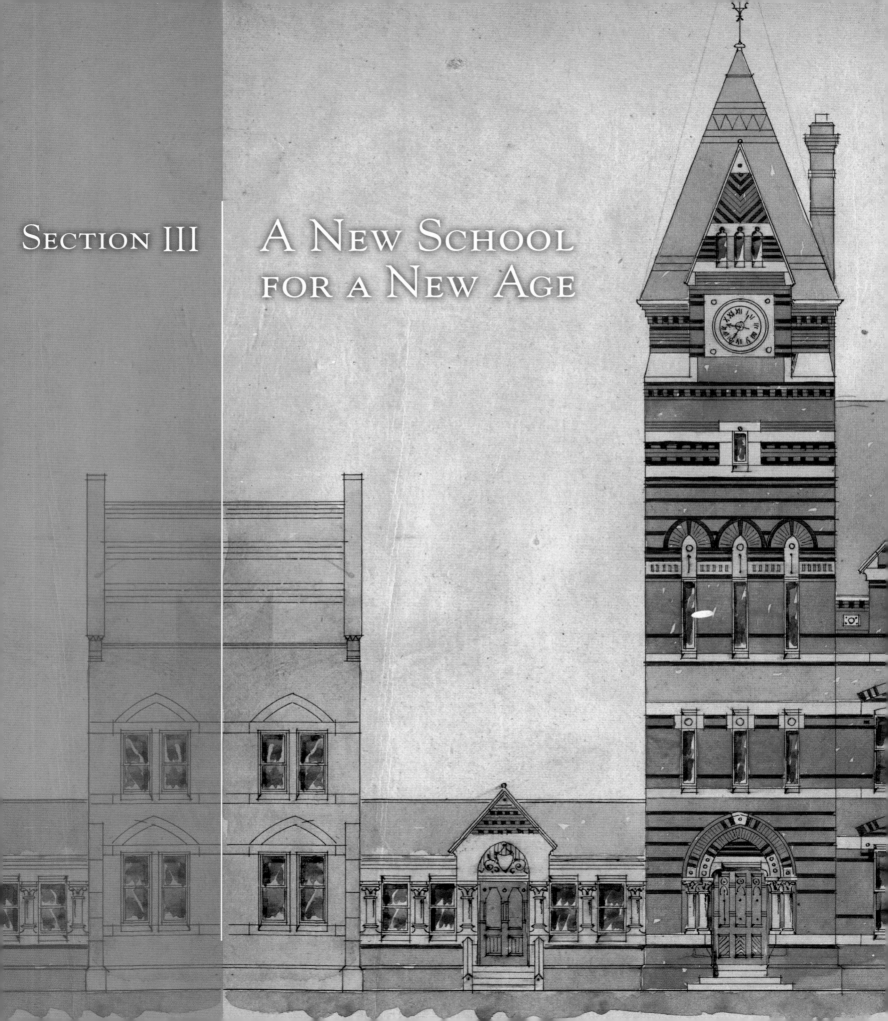

Section III A New School for a New Age

7 | REFORM AND RENEWAL 1835–90

Upon arrival at Felsted, the new incumbent would find an empty Schoolroom: Squire's last boy had been removed some time before his Master saw fit to resign his sinecure at Felsted and take up a lucrative parish living at Ashen in Suffolk. To put the gravity of the task in perspective, we must consider the case of Rugby School, a foundation but three years younger than Felsted, and whose history had followed a similar graph of highs and lows. By 1828, when the great reforming headmaster, Thomas Arnold, was appointed, Rugby too was in the doldrums, comparatively speaking. An urban establishment, it had long had the benefit of trunk road communications and a good academic record, yet Arnold found there all the vices and corruption that were blighting so many of the better supported 'great schools' like Eton and Harrow. Rugby School was by no means moribund (though numbers had been falling steadily since the turn of the century), but it was assuredly sick at heart. Arnold was without doubt a far greater scholar and educationalist than was Thomas Surridge, upon whom Finch had settled his choice as Squire's successor, though essentially their tasks were one and the same: to save their school and in so doing assure the survival of the classical tradition in English education. It will therefore come as little surprise to know that in Arnold's case nominal success was quickly achieved; with Surridge the Fates would deal less kindly.

THOMAS SURRIDGE (1835–50)

Desperate measures are often the only solution to desperate situations; in his first appointment to the Felsted Mastership and Chaplaincy, George Finch would appear to have thrown caution to the winds. In the person of Revd Thomas Surridge, the Patron had found a most extraordinary individual, and one likely to prove either the salvation or, more probably, the final extinction of the School. Surridge seems to have presented himself as an able scholar, having risen by dint of his own intellectual worth from the most humble of beginnings in the Irish skilled labouring class. Educated at Trinity College, Dublin, he won a scholarship and graduated successfully in 1810, taking holy orders the same year. He embarked on a 23-year career in the Royal Navy, and was appointed chaplain to a succession of fighting ships, though generally serving his time in shore establishments in Portsmouth and Valetta, Malta. Upon leaving the Navy, Surridge acquired two law degrees from his old university, by purchase rather than study, if the evidence does not mislead. Thus effectively, if unethically, equipped for an academic career, he set about finding employment as a schoolmaster. Patron Finch may well have been seduced by the candidate's breezy bonhomie and military swagger, hoping no doubt that a successful self-publicist might turn the fortunes of the School around.

Initially, all seemed to bode well for the new era: Surridge set about advertising for pupils in a businesslike and enthusiastic fashion, intending to begin classes in the autumn of 1835. The local response was indeed encouraging. However, the slow but inexorable march of the legal process was threatening to lay a crushing boot upon the affairs of the 'heirs and successors temporal and spiritual' of Richard, Baron Riche of Leez.

The Charity Commission's report came as an unwelcome intrusion at the worst possible tide in the affairs of Felsted School. In essence, the Commissioners wished to know why a foundation that drew a considerable income from its endowments had in living memory and beyond educated but a handful of the 'ffree scholars' designated in the Foundation Deed as the projected recipients of the charitable funding provided for them by ancient statute. There could be no glib response then, as in our own times, to so fundamental an enquiry: what had become of Lord Riche's pious intentions for his 'ffree schole at ffelsted fforever', which for so long had catered almost exclusively for fee-paying boarders of the 'middling sort'? Patron and Master were hard put to rebut the implied criticism, and wisely chose to attempt a subtle reinterpretation of their statutory obligations: henceforth the School would accept free scholars of appropriate academic promise for tuition in modern subjects as well as Latin and Greek. It was hoped that now the School could recruit more freely from the Essex-born poor, thus fulfilling the Founder's will and also shaking off the unwelcome attentions of the Commissioners. New advertisements appeared in the leading Essex newspapers in July 1839; in the following December, Surridge wrote a lengthy epistle, which he circulated to all the clergy and gentry he could identify, setting out the new style of education he was proposing for the School and calling upon them to nominate candidates for admission as free scholars under the new arrangements. A flavour of Surridge's orotund style and pseudo-messianic notion of the School's future may be gleaned from the following extract: 'The School-Room having lately undergone a thorough repair, is now comfortably, commodiously and handsomely fitted up, and ready for the reception of Pupils, for whom every measure, within our power, calculated to encourage their pursuit of the higher order of Literature, or to fit them for the active and respectable walks of life, will be studiously adopted.' Where Arnold was steadily renewing the vigour of Rugby's classics tradition, Surridge was fighting a largely unsuccessful battle to fill his country schoolroom with local boys, by offering the writing of English and elementary mathematics. Thomas Carlyle, writing in 1845, speaks of 'Felsted in Essex, where there is still a kind of School or free-School, which was of more note in [Oliver Cromwell's] days than now.'

Surridge was no diplomat either. With a failing school in his charge, he picked a fight with the Vicar over the gallery at the west end, which for a great many years had accommodated very few pupils. In short, the fashion for installing organs in churches had reached Holy Cross, and the gallery was the obvious site for such an addition to the furnishings. Surridge drove a hard bargain over the precise amount of space he would be prepared to cede for the organ's installation. He fought with his Ushers, too: in 1842, he required Revd James Crocker to be pensioned off as 'not competent to perform his duties from indisposition'; then, almost immediately, Surridge

Thomas Carlyle, by Sir John Everett Millais.

petitioned the Patron for the dismissal of the replacement Usher, Revd R.K. Kirby, the charge this time being that he 'persistently disobeyed orders'. In fact, Surridge had tried to lay the blame at Kirby's door for his own failure to attract any significant numbers of new pupils to the School, and this was the only way he could extricate himself from the consequences of his prevarications.

All the while, a lengthy wrangle was trickling its way through the notoriously time-sapping Court of Chancery (so tellingly characterised in Dickens's *Bleak House* in the interminable ramblings of the Jarndyce and Jarndyce case). The more recondite aspects of the Foundation's funding had been audited and found wanting by the Charity Commission; it was now in the province of the lawyers to sort out a new

Architectural details: School House (above), Dutch Block (right) and Grignon Hall (far right).

scheme for the proper execution of the Foundation Deeds. In particular, it was of the utmost priority to ensure that all rents and monies due to the Foundation were accurately assessed and efficiently collected; many past years of inefficiency and peculation, not to say downright abuse of the funds, must be ended, so it had been decreed.

In the first place, Surridge had to go. He accepted a severance package that included a substantial £1,000 lump sum, and an annual pension of £250; he was probably rather better paid once he had retired than while he was employed by the Foundation. In terms of pupil numbers, his early optimism and energy had proved but vain posturing; his legacy exactly matched that of his predecessor: not one boy's name remained upon the Felsted School roll.

By mid-year of 1850, Revd Surridge had departed, leaving Felsted School in no better state than he had found it upon arrival 15 years before. Despite his innovative attempts to rebrand the education on offer, the early successes of his campaign were never consolidated, and the Schoolroom stood cavernous and silent once more.

Elsewhere, however, a significant revolution was burgeoning in the world of English education, which Felsted must be part of or fade from view once and for all. The Endowed Schools Act of 1840 had come as something of a boon to the ancient grammar foundations, hidebound theretofore by the statutes of their founders and compelled to deliver the classical curriculum in a world increasingly oriented away from the dead languages and towards the practical skills set that was becoming ever more important in the fast developing Industrial Age. Thomas Arnold at Rugby School had broadened the curriculum to include modern subjects such as English and mathematics, and reformed the ethos of the boarding side of his school. Out went the antiquated and largely unsupervised dame lodgings; in came housemasters and a system of prefects to moderate and control the worst excesses of mob rule endemic among adolescent boys left to their own devices. Rugby's popularity and renown was revived almost overnight. New ranges of impressive buildings by Hakewill and Butterfield were commissioned, and numbers of boys rocketed – unmistakeable evidence that the right man

Far left: *Thomas Arnold* by Thomas Philips, 1839 and (right) *Nathaniel Woodard*.

and the right ideas could transform the fortunes of an ancient foundation and forge a new school for the dawning Victorian Age. Perhaps Felsted too might find a way to follow this far-sighted and radical lead?

A further significant development in the wider context of educational reform was the exponential growth of the wealthier echelons of the new middle class; business, trade and manufacturing industries had brought great rewards to those bold enough to take the risks of entrepreneurial gambles. There was a rapidly expanding clientele, hungry for the sort of education that would cement their claims to respectability and hasten the achievement of parity of esteem with the upper classes, whose hegemony had been long sustained by the exclusivity of their educational experience in the hallowed halls of a handful of so-called 'public' schools. Besides, there was a British Empire in the making, which would require a force of suitably prepared officials to take on the responsibilities of colonial government in the newly acquired territories. The second half of the nineteenth century would see the rapid expansion of the boarding public school as the breeding ground for this new cadre of Englishman. By the

mid-1860s, the proprietary schools, founded by subscription or direct investment by business consortia, were making their name in the educational firmament: Cheltenham (1841), Marlborough (1843), Brighton (1845), Lancing (1848), Wellington (1859), Clifton and Haileybury (1862), Cranleigh and Malvern (1865) are the best known of this new breed, which built upon the old established mintmark, but adapted and innovated, too. Ancient foundations also found the confidence to build and adapt: Repton, Uppingham, Oundle and Sedbergh were soon striving to compete for pupils and parity of esteem. There was an unprecedented boom in building works in schools throughout the land, and the Gothic Revival style was everywhere to be seen. The expanding railway network was facilitating travel to and from the far-flung locations. A rural school could compete on equal terms with its urban rivals, so isolation of situation could be promoted as a positive asset; Canon Woodard, whose three foundations in Sussex were the first of many, made a virtue of the remote sites he chose for Lancing, Hurstpierpoint and Ardingly Colleges. Felsted was certainly a far-flung outpost; but the railway was coming …

The cricket XI of 1867.

ALBERT H. WRATISLAW (1850–5)

In seeking to repair the damage left in the wake of Surridge's ignominious retreat from his post, Patron Finch chose Revd Albert Henry Wratislaw, at the time of his appointment Fellow and Tutor of Christ's College, Cambridge. Felsted School might well be empty of pupils, but its former glory could still command attention in the highest academic circles, even then.

Wratislaw was a product of Rugby School, and he had been there in the Arnold era, so the new wine of the modern educational theory and practice was surely in his blood. A Cambridge polymath, Wratislaw had achieved a top First in the Classical Tripos, before devoting his time to the study of Slavonic languages, in which he was to become one of the experts of the age. During the two years that elapsed between his appointment to the Mastership at Felsted and his

inauguration into the post, Wratislaw continued to teach the undergraduates at Christ's; meanwhile the Felstead Charities Act was finally promulgated in Parliament and passed into law in August 1851.

After 15 years of stagnation in Chancery, the new scheme for the Felsted Foundation could be put into effect. In brief, the Act provided for a radical change in the governance of the School and associated charitable foundations. After the best part of three centuries, the Patronage was abolished; a Board of Trustees, to comprise 11 members, was set up, and responsibility for the Foundation's financial affairs vested in the Trustees. At the same time, the endowment income was consolidated, and the long outmoded herring dole commuted into cash payments, to be distributed to the needy parishioners of Felsted and Waltham as before. Once new purpose-built accommodation (to include a new School Hall and boarding house) could be provided for the reconstituted School, the original Schoolroom would be sold. Wratislaw's reign could now start in a climate of optimism: it would not be long before Felsted should find its place restored in the front rank of modern public schools.

Wratislaw had been appointed Chaplain and Schoolmaster; as he took up residence in Felsted House on the Chelmsford Road, he was henceforth to be styled Head Master of Felsted School, with a Second Master, Revd J.H. Backhouse of Manchester Grammar School and Brasenose College, to assist him. As numbers grew steadily, an Usher, now titled Third Master, was soon appointed. The new Scheme allowed for a wider-ranging curriculum, which soon proved to be to the liking of the public, who were won back to the Felsted fold by the promise of the Trustees to 'give the boys a sound moral, religious and useful education.'

But there were disappointments to be faced: the appeal of Felsted, without the attractive premises envisaged by the lofty but unrealistic plans first mooted, was of limited scope, and parents were initially inclined to view the School as a staging post towards larger and more securely established public schools. In short, there being no system of preparatory schools yet in existence, it was expedient for parents to seek a sound start for their sons in a local school of lesser standing. Wratislaw must have found this situation both galling and frustrating, to say the least, given his stellar academic qualifications, his personal ambition and the promises he had counted upon of a swift expansion of his kingdom. Nevertheless, he set his mind to the matters in hand: he instituted regular form orders, appointed prefects and encouraged athletic sports (cricket and boxing in particular) and military drill, despite having few pupils older than 13 years of age. He was importing all that he had found to be the best of Rugby's ethos and practice: the first cricket match was played against the village, and later a school match versus Brentwood resulted in a crushing victory; an athletics competition was also inaugurated.

But progress towards fulfilling the early hopes of achieving a status and style commensurate with the appellation 'public school' was very slow indeed. The Trustees proved unwilling to commit themselves to the considerable financial risks entailed in the building of a new School House, and Wratislaw lost patience. There were now upwards of 70 boys in his charge, most of them boarders, and there was no room for increasing numbers. Informal arrangements, such as had been acceptable in the seventeenth and eighteenth centuries, could not be entertained in the nineteenth. Wratislaw saw himself at the head of a school of 150, and he could see no credible signs that the Trustees were contemplating the expansion he had been promised. So in October 1855, he resigned, having accepted the headship at Bury St Edmunds Grammar School, an ancient foundation like Felsted, but with a plentiful supply of local boys eager for the knowledge he could impart. He took a number of his Felsted pupils with him, too, further emphasising to the Trustees the debilitating consequences for the School's fortunes occasioned by their pusillanimous delay. They appear to have resolved to learn from their mistakes, however, and acted decisively to recover the lost ground. They appointed a locum tenens Sixth-Form Master, in the shape of Revd J.E. Tweed, a former Chaplain of Christ Church, Oxford, and made Backhouse interim Head Master, pending a satisfactory outcome to their precipitate search for a permanent replacement.

Wratislaw can fairly be said to have put in train the revival of Felsted School, but it would fall to his successor, Revd W.S. Grignon, to consolidate the precarious position the inexperienced and overcautious Trustees were to bequeath to him.

William S. Grignon (1856–75)

Revd William Stanford Grignon came to Felsted in January 1856. A Scholar of Trinity College, Cambridge, Grignon had ample academic achievement to back up his application for the post at Felsted. He had remained at Cambridge after graduation in 1846, teaching undergraduates on an informal basis in Trinity, and hoping to gain the fellowship he had narrowly missed being awarded directly after his final Tripos examination. He then took up an assistant master's appointment at one of the emerging proprietary schools, Brighton College, from whence he proceeded to accept the headmastership of the Sheffield Collegiate School, an establishment of marginally greater antiquity, but of equal thrusting ambition in the prevailing atmosphere of expansion and experimentation in secondary education.

Grignon had all the attributes the Trustees were hoping to attract to the Head Mastership – apart from physical stature, it would seem, for he stood no taller than five foot

Revd W. S. Grignon.

School House, c.1867.

four inches. What he lacked in height, he certainly made up for in personal dynamism and ebullience; he stormed into his duties like a diminutive, electrically charged cyclone. The Trustees were bullyragged into getting the building work started and the day-to-day finances overhauled. Chancellor, son of the Chelmsford architect who had transformed Ingram's Close into the New School House, was engaged to turn that building into the 'Old' School House by constructing a new School House complex on land acquired by the Trustees for the purpose. A boarding house, to be supervised by the Second Master, Revd Backhouse, was completed by August 1860, at a cost of £1,653; and the Head Master's new residence (many years later to be named Stephenson's) was ready for occupation by Grignon and his family by the end of the same year. Ingram's remained for the time being to accommodate further boarders, as numbers were again rising steadily from the 67 boys Grignon had faced on his first morning in the Schoolroom in the centre of the village.

The distance between Head Master and Second Master was reduced by the construction, first, of a new school hall with a covered playground beneath (completed in 1863); and then, after three years' work, the splendid School House was ready for occupation, thus completing the iconic range we know today. In common with much of the scholastic accommodation that was coming into being on campuses all over the country, Chancellor had taken for his template the hostel system. This design, adopted by Woodard in his foundations, is probably best demonstrated in the Quad at Haileybury, where the original Imperial Service College had been instituted. In brief, a range of buildings of at least three storeys' height, sometimes placed around a closed quadrangle, is constructed: the ground floor is given over to classrooms, common rooms, kitchens and dining areas; while sleeping quarters for staff members, pupil dormitories and communal washing facilities are arranged on the floors above.

'The Felsted Flyer' at the station.

Grignon now had the space to expand his numbers considerably, something the ailing finances of the School badly needed, for by the time of the opening of the New School House and the sale of the Old Schoolroom, Grignon had been compelled by dire necessity to take over the duties of House Steward (Bursar in today's nomenclature), the Trustees having reproached Grignon himself for the inadequacies of the person they had appointed for the task. It should come as no surprise to discover that the Head Master was an accomplished accountant; he managed the School's expenditure to good effect, and turned a worrying loss into a healthy profit in the first year of his stewardship. Certainly, Grignon was a tireless worker for the School's best interests; he understood that to compete with the best, you had to see yourself as a worthy rival – this Grignon adopted as his mantra. He introduced military training and founded a Volunteer Corps, which joined forces with other such corps in the locality, for field days and drilling and shooting competitions. He encouraged sports matches against local clubs, London hospitals and Cambridge colleges, and he strove hard to arrange fixtures with other schools, knowing the value of such contacts with those you are striving to emulate.

In February 1869, the branch railway line linking Witham on the Great Eastern Railway's Norwich line to Bishop's Stortford station on the main Cambridge line was opened to passenger traffic: Felsted village had its station and Felsted School could now draw its clientele from far and wide.

By the time the Taunton Commission was reporting, in 1869, upon the findings of its investigations into the state of the older endowed schools countrywide, Grignon was well advanced along the road to forging anew the reputation of Felsted. So much so that he was among the leading headmasters to be invited by Edward Thring of Uppingham to discuss the formation of a defensive association, to be known as the School Society and Annual Conference, in a bid to counter the Commission's importunate activities, which had as its *raison d'être* an inquiry into the feasibility of the state incorporating all such schools into a consolidated secondary education provision. Thring's invitation was accepted by a dozen heads, including Grignon, who met at Uppingham in 1869, to debate their response to the threat they and their schools might face. Those present deemed the meeting worthwhile and further annual meetings were held thereafter, as the Headmasters' Conference (HMC) came into being.

to embrace the benefits on offer. Rugby football had gone, for the time being, and (in common with many other schools at that time) a hybrid own-brand of team football (with resemblances to the Eton Field game played to this day) was developed. Matches against other schools could not be entertained until codified rules had been set down, and that time was a decade and more in the future. But cricket was thriving, and Grignon himself played in the XI, when the opponents were the adult teams put out by the clubs of local towns and villages. For boys not particularly athletic or competitive there were the time-honoured country pursuits of their forebears to fall back upon: rambling, rabbit-snaring, bird-nesting and fishing. The mill pool swimming place on the Chelmer River was as well frequented as it had ever been. Old Felstedian G.G. Coulton, who attended the School in Grignon's time, writes fondly in his autobiography that 'Felsted gave us, as compared with other schools of the same class, a sort of healthy freedom.'

Grignon allowed theatricals to be performed on special occasions, especially in the week approaching the Christmas

Grignon was no doubt cheered and inspired by his inclusion in the august band of headmasters of the resurgent endowed grammar schools; his wholehearted encouragement of the boys' all-round education speaks of a disciple of the fast-growing *mens sana in corpore sano* creed sweeping the boarding school world. 'Muscular Christianity' was Thomas Arnold's legacy, and Felsted was as keen as any youthful community

A selection of *The Felstedian* magazine covers (above); the first edition, on left, appeared in 1872 and the Chapel *c.*1910 (right).

recess, and there was a well-supported tradition of choral music, though instrumental music was yet to emerge as a recognised activity. The Volunteer Corps had acquired a fife and drum band by the early 1870s, too. In 1872, Grignon sanctioned the institution of a School newspaper, and *The Felstedian* was born the following year. And all the while, the Head Master was expanding his fiefdom, in buildings and territory, such that Felsted had, by the end of 1873, all the physical attributes of a well-established public school. Grignon's last great project was the provision of the School's own place of worship.

The pupil numbers had by 1870 far exceeded the available benches in the Holy Cross gallery and there was no room to accommodate the boys in the main body of the nave. After an unsatisfactory period during which Grignon held his services in the new School Hall, he prevailed upon the Trustees to sanction the building of a chapel, provided that a suitable sum of money could be raised by subscription to fund the project. Grignon had a staunch ally in Revd Rowe, who showed tireless energy in rounding up contributions from parents and other benefactors. By February 1872 the work could begin: the plans, again by Chancellor, were realised by contractor James Brown, and the new building was ready for consecration on Founder's Day, 1873. The design was simple and the interior originally furnished in semi-collegiate style, with inward-facing pews for the Masters, who could the better supervise the forward-facing boys' behaviour during services. A fine Henry Willis organ was installed a few months later, thus completing the project with a characteristic Grignon flourish.

In setting down the catalogue of Grignon's contribution to the renaissance of the Renaissance foundation he had come to save, we should remember that, like all his predecessors to date and a fair number of his successors, the Head Master's first duty was to teach the Sixth Form: his academic oversight of the top 20 to 30 scholars in the School would have kept him in the Schoolroom for a good proportion of the working week, leaving only the out-of-class hours free for administrative and pastoral concerns. He was also expected to fulfil the responsibilities of School Chaplain, and was still acting as Bursar and overseer of the construction projects undertaken throughout his period at the helm. It cannot, therefore, be wondered at that he grew deeply incensed at the Trustees'

The Chapel organ today.

reluctance to give their Head Master their backing when a major row developed between Grignon and his Sixth-Form assistant, Revd H.C.P. Jones. The latter fulminated a complaint to the Trustees that Grignon had passed him over for a deserved promotion (and, one assumes, a pay rise), and canvassed support among the other Assistant Masters. Such insubordination should have been swiftly crushed by the summary dismissal of the unruly faction; in the event, the Trustees demurred, and a full-blown crisis resulted.

Sensing that Grignon's position was weakening, Jones pressed his advantage: he had the texts of his acrimonious exchange of letters with the Head Master printed and passed copies to all the Trustees, at least one of whom, Archdeacon Ady, supported the complainant. In the event, the Trustees had to come down for the Head Master, and Jones was dismissed. Three more Masters resigned in sympathy, and Grignon's authority was for the time being restored, but his resentment of the Trustees' bad faith led him to raise the stakes considerably. He resigned the House stewardship forthwith, and adopted an aloof disregard for the Trustees, communicating only in writing and as infrequently as possible. A.C. Veley, Clerk to the Board of Trustees, took on the role, though the practical duties of the post were delegated to the House Matron, Mrs Groome. Grignon further isolated himself by informing the parents that he would no longer deal with financial or domestic matters, which, he went on to stress, should be addressed to Veley or Mrs Groome directly. Having thus declared a covert war on his Trustees, Grignon unwisely contrived to hand the initiative to his enemies by publishing his grievances against them in an open letter to the *Chelmsford Chronicle*. Such public insubordination could not be tolerated: Veley, in particular, set about collecting the requisite ammunition with which to assail the recalcitrant and mutinous Head Master.

The accounts were scrutinised and discrepancies unearthed: to Grignon's detriment, it was demonstrated that expenditure was outstripping income, a most damaging flaw in the Head Master's management of the School, so it was alleged. An outbreak of scarlet fever proved the final bone of contention: the Trustees ordered Grignon to turn Backhouse's boarding area into an infirmary, so that boys suffering from the illness could be isolated from their peers in the School House

Revd A. W. Rowe (Master, Housemaster and Acting Head Master 1859–89).

dormitories. Grignon was compelled to suspend the admission of new boys for an indeterminate period, thus reducing numbers in the School and consequently exacerbating the cash flow embarrassment he was keen to allay. His vehement protests went unheeded, as Veley primed his five fellow Trustees against him. At a meeting to which Grignon came expecting to present his case for reversing the Backhouse's decision, he was informed of his dismissal. Revd Rowe was given charge of the School, pending the appointment of a successor, though the Trustees decided to await the promulgation of the new Felsted School Scheme, which had at long last crawled its way towards the statute book.

With Grignon's departure, the final salvoes of the war could be exchanged. Grignon published a lengthy diatribe against the Trustees, who replied in kind. A committee of Old Felstedians led by G.C. Calliphronas, recently elected to a fellowship at Gonville and Caius College, Cambridge, and (separately) a group of parents rallied to Grignon's support. A petition was organised to prevail upon the Trustees to grant a pension, but too much acrimony had been unleashed for there to be any prospect of the Trustees agreeing to such a request. In the end, Grignon left with a handsome testimonial fund of some £400, levied by his supporters, and the Trustees set about the delicate task of repairing the damage to their reputation and that of Felsted School, whose name had been dragged through the mud by the dispute, even to the extent of a vituperative exchange of questions in the Chamber of the House of Lords. The last word on the matter was uttered by Lord Campbell, who hoped that the Government would persuade the Charity Commissioners 'to frame a different class of schemes and prevent such a scandal as the Felstead case from occurring in the future'.

So Grignon's 20 years of tireless striving came to an ignominious and acrimonious conclusion; but his legacy of significant achievement and progress for the School is undeniable. Nevertheless, it is fair to say that by 1876 Felsted might well have been further advanced along the road to full acceptance among the best public schools of the later Victorian period had Grignon been a great, rather than a merely successful Head Master. It would appear that he lacked the truly incisive flair for leadership and vision that might have served Felsted even better: he could not delegate

and he could not rise above the petty personal grudges that can plague the insular and claustrophobic environment of a country boarding community. There is no doubt that he was popular with his boys, and that in return he gave himself over to their welfare unstintingly; it was in his working relationships with the Trustees and the staff of the School that his failings were most acutely damaging to his cause. Nevertheless, Felsted School was on the map again, and much of what Grignon had bequeathed would serve his successors well as the century neared its close.

Delaval S. Ingram (1876–90)

In Revd Delaval Shafto Ingram, the Trustees found a safe pair of hands, something the School badly needed after the upheavals of the Grignon fiasco. Revd Rowe had held the School together manfully, but the fallout had been severe. Boys had been removed in protest at Grignon's treatment, and several fellow heads had demonstrated their solidarity with their wronged colleague in the national newspapers. Ingram had to act swiftly to repair the damage to the good name of the School. Despite all his efforts, Grignon had

barely succeeded in broadening the Felsted catchment area (as we might term it today), and for all his promotion of sporting contacts for his boys, the School remained relatively remote and unrecognised by the rivals he had sought to emulate. There was serious work to be done, and Ingram was the man for the job. A strong academic, he had been a pupil at Giggleswick School in North Yorkshire, an establishment very like Felsted in many ways, from whence he had proceeded to St John's College, Cambridge, where he took a First in Classics. Having begun his teaching career as an Assistant Master at Tonbridge (where he married the daughter of Mr Welldon, the Headmaster), he had served at Tiverton Grammar School (now Blundell's School) as Second Master. His background and family circumstances could not have prepared him better for the challenges he would face at Felsted, a school with strong similarities to those he had himself experienced before his arrival. His own personal enthusiasm for sports and community activities was seen to good effect from the first day he stepped foot on Felsted territory. He was a vigorous 36-year-old, and keen to show his 'lads' that they had a Head Master to be reckoned with: he

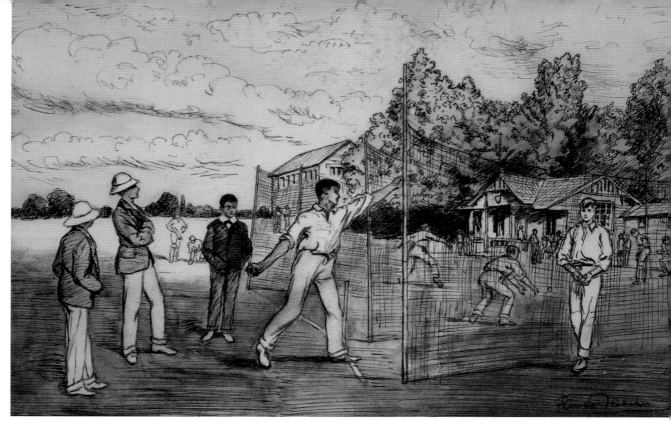

School's eyes to the wider community, and vice versa. It
was also a great fillip for Ingram to have the new Scheme at
long last applied to the School's governance. The Trustees
were abolished and a Board of Governors installed. Where
the proposed Scheme had stalled in the House of Lords in
Grignon's time, it was now signed into law by Queen Victoria
herself, at Balmoral, on 23 October 1876. Responsibility for
dealing with the many similar proposals for endowed schools
across the country having been taken over by a Committee of
the Privy Council, and there being no dissenting voices raised
against the Felsted Scheme, it was sent for royal assent, and
that was that.

Once the fractious relationships within the School's
management structures, so damaging to the latter years of
Grignon's reign, had been ironed out, by the new Scheme
provisions and by careful and thoughtful negotiations between
Head Master and Governors, Ingram could get on with his
work. By 1877, he had reformed the school year to comprise
three terms, and started football and shooting matches
against other schools. In 1879 a new cricket pavilion was
built (now the Chaplaincy Centre), and from 1880 onwards
there were lawn tennis fixtures with local clubs, too. In 1883,
a gymnasium was built (now the Hunt Theatre), and boxing
and fencing began at the School thereafter. The ad hoc fives
court, established in Grignon's time, was refurbished and
covered in, with a gallery for spectators added. Instruction
for the physical training drills and gymnastic exercises, as
well as coaching for the shooting team, was provided by the

knew how to win the boys' respect, but he also understood the
value of charisma in a headmaster's day-to-day relations with
staff and students alike.

Among Ingram's early innovations were to institute an
annual Speech Day; the first was held on 27 June 1876, his
first Summer Term. This and his decision to hold confirmation
services in the Chapel brought parents and relatives of the
boys into the School: a significant step towards opening the

employment of an ex-Rifle Brigade Sergeant named Green. His successor, Sgt Dimmock, began senior and junior boxing competitions, for which trophies were awarded.

Lest it be thought that Ingram had eyes for the sporting bloods alone, it should be added that he was instrumental in setting up the School's first contacts with London's Docklands slums, by sanctioning the subscription fund which led some years later to the building of the Ascension Church and the establishment of the School Mission, which endures to this day. Ingram was no slouch when it came to encouraging the academic prowess of his lads: he made sure that the newly instituted Oxford and Cambridge Schools Examination Board were invited to examine the Felsted boys on a regular basis; where beforehand there had been only sporadic visits by visiting dons, there was now a formalised inspection of the School's work, a development that brought kudos to the School. The building in 1879 of a separate Infirmary (now Gepp's House) enabled Backhouse's (which had served as the 'San' since the scarlet fever outbreak in 1873/4) to revert to its former purpose as boarding accommodation, and Ingram decreed that the Sixth Form should be housed there, an innovation replicated to a certain degree more than a century later by the major reorganisation of the House structure in 2008, which reserved Windsor's House for the Upper Sixth boarding boys in the School. But there was no House system in Ingram's day: a bachelor Master might have oversight of four or five dormitories at any one time, and heavy reliance was vested in the prefects to maintain good order.

Ingram addressed himself to the matter of broadening the curriculum, too: he instituted an alternative programme, to include German and Modern History, to run parallel to the Classical Forms in the Middle and Upper School; he appointed G.H. Williams to take charge of this new Modern side. Revd W.F. Evans, of Jesus College, Oxford, joined the teaching staff as the first specialist Science Master. The School's Natural Scientific Society had already come into being in 1877, founded by the veteran schoolmaster, Revd Rowe, and supported by the Governors, who included the Cavendish Professor of Physics at Cambridge, Lord Rayleigh. Of comparable establishments, perhaps Oundle alone, under Sanderson, some 20 years later, might claim to be as well advanced in the promotion of the sciences as a valid branch of the secondary school curriculum,

by which time a fully functioning Science Block had seen the light of day at Felsted School.

By the time Ingram resigned to take up a parson's living at Great Oakley, aged just 50 years, the tide of successes was beginning to ebb at his School. Numbers were dwindling steadily, as the new vogue for preparatory schools was emerging, and younger boys no longer came to Felsted for the duration of their schooling. Despite its strong academic tradition, its wide-ranging extra-curricular programme and growing reputation as a cradle of doughty sportsmen, Felsted had yet to kindle any lasting favour with the boarding school-frequenting classes beyond the confines of Essex and Suffolk. Nor could the School call upon reserves of local day boys to fill up the roll: Felsted had outgrown its humble grammar school antecedents, but had yet to reach full fledging in the world of the Victorian public school.

Boys in House Room at Windsor's by Hanslip Fletcher, *c.*1913.

8 | A Place at the Top Table 1890–1933

The educational map of Britain had changed irrevocably by 1890. Forster's Education Act of 1870 had established plans for an integrated state education system that was gaining significant ground, especially in the provision of universal elementary schooling for the wider populace. Perhaps Felsted could tap into this developing reservoir of basic literacy by reviving its ancient precedent as the provider of free grammar school education to the sons of the Essex poor? Certainly, despite the sterling efforts of its last three Head Masters, the School's survival into the next century remained uncertain. Ingram's last eight years had seen numbers fall by nearly half, from a peak of 222 to 121, barely sufficient to guarantee financial viability. The Governors must have despaired to see their School's popularity so vulnerable to the vagaries of fashion and parental whim. As on so many previous occasions, the appointment of a Head Master worthy of the challenge was not a task that could be shirked, nor was there any leeway for error of judgement: once again, it looked likely that Felsted School might join the legion of ancient foundations already lost to history or compelled by straightened circumstances to accept the 'Queen's shilling', as the state's newly established Board of Education sought to add a secondary provision to its growing hegemony.

Herbert A. Dalton (1890–1906)

In the person of Revd Herbert Andrew Dalton, the Governors could not have made a more auspicious appointment; it can safely be asserted that Dalton's stewardship of the fortunes of Felsted School was instrumental in securing the School's place in the foremost rank of English boarding public schools. He was a builder and a reformer, whose personal dynamism was to alter the course of Felsted's recent erratic progress irrevocably for the better. By the time of his departure in 1906, the School's landscape had been substantially changed, and the style, ethos and expectations radically transformed.

Dalton's father, the distinguished cleric Revd C.B. Dalton, had been a Felsted pupil under Squire, and his mother was a sister of Bishop Blomfield, Bishop of Colchester and a Governor of the School. Lest the charge of nepotism be levelled, let it be affirmed at this juncture that the new Head Master's claims for preferment raised him head and shoulders above his rivals: he had been an Open Scholar in Classics and taken a double First at Corpus Christi College, Oxford; had won a Studentship at Christ Church, Oxford; had served as Headmaster of St Edward's School, Oxford; and, most recently, had been Sixth-Form Master (that is, Second Master) at Winchester College. His academic qualifications could not have scintillated more brightly, but it was in his inherent brilliance of vision that Dalton's contribution was seen to best advantage: he knew how the most successful schools worked, and his ambition was to make Felsted one of that elite constellation. He began at once: by the end of his second term in office, he had imported the House system from Winchester, convincing the Governors that the personal oversight afforded by a House Master, allied to the *esprit de corps* engendered by continuity of fellowship and accommodation, would breed loyalty and good behaviour, alongside improved academic diligence. He reorganised the domestic arrangements within School House, separating the duties of Matron and Housekeeper, such that health and catering matters were no longer compromised by confusion. He allocated Backhouse's for the accommodation of the youngest boys, but planned in the longer term to inaugurate a separate preparatory department, once funds became available. A short year after taking up the reins, he had installed electric lighting throughout the School, a truly inspirational and revolutionary innovation.

Felsted School's star was again most conspicuously in the ascendant: by 1893, Dalton had over 240 boys under his sway, double what he had found upon arrival. Later that

same year, he persuaded the Governors to devote funds for the acquisition of the lands of Garnon's (or Garnetts) Farm, which lay within the Mile, and thus the playing fields were increased by some 26 acres. Crucially, too, he brought about the purchase of the fields behind Lawsells, the venerable old dwelling house opposite Ingram's Close; on this site, two years later, would arise the Junior House, the Felsted Preparatory School of our day in embryonic form. We have noted that Dalton was a builder and reformer, and we have seen just how rapidly he had made his mark on the fabric and morale of the School. He saw the need for a larger infirmary and secured the Governors' approval for this project. By 1896, Dalton had overseen the construction of an indoor swimming pool, if not perhaps the very first such an amenity to grace a public school campus, then surely one of a tiny few to remain in operation to this day in its original Victorian edifice.

The Head Master's dramatic early successes in terms of resuscitating the failing pupil numbers brought problems of how the increased population could be satisfactorily accommodated. Finances were still very tightly committed, and capital expenditure seemed out of the question, for the time being. However, Dalton was a canny manager of

men; having cast his spell over the Governing Body, he proceeded to weave his magic elsewhere. His scheme for a new preparatory department would certainly have foundered had the funding been left to the School's own finances, but the Head Master knew a thing or two about private initiatives in this regard: he cajoled C.M. Miller, one of his recently appointed Assistant Masters, to raise the capital for the project, which he duly did – the clinching proviso

Elwyn House, with Queen's Square on left (top) and swimming pool of 1896 (above).

The Junior House, 1911, with F. Jacob (Master 1907–33) seated centre.

being that Miller would run the Junior House as his own fiefdom, while the Governors indemnified him against loss by taking an option to purchase the building at a later date. Dalton's methodology proved very sound indeed: the Junior House opened in January 1895, with 35 boys, including the Backhouse's contingent; by the following Summer Term, when Miller left to start his own preparatory school elsewhere, the full complement of 50 pupils had been achieved. Miller was happy to lease his investment to the Governors, who thus did not have to buy him out for the time being. A similar process was invoked five years later, when further expansion was desired: Revd R.F. Elwyn, Housemaster of 'C' in School House, financed the construction of his own out-House, across the cricket ground from the main buildings, migrating there in 1900 and taking with him a quorum of senior boys to get the new colony going. At the same time, Old School House was closed to pupils, and began a new incarnation as staff accommodation and offices – not the last of many metamorphoses over the long history of Ingram's Close.

Of all Dalton's many considerable legacies, there is one that perhaps towers above the rest for sheer brilliance of vision.

In common with fellow heads throughout the land, Dalton had been wary of the growing desire by central government to muscle in on the successful secondary schools in the private sector, with a view to incorporating as many as possible into a reformed state system. After Forster's Elementary Education Act had come several parliamentary inquiries, which hinted at a takeover bid in the not-too-distant future. Felsted's Head Master went on the defensive: he invited the Oxford and Cambridge Schools Examination Board to inspect his School, and received a glowing report on the work of the pupils. However, there were adverse comments aimed at the fitness of the physical accommodation within which that work was being accomplished. In particular, the provision for the teaching of science was described as inadequate, since practical work was impossible in the constrained environment of traditional classrooms designed for formal instruction by a lecturing 'beak'. Dalton set about acquiring for the School its first purpose-built laboratories. In the Revd Canon H.E. Hulton, Vicar of Great Waltham and a recently appointed Governor, the Head Master found his perfect ally: Hulton gave his blessing and a considerable capital sum (£925, well over half the requisite

The Engineering Workshop by Hanslip Fletcher, *c.*1913.

amount) towards the fulfilment of the project. The oldest laboratories (to the left of the Science Block's main corridor) we know today date from 1899, and Dalton foresaw the vital importance of the sciences in providing at Felsted the *sine qua non* of a rounded education in the new century.

Head Master Dalton had firm ideas about how an establishment such as Felsted School should present its public face, too. He revised the uniform to include top hats and formal suits for Sunday wear, and devoted funding to the Rifle Corps, its Drum and Bugle Band, and to promoting the 'foreign' matches which had started rather tentatively under his predecessor's aegis. Cricket and soccer were well established by 1901, and hockey was being played seriously at the School, too, with matches against clubs and schools keenly anticipated.

The School was assuredly gaining regional attention once more, but Dalton's work was not yet done. The opening of the new Science Block had prompted thoughts for a more

imposing main hall, and dedicated classrooms to replace the cramped and unsatisfactory accommodation in School House and Backhouse's, where teaching rooms doubled up as House common rooms when not in use for teaching. Plans for a splendid 'Big School' were drawn up by the School's architect, Sir Arthur Blomfield, in 1899; an appeal was set up to raise the funding, which was only partially successful, such that the construction of the hall was shelved for the time being, and a smaller building (now called the Dutch Block) was completed.

Inevitably, it was Dalton who instigated the delightful and perhaps unique tradition at Felsted of naming the teaching rooms after notable figures in the School's long history: Founder, Governors and distinguished Masters and Old Felstedians are thus touchingly memorialised to this day.

The Grignon Hall project was continued two years later, with the dedication of the foundation stone on Speech Day 1902. By that date, the Old Felstedian Society had been founded and two editions of the *Alumni Felstedienses*

published (1890 and 1897). Dalton's long-held hopes of providing satisfactory accommodation for the practical skills of Engineering and Carpentry came to fruition with the construction of a large, hangar-like workshop (complete with an industrial-style pulley system to power the many lathes from a centrally generated source) just to the east of the laundry-cum-swimming pool-cum-Science Block site along the Stebbing Road from School House. Felsted's Army Class, in particular, must have found their new abode very much to their taste, after having had to squeeze into a long, narrow shed attached to the rear wall of the Gymnasium (now occupied as 'green rooms' for the Hunt Theatre). As before, the Head Master made good use of the reports and suggestions received from the Board of Education inspectors who visited Felsted in October 1903, to put pressure on the Governors to see the School's physical expansion his way.

In the wider sphere, too, Dalton had his antennae well primed: there had been a growing trend among the leading public schools to set up and maintain missions in deprived inner-city areas in London and the great industrial centres of the Midlands and the North of England. If Harrow, Rugby and Eton could have their community good works formalised in this way, then why not Felsted? Early in his reign, the Head Master had pledged strong support to the first Docklands Missioner, an Old Felstedian named Revd T.H. Gilbert, whose work began in 1891. The School's connections with the parish in Custom House developed steadily over the next dozen years, culminating in the establishment of a new Ascension Church, funded by Old Felstedian subscription, designed by Old Felstedian architect J.E.K. Cutts (1862–5), and consecrated in June

1904. This close relationship endures to this day, of course, as modern-day Felstedians follow in their forebears' footsteps in as worthy a cause as any embraced by their School over the centuries.

In spite of the expansionist vision of the Head Master, all had not been going entirely to plan: the numbers suffered another fall in the early years of the new century, for no clear reason, it would appear. The Governors had appointed Dr E.B. Trow as Bursar, the first such in the School's history, in 1903; henceforth, the finances could be monitored by a competent professional, whose oversight of the purse strings might help the School to weather yet another dip in its fortunes. Part of the problem lay with the Junior House, where the House Master, A.V. Gregoire, had run out of steam: when he resigned his post there were only 24 boys in his care – a shortfall of 50 per cent was a serious failing, and one likely to send unwelcome ripples through the School roll in the coming years.

Once again, the spectre of a falling roll was beginning to cast a shadow over the School's strong recent resurgence; it would, however, fall to Dalton's successor to address the matter: Dalton had accepted the appointment as Headmaster of Harrison College, Barbados, where he felt his wife's failing health might be succoured. Revd H.A. Dalton left the School in the summer of 1906; his legacy is all-pervasive on the campus of Felsted today, and his memorial is to be found in the Chapel pulpit, which displays the arms of his schools and colleges for all to see.

Top right: Revd Herbert A. Dalton, Head Master (1890–1906) and (below) the Chapel pulpit, showing Revd Dalton's coats of arms.

THE DEVELOPMENT OF THE HOUSE SYSTEM AT FELSTED

Though Felsted has never claimed to be one of the elite group of ancient grammar school foundations, it nevertheless has seen periods of national renown, notably in the seventeenth century, when substantial numbers of boarding pupils were taken on by Schoolmasters Holbeach (1627–49) and Glascock (1650–90) for scholastic instruction. These 'foreigners' were generally accommodated by local families, much as had been the practice at Shrewsbury and Westminster, two schools of comparable antiquity. When in 1800, at the instigation of Head Master Carless (1794–1813), substantial extensions were added during renovation works to his accommodation at Ingram's Close, a significant number of boarders could be housed under the Head's own aegis and to his own personal financial advantage.

The burgeoning boom in residential schooling occasioned by the reforms initiated in the early 1840s by Thomas Arnold, Head Master of Rugby, was to prove a great opportunity for Felsted, the pupil numbers having dwindled to such an extent that the school had been closed for several years. Once the requisite parliamentary sanction had been given by the Felsted Charities Act of 1851 for a change to the School's foundation statutes, the way forward was open for the major development in buildings and the expansion of the School's horizons as a regionally important 'public' school. Head Master Grignon (1856-75) can justly be regarded as the second founder of the school; he it was who oversaw the major building scheme that brought School House into being, between 1860 and 1867. Within the imposing structure, provision was made to accommodate well over 300 boys, but in dormitories, not 'houses': the hostel system then being the most cost-efficient organisation for a medium-sized residential institution. Old School House (known then as Rowe's, but now recognised again as Ingram's Close and home to the present Medical Centre) was kept open as an overspill hostel until its closure in 1900. Reports in *The Felstedian* magazines of the period, however, give plenty of evidence that the boys themselves enjoyed the competition of quasi-house match engagements; but such football and cricket matches were of an informal 'pick-up' nature, without ever giving rise to the strong loyalties associated with the House matches of later times.

Upon his appointment in 1890, Head Master Dalton made immediate and radical changes to the organisation of his pupil body: he made provision for the separate accommodation of the youngest boys (under 13 years of age) in Backhouse's (now part of Windsor's) and made plans for a separate Junior House across the Braintree Road (the forerunner of the present Felsted Preparatory School), which opened in 1895. Most crucially, he reorganised the living spaces within the School House into four distinct areas, which became known as A, B, C and D Houses. For the first time in the School House's history, individual Masters were designated as Housemaster to a particular all-ages grouping of pupils, and the system Dalton had observed in operation at Winchester was soon effectively imported to the Felsted scene. In due course, two further out-Houses were added: Elwyn's (E) in 1900 and Ingle's/Follyfield (G) in 1928. After the Second World War, two of the four houses in School House, Gepp's and Stocks's, were moved out to new accommodation elsewhere on the campus; and Deacon's, a seventh boys' house, was opened in 1960. The advent of Sixth-Form girls in 1970 saw the opening of Manor (M), originally in the village itself; Garnetts (N), the second Sixth-Form girls' House, opened in 1984.

Stocks's and Follyfield were converted in the mid-1990s to accommodate girls; in 2008, Mont's and Manor became day Houses. A fifth girls' House, Thorne (T), opened in 2010.

Housemaster Revd R.F. Elwyn with House cup-winning footballers, 1902.

The Common Room, 1922 (above) and the original Grignon Hall of 1902 (right).

Frank Stephenson (1906–33)

In appointing Revd Frank Stephenson to the Headship of Felsted in February 1906, the Governors once again proved their acuity in judging both the man and the task for which he was destined. Stephenson was a fine scholar, as indeed had been all of his predecessors in the post, but he was also a well-rounded and balanced schoolmaster; his previous experience was particularly relevant, since he had served as Sixth-Form Master (that is, senior Classics Master) at Rossall School in Lancashire and Cheltenham College; both were successful examples of the new breed of proprietary public schools that were finding increasing favour with the middle-class clientele at the turn of the twentieth century. Rossall had been founded on the isolated Fylde promontory north of Fleetwood, and the 'hostel' or dormitory system (which Dalton had reformed at Felsted) was in operation for the boarders. Cheltenham, perhaps the leading light of all the new elite, had modelled its organisation on the separate boarding house regimes of the ancient collegiate schools, such as Eton and Winchester. Thus Stephenson came with a working knowledge that he could apply to the 'mixed economy' he found at Felsted, where one out-House, Elwyn's, was already bidding fair to eclipse the

four somewhat arbitrarily formulated 'Houses' accommodated within the confines of the School House buildings.

A product of the City of London School and Christ's College, Cambridge, Frank Stephenson was a man in his youthful prime, aged 34, when he arrived at Felsted. Newly married and full of ambition, Stephenson set about restoring the School's flagging fortunes. He found 216 boys, nearly a quarter of them in the lowest forms, so Dalton's last efforts at recruitment had just about turned the tide of falling numbers, and Stephenson could begin his work with a promising cohort of youngsters to mould. As we shall see, they were to prove an outstanding group of alumni, by all the measures one might apply.

The first problem to be addressed, however, was the question of the Junior House: it was just not paying its way, probably because its precise purpose had not been defined, and its direction had in recent years been left in the care of the School doctor. Stephenson realised early on that for the preparatory department to succeed, it must be staffed with Masters of proven worth, and not simply entrusted to junior men who happened to be married. In a decision of inspirational sagacity, he appointed a rugby international, Frederick Jacob, whom he had known as a colleague on the staff at Cheltenham, to take charge of the Junior House; the transformation was immediate. Jacob saw his role more as a headmaster of a preparatory school; such institutions

were springing up in ever-growing numbers in the years immediately preceding the First World War. Jacob's boys might not necessarily, therefore, see themselves as 'waiting to be old enough to get into Felsted proper'. Jacob inculcated a sense that even youngsters can be given leadership opportunities, and to that end he introduced the Leagues system still in use today at Felsted Preparatory School. The Leagues provided for inter-House challenges such as would be encountered later in their schooling, but on a smaller and more intimate scale. For the first time, the Junior House had its own ethos and integrity, and this would prove crucial in the coming years, as competition for younger and younger pupils became ever fiercer.

Stephenson's other strong instinct was that to compete successfully with the emerging proprietary public schools, as well as with the ancient foundations that had taken up the government's offer to become state-aided, Felsted's academic reputation was in dire need of enhancement. That was not to say that the School did not produce scholars and prizemen at the Universities of Oxford and Cambridge: over the recent decades there had been many. What Stephenson believed, and what he urged upon the Governors to agree, was that offering entrance awards at the outset of a boy's time at Felsted would bring opportunities for publicity which could only enhance the School's name in the wider academic sphere. Stephenson also determined to follow Dalton's lead in broadening

further the curriculum: he instituted a four-stream academic system, which allowed boys after the first year to determine their future schooling by their interests and aptitudes, something that seems to us to be an utterly sound educational principle, but which in Stephenson's time was somewhat groundbreaking. With an Engineering side now in place to complement the Army Class and the Classical and Modern sides already well established, Felsted could now offer a fully rounded programme. Assuredly, the School's breadth of curriculum would enhance its attractiveness in the public-school marketplace.

Dalton's building spree had left the Governors with a significant debt to be managed, but Stephenson, too, was a builder. He determined to press on with the Big School project begun by his predecessor in 1902. The site had been earmarked and the foundation stone laid, but subscriptions to the fund had more or less dried up, so the project had made no further progress. Stephenson seized upon the opportunity afforded by the death, in January 1907, of former Head Master Grignon, to focus attention and fund-raising more effectively. Notwithstanding the reverence in which Grignon's memory was held by so many of his past pupils, the required sum was very slow to materialise. By Speech Day 1908, it was felt that a start must be made, and the Governors prevailed

Evening 'prep' in the School House hall.

The Junior House cast of *The Abbot of Leez*, performed as part of the 350th anniversary celebrations, 1914.

upon the builders, Walter Lawrence of Waltham Cross, to carry out Blomfield's plans at a parsimoniously economical cost of £3,200. In the event, the Grignon Hall was erected and opened on Speech Day 1910 by the Earl of Warwick, a distant descendant of Lord Riche. Once the new Big School, furnished with the desks from the School House schoolroom, was fully operational, the vacated space could be turned into a commodious dining hall, thus allowing smaller dining rooms elsewhere in the building to be used exclusively as House common rooms: the awkward impracticalities caused by the outmoded hostel-style multi-purpose spaces were at long last being superseded. The School House dining hall continued in that role until centralised catering was transferred to the Lord Riche Hall in 1989, after which it saw service as an examinations hall, then as an art gallery, and subsequently was converted into the Sixth Form Centre we see today.

Stephenson demonstrated his financial acumen, too, in causing to be acquired for the School the ownership of the Junior House, bought from Miller, from whom it had been leased, for £4,550; and from Elwyn, who was leaving to take over as Headmaster of the King's School, Rochester, he secured for the Governors a lease on Elwyn House for the time being. The four cottages known as Queen's Square (two of which now constitute the main cricket pavilion) were also purchased, along with the substantial strip of land fronting the Braintree road between Elwyn's and Garnetts, where the new state-of-the-art cricket nets are now situated.

Astute appointments to the staff meant that certain activities most likely to raise a school's standing among its peers, such as academic and sporting excellence, were

Felstedians visit the grave of Capt. J.L. Green, VC at Foncquevillers, France.

FELSTED'S FIRST WORLD WAR HERO: CAPT. J.L. GREEN, VC, RAMC (OF *c.*1902–6)

When Germany's forces marched across the Belgian frontier on 4 August 1914, Felsted's leavers were thoroughly well prepared for the Army they would be flocking to join, though not for the style of mechanised slaughter they were to face on the Western Front in France and Belgium.

One such was Capt. John Leslie Green, RAMC; battlefield medical officer and Felsted's second Victoria Cross hero. The citation for his posthumous award (dated 4 August 1916) reads:

For most conspicuous devotion to duty. Although wounded himself, he went to the assistance of an officer who had been wounded and was hung up on the enemy's wire entanglements, and succeeded in dragging him to a shell hole, where he dressed his wounds notwithstanding that bombs and rifle grenades were thrown at him the whole time. Capt. Green then endeavoured to bring the wounded officer into safe cover and had nearly succeeded in doing so when he was himself killed.

admirably well catered for. Indeed, Stephenson was able to report with justifiable pride on Speech Day 1914, that both Presidents-elect of the Oxford and Cambridge Unions were Old Felstedians. This, of course, was the occasion of the 350th anniversary of the Foundation; the cheerful throng enjoying the celebrations, the Masters, the boys and their parents, and all the guests, were blissfully unaware of the terrible violence about to engulf them all. By the cessation of the looming hostilities, 249 Old Felstedians would have given their lives in the conflict that history came to know as the Great War to end all wars. Stephenson, like so many of his fellow headmasters of the time, would have to face the heart-wrenching task of announcing the mounting losses in Assembly and Chapel; more often than not, the victims' names would have been those of recent leavers, but a few short months older than those who heard their Headmaster's grieving pronouncements.

The period of the First World War would bring into ever-sharper focus the moral, physical and military training received in the Edwardian boys' public schools; young men with Officers' Training Corps experience were fast-tracked into active service as subalterns, whose life expectancy once they entered the front line as infantry officers could be numbered in weeks rather than months. Names recorded in the 'Valete' pages of *The Felstedian* could all too often reappear in the 'Killed, Wounded and Missing' lists in editions of the School magazine published but a few months thereafter, so swift and sure was the carnage to claim its front-rank victims. In those pages, too, may be found the School's acknowledgement of the second Victoria Cross to be awarded to an old boy: Capt. John Green of the RAMC, for 'Most conspicuous devotion to duty' in the face of the enemy. Henry Newbolt's somewhat mawkish eulogy in 'Vitaï Lampada' of the cricket-loving boy/officer rallying the ranks with the immortal cry, 'Play up, play up, and play the game!' was to prove all too prophetic for the products of Felsted School and its ilk.

The game to play, apart from cricket was, of course, rugby football. There had been undercurrents of agitation at Felsted for the introduction of this code for a number of years, which had been resisted by successive Games Committees, who favoured the retention of soccer on the grounds of its having long been the winter game at the School. But hockey had already eclipsed soccer in the inter-school and club successes it had recorded in the first decade of the 1900s, so in the end, the enthusiasm of the 1917 cohort of footballers to follow William Webb Ellis and 'run with ball in hand' carried the day. By 1919, Felsted was gaining recognition as a doughty opponent in rugby as in all other sporting competitions with its rivals, and a strong fixture list was soon undertaken, which included matches against established rugger schools such as Haileybury and Mill Hill, and with the Harlequins and Rosslyn Park, two London club sides of high renown. Old Felstedian teams were also making their mark on the South Eastern club scene, with extensive fixture lists for cricket, rugby football and hockey well established by the mid-1920s.

As life returned to something akin to normality after the war, Stephenson again turned his attentions to the consolidation of the progress made during the first decade of his time at the helm: crucial territorial acquisitions were made, including Garnetts farmhouse and Prysties field beyond the Stebbing Road; most important perhaps, was the purchase

GUNNER H.L. HULBERT, US MARINE CORPS (OF 1880–3), CMH, DSC, NAVY CROSS, CROIX DE GUERRE

Henry Lewis Hulbert of the United States Marine Corps was killed in action at Mont Blanc Ridge, France on 4 October 1918. At the age of 51, he had returned to serve his adopted country, the US, despite his advancing years. In earlier US Marine service he had shown sustained conspicuous bravery in the Philippines campaign of 1899, repeatedly attacking the enemy positions single-handedly, while protecting two wounded senior officers in his section. For that action he was awarded the Congressional Medal of Honour, the US equivalent of the Victoria Cross. Hulbert is certainly Felsted's most decorated military hero. A US Navy destroyer was named the *Henry L. Hulbert* in his honour, in 1919.

First World War memorial by Frank Salisbury at the west end of the Chapel (above); plaque above south entrance to War Memorial classroom block (top right) and the burnt out shell of the Grignon Hall after the devastating fire of 1930 (bottom right).

in 1925 of Elwyn House, for a very reasonable £7,000, and for a paltry £400 the Old Schoolroom in the village.

Stephenson was a builder, too: he saw to the much-needed extension of the Chapel, in which an elaborately carved Great War memorial panel was placed under the three high stained-glass windows at the west end, to the left of the south entrance door of the original Victorian building. He shepherded through the realisation of the War Memorial block of classrooms, opened on Speech Day 1924; the range continued the line of buildings from the Grignon Hall towards Dalton's science laboratories, and included a purpose-built library and museum. This project had originally been mooted by the Old Felstedians in 1918, even before the last shots of the hostilities had been fired.

The First World War produced a palpable rise in the popularity of the boarding school experience, and so it was with Felsted. By early 1920, the School was full, and the waiting list crammed with eager postulants; Stephenson

sought to capitalise on this good fortune by opening a new boarding House. In 1923, the Governors had prudently purchased a large field opposite Elwyn's on the Braintree Road, which was long thought of as an ideal site for building development, either as additional space for the Junior House or, as in Stephenson's latest scheme, as a suitable site for a proposed new out-House. Follyfield cost £19,000 to build, and was opened in the Summer Term of 1929.

With one of those strokes of cruel fate, so crushing in their unerring aim at our most susceptible concerns, it was Stephenson's greatest building achievement that fell victim to the ravages of an unprecedented conflagration. In the early hours of Sunday, 2 March 1930, the School was awakened by alarm calls to find the Grignon Hall ablaze. Boys joined the professional firefighters in attempting to quell the flames, but all to no avail. Devastation and ruin prevailed. With characteristic fortitude, Stephenson rallied his troops and set

The Stephenson Gate, built in 1938.

about the reconstruction work at once. It can only be guessed how much disruption to the orderly business of education must have been occasioned by the overnight loss of the main school hall and all eight teaching rooms in the Dutch Block. Happily, the Bury had become available for the School's use, and teaching groups could be accommodated there: a welcome relief from the hurried return to the hostel regime of using House common rooms for lessons. The established School architects, Chetwood and Grant, produced an enlarged and remodelled design for the main School Hall, which included a corridor on the east side linking the stage and green room (now Rendall classroom) and the Dutch Block concourse. Phoenix-like, the new Grignon Hall arose from the ashes, and was rededicated on Speech Day 1931.

By 1933, Stephenson's erstwhile robust health had broken down, and his own devotion to duty had to some extent compromised his personal well-being: he never gave an inkling to his pupils that he had long been suffering from the debilitating effects of diabetes, a condition then largely thought to be untreatable. In typically selfless style, he resolved to hand on the torch to a younger man, and his resignation was tendered early that same year. Before he

departed, however, he was able to attend one further opening of a new building of iconic status in our own times, the J.W.H.T. Douglas Memorial cricket pavilion: the two central cottages of the ancient Queen's Square had been refurbished at the instigation of P.R. Wilson, Chairman of the Old Felstedian Society and a School Governor, and were fitted out with changing rooms and showers to suit their new purpose. A living area was also included, to be occupied by one of the School handymen. That area, as with so many others over the years, has seen a sea change, accommodating as it does now the Archives of Felsted School.

It is beyond question that Revd Frank Stephenson's hand is everywhere in evidence on the modern Felsted scene. His buildings are the most obvious memorial to his incalculable contribution over the 27 years of his Headmastership, and the Stephenson Gate, erected in 1938, two years after his passing in November 1936, is a permanent reminder of his stewardship of Felsted School, as indeed is the name by which the house occupied by his successors in the post of Headmaster is known. But Stephenson's influence upon the academic and cultural ethos of the School runs much deeper than mere bricks and mortar boards.

SECTION IV | OLD WAYS DIE HARD

9 | LAST RITES FOR THE SONS OF EMPIRE
1933–47

It must have seemed to those who had endured the terrible sufferings of the First World War that the hard-won victory must bring some long-term rewards to those who had endured so much. When Revd Stephenson and his colleagues resumed their labours at Felsted, their sadness at the lengthy list of casualties may have been partially assuaged by the sense that right had prevailed and that the products of this and other public schools had more than done their bit to secure the future of the nation, the Empire and their way of life.

However, the changing political landscape following the ravages of the First World War must have been viewed with increasing unease by those who had always believed themselves to be the undisputed backbone of the nation's leadership. By 1933, just as the Felsted School Governors were faced with the task of finding a suitable successor for Stephenson, the Wall Street Crash and subsequent Great Depression had shattered the economic security of western nations, and the ensuing social upheavals throughout Europe were brewing renewed conflagration: Adolf Hitler's rise to absolute power in Germany had begun in the ashes of the Reichstag fire in February of that very year.

JULIAN K.J. BICKERSTETH, MC (1933–43)

Felsted's standing in the first rank of schools at the time can be inferred from the long list of 56 candidates who applied for the post of Headmaster; of these, no fewer than 32 were already serving headmasters, but only seven of the applicants were in holy orders. Significantly, the pedagogical profession was no longer considered to be the exclusive preserve of clergymen;

nor did able schoolmasters who lacked the clerical imprimatur feel themselves to be debarred from throwing their hats into the ring for head magisterial promotion. Nevertheless, one of the cassocked seven stood head and shoulders above all 56: Revd Kenneth Julian Faithfull Bickersteth, of Rugby School and Christ Church, Oxford, had been decorated for gallantry on the Western Front, where he had done sterling service as a battlefield chaplain, and he was currently serving as headmaster of a leading Australian public school, St Peter's Collegiate in Adelaide. In the course of 13 years at the helm, he had contrived to raise the pupil numbers and overseen the building of a splendid War Memorial Hall, thus consolidating his school's pre-eminent reputation. In the wider spheres of influence open to Bickersteth, he was instrumental in establishing ➤ *p. 85*

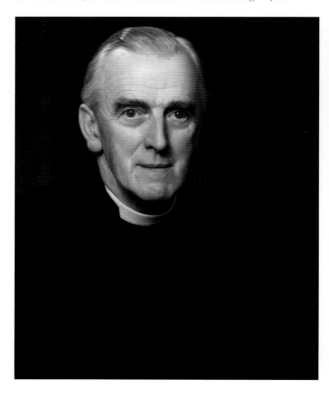

Right: Revd K.J.F. Bickersteth, Headmaster (1933–43) and (opposite) slow march from Chapel to morning 'swots', showing Old Fives Court in background.

Of the many features of Felsted that its former pupils of a certain age will recall with the utmost affection, the Bury and its associated society areas and meeting rooms will certainly rank among the foremost. A most unusual facility, perhaps unparalleled anywhere in the English public school world, for well over 50 years, the Bury was the locale where the presiding genii of Felsted's many and varied clubs and societies held sway. The commodious and civilised environment provided a haven of quiet intellectual and creative activity, sufficiently remote from the hurly-burly of daily life in a busy boarding community. For boys of an earlier and more robustly athletic age, whose talents and interests were not of a sporting nature, the Bury held a particular magic, which, for a variety of reasons, faded rather fast in the latter years of the last millennium.

The concept of a clubs and societies headquarters, accommodated in a separate building and overseen by an enthusiastic and avuncular schoolmaster Warden, was embraced whole-heartedly by Headmaster Bickersteth, who recognised the potential to be developed in Colonel Phillott's attractive property, which had come into the School's ownership in 1930, complete with its eclectic collection of

furniture and contents. Bickersteth's brother, John Burgon Bickersteth, was well advanced in his lengthy incumbency as Warden of Hart House, an innovatory facility at the University of Toronto, where students could find respite on campus from the rigours of lecture room and playing field, while developing their intellectual and creative extra-curricular interests.

As the first edition of the *Bury Report* attests, Colonel Phillott's gift 'endows the School life with a rare sense of expansion, a keenness in pursuits that sweeten leisure and rise above mere hobbies'. With changing fashions abetted by the ever-advancing technological revolution, the student of today is likely to find the concept of an 'out-of-school' activities centre less of a draw. Felstedians today enjoy a range of society and cultural activity as wide as ever, despite the Bury's dwindling appeal. The time of the famed Bury Expeditions Days is no more. These biennial occasions, when the entire school set off in a fleet of buses for distant destinations, under the aegis of one of 40-odd societies, are long past; but the number of trips has increased exponentially. No longer does the boarding school pupil endure a long exile from the world during the term-time weeks.

The Bury itself has evolved in recent times; now partially given over to provide private quarters for the Deputy Head, its public spaces have contracted somewhat. The Music and Breda Rooms retain their stately grandeur and continue to serve most admirably as venues for debates and scholarly talks by visiting grandees and such; but the busy bustle of model railway-making, the rustle of photographic dark-room derring-do, and the repetitive clanking of the offset-litho press printing the next term's calendar, to name but three, have long been stilled.

Clockwise from top left: David Plested's watercolour of the Felsted Bury; Bury Members' Room, 1938; Bury Press in action; detail from the *Bury Report*, 1935.

the Australian branch of the HMC, served as a Member of the Council of the University of Adelaide, and found time to act as Senior Chaplain to the Australian Armed Forces. Bickersteth was a man of charisma and wide-ranging experience, who could bring to the Felsted scene a *je ne sais quoi* of exotic cachet, as well as sound scholarship and proven leadership experience; not to mention the 'go-getting' elan associated with colonial administrators.

Revd Bickersteth, like Stephenson before him, was keen to ensure that building provision kept pace with the changing requirements of a modernising educational philosophy. The Junior House was a case in point: the concept of an established feeder preparatory department had been slow to take root in the gubernatorial perception; not least, perhaps, because under Jacob, the 'Muscular Christianity' element of the regime had greatly outweighed any academic focus that Headmaster and Governors might have desired. A further factor likely to vitiate good learning was the ad hoc arrangement regarding part-time secondment of Masters from the main school, who took their turn in the classrooms 'across the road'. With the Revd A.C. Telfer (newly returned to Felsted after a six-year absence as Headmaster of Ludlow Grammar School) and his wife now in charge, a more scholarly and rigorous curriculum could be instituted and a more congenial 'family' atmosphere promoted among the boys. By the Autumn Term of 1936, 80 youngsters were being taught by a dedicated staff of five graduate Masters. A substantial new extension, with dining hall, classrooms and dormitories to accommodate an expanding pupil roll, had been constructed along an aesthetically pleasing cloister colonnade to the west of the original building. The Junior School, Felsted, was taking shape, although it would continue to be known officially as the Junior House until 1956.

Further additions and adaptations to the School's physical infrastructure made under Bickersteth's percipient aegis included an enlargement of the Infirmary (subsequently renamed the Sanatorium), which a later Headmaster would deem sufficiently capacious to accommodate an entire boys' House, once the exodus of Gepp's from School House had been mooted in the mid-1950s. Provision thus completed to succour the sick, Bickersteth turned his attentions to the healthy: *corpus sanum* was catered for by the wholesale

Common Room teaching styles: M.R. Craze (top) and O. I. Simpson (above).

refurbishment of the School House dining hall, and by the opportunities afforded for healthy recreation by the erection of a pair of Gradidge squash courts (sandwiched now between the new squash courts and sports hall of 1978). Just beyond these, on the corner of the Stebbing Road and Garnetts Lane, were laid down the hard-surfaced tennis courts-cum-hockey 'quad', to provide all-weather facilities when the grass playing areas became waterlogged.

Mens sana, however, was ever the first priority for Bickersteth: as one of his early reforms of the curriculum, the Headmaster had abolished Stephenson's 'Army' and 'Engineering' streams, believing fervently that such terminology was apt to detract from the School's academic reputation among prospective parents and headmasters of preparatory schools; but also he thought it unwise to sanction officially the labelling of the less-academic boys as unsuited to any but practical courses. Henceforth, boys would be setted by ability for mathematics and other non-English subjects, an innovation which allowed for specialist science teaching in the lower forms, and permitted a wider range of options for those aged 15 or 16 who had successfully negotiated the School Certificate examination. Very much the formula, *mutatis mutandis*, prescribed for successful timetabling in our present times. Numbered among the most influential and long-serving of Bickersteth's appointments to the staff are to be found O.I. Simpson, M.R. Craze and G.A. Mason, all of whom did sterling service in many roles.

In pursuance of his desire to allow a broader curriculum in the lower years, Bickersteth had lobbied the Governors successfully for a large-scale redevelopment of the 1899 Science Block, which by the mid-1930s could no longer provide adequate resources for specialised laboratory-based science instruction. In Stephenson's latter years, Felsted had begun to

send a steady stream of accomplished young scientists to the Universities; for Bickersteth it was axiomatic that this happy trend must be maintained and, where possible, enhanced.

It was Dr S.A. Courtauld, the Chairman of Governors, who proffered the capital needed for the project; this was a most generous gift to the School, not least because just two years earlier he had financed the aforementioned dining hall refurbishment in School House. By the Summer Term of 1938, the new junior science laboratories were ready for occupation, with a purpose-designed Art School on the first floor; the original rooms were refitted for use as specialist Sixth-Form teaching spaces. The official opening ceremony, carried out by Lord Rayleigh, FRS, OM, on Speech Day, was lent a suitably cutting-edge aura: the unlocking mechanism on the main doors was operated by a photo-electric cell and activated by an accurately focused torch beam. Lord Rayleigh, a scientist of the first rank himself, was no doubt charmed and delighted by the stagy hocus-pocus.

Despite the many far-reaching reforms he wrought in the academic and cultural life of the School, it is for one particular phase of his administration of Felsted's affairs, coming as it did just as his time at the helm was drawing to its close, that Headmaster Bickersteth will be most rightly feted by posterity: his brilliant management of the School's enforced exile from Essex during the Second World War.

As had been the case for his predecessor in the summer of 1914, those thronging the grounds and filling the Grignon Hall and surrounding marquees for Bickersteth's triumphal 1939 Speech Day had viewed the immediate future with blissful insouciance. In his address, the principal Guest of Honour, Mr Duff Cooper, MP (who had resigned his Cabinet post as Secretary of State for War over the Munich humiliation the previous autumn), had spoken of his own certainty that a European conflict was becoming ever more likely; but he assuaged the rising anxieties of his audience with the addendum: 'However, I should hope that here in this quiet corner of Essex you are as safe as anywhere in England.' The Headmaster, replying, added the following comforting words: 'Since last year, the Governors have been compelled to consider carefully the position of the School in the event of war … and have decided that there would be no need for us to move.' Had Bickersteth's thoughts and plans been accurately reflected by what he said on that occasion, there is the greatest likelihood that the School's story might have mirrored that of establishments less well-directed or indeed less fortunate,

Above left: Bust of Dr S.A. Courtauld, Chairman of Governors, sited in the Science Block lobby, alongside the marble plaque commemorating his generous funding of the new laboratories and (above) chemistry lesson c.1951.

87

Common Room caricatures by Graham Keeping, 1935.

like Weymouth College and several others, whose wartime emergencies were to prove their conclusive demise. Post-war generations of Felstedians owe the deepest debt of gratitude to Canon Bickersteth, as he later became, for his foresight and persistence in planning for the worst case in private, while showing to all and sundry an optimistic facade.

It is greatly to his credit that when impending disaster struck the British Expeditionary Force in France the following May, the Headmaster had a viable strategy for evacuating his school ready for implementation at the shortest notice. It is no small matter to remove the physical impedimenta necessary for the smooth operation of a boarding school of 400 boys to a place of relative safety; much more problematical is to have access to suitable accommodation for such an invasion. Felsted School was in luck: its Headmaster could call upon the good offices of a family friend, Mrs Dorothy Trafford, whose son, John Lionel, had joined Gepp's in 1938, and whose property holdings near Ross-on-Wye in Herefordshire extended to four sizeable country houses, all within a very few miles of each other. Small reading parties of Felstedians had already been availing themselves of Mrs Trafford's hospitality

at Hill Court, so Bickersteth and several senior Masters were fully conversant with the possibilities and the pitfalls of a mass migration to Ross, should the need ever arise.

Arise it did, for the evacuation of the troops from Dunkirk had left the hostile forces of the Third Reich a few short sea miles from the Essex shores. Brigadier C.J.S. King (OF 1904–8) was said to have expostulated emphatically that the School could no longer remain in situ, now that East Anglia was the front line of our island's defences. A phone call from the Ministry of War and the arrival of an advance party of the Royal Engineers shortly thereafter had left the Headmaster and the Governors little room for manoeuvre; besides, when Bickersteth cast his eyes through his study window, his gaze was greeted by the apocalyptic sight of the famous Felsted cricket ground on the Front now doing duty as a parking area for heavy army lorries, and bayonet-wielding sentries prowling his demesnes.

The die was cast: the boys, all but a working party of 50 seniors, were sent home with instructions to reconvene after a fortnight's break in the terra incognita of hilly Herefordshire. The great adventure had begun.

'FELSTED-ON-WYE' (MAY 1940 TO MARCH 1945)

It is hard to imagine just how deeply unsettling it must have been for the youngsters hunched over their Latin proses and simultaneous equations in the Dutch Block to hear the loud revving of the military vehicles pouring through the Stephenson Gate on that fateful afternoon in late May 1940. The invading troops were 'friendly', no doubt, but their intentions were soon made plain: this is our place now; you lot, clear off, pronto.

Headmaster Bickersteth's evacuation plan had to be implemented forthwith. The School's myriad nooks and crannies had to be cleared of all furniture and other portables, and what could not be transported to Herefordshire must be stored where it would escape the Army's predatory attentions. Astonishing to relate, within barely a week of starting the colossal undertaking, the dedicated task force of Masters and senior boys had cleared the dorms and day rooms throughout the School, stacked the classrooms along the Memorial Block corridor to the rafters with impedimenta not required on the journey, and assembled everything earmarked for transportation in the Grignon Hall. It took just a week more for Mrs Trafford's four Herefordshire country houses to be kitted out with the beds, 'tabbies', lockers and desks necessary for school life to resume something resembling a normal routine.

'For those who would grumble and complain – and it is not always difficult to find causes here – we would stress the amazing good luck and good management that has brought us entire from one side of England to the other. Had we been a little too late, had things gone slightly differently, had this or that happened *we should in all probability no longer be a school*' (emphasis added). Thus commented the Editorial of *The Felstedian* magazine of July 1940, not only voicing the community's collective sigh of astonished relief as its exile began, but also hinting at the underlying toils and tribulations to be endured and perchance overcome.

From the top: Canon Ffrome Court; Goodrich Court and Pen Craig Court.

The main house, Goodrich Court, was a Victorian pile in the baronial style: towers, turrets and machicolations presented to the outside world; within, the interior was, to all intents, a private museum, with valuable tapestries adorning the walls and suits of ancient armour guarding the staircases and public rooms. A member of staff who took part in the migration wrote of the experience thus: 'The Masters and boys forming the advance party found [at Goodrich] a house whose interior resembled a private museum, so the first task was the removal of all the furniture that was far too valuable to leave around in a school ... Eventually, by Monday, June 10th, only thirteen days after our removal had been ordered, the house was more or less ready for the reception of the school.'

Once the Louis XV furniture had been removed to safety and the Felsted bric-a-brac installed, the place soon assumed the lived-in familiarity of School House: Gepp's, Stocks's and Mont's were soon in possession, albeit that their sleeping arrangements in large marquees in the courtyard promised a somewhat draughty time of it, once the summer season had run its course! Teaching areas were commandeered and Masters' quarters allocated in the upper floors. The cramped living conditions of the boarders were eased a few months later when the stable block had been adapted to house the Gepp's dormitory and a more-than-adequate science laboratory.

Elwyn House found themselves masters of a delightful Georgian home, Pencraig Court, just three-quarters of a mile from Goodrich, where H.E. Reekie, the future Headmaster, marshalled his troops and began digging for victory in the kitchen garden. More problematical were the lodgings allocated to Windsor's and Follyfield: Hill Court, a delightfully proportioned Queen Anne country house stood but a mile as the crow flies, from the main centre of the

(Clockwise from top) Scouts' bridge over the Wye; Great Hall, Goodrich Court; 'swotting' in panelled splendour, 'Felsted-on-Wye'.

School at Goodrich Court, but was a tedious three-and-a-half-mile trudge for its boys, since the Wye River separated them from their lessons and their dining hall. P.G. Rendall, Housemaster of Gepp's and Scout-master, resolved the problem. By the following Spring Term, a suspension bridge had been constructed to carry a walkway over the river, thus shortening the journey to a bracing half-hour each way. Some boys were known to ride their cycles across the swaying contraption, when the gaze of authority was averted! Felsted's Wye Bridge was not to be permitted to outlive the School's occupation of Hill Court, but the achievement itself bears solemn witness to the wonderful spirit of innovation and adventure instilled by the exigencies of exile.

The Junior House, too, found a temporary refuge in the Herefordshire heartlands, at Canon Ffrome Court, near Ledbury, some 30 miles distant from Ross-on-Wye. There, Revd A.C. Telfer and his staff soldiered on regardless, enjoying so much their idyll in the Welsh Marches that they lingered there a term after the main School had made the return to Essex in March 1945.

Within a very few short weeks, Felsted was securely ensconced in its new homes, and business as usual was the order of the day. Certificate examinations had to be taken almost at once, and no discernible diminution in standards was noted. Boys and Masters adapted quickly and transformed their new abode into a facsimile of their traditional purlieus: the Bury societies were soon revived, a plethora of theatrical and musical entertainments were produced, issues of *The Felstedian* were published, and sporting contests were arranged against opponents near and far. Rugby, hockey and cricket were soon thriving: pitches were fashioned within the Goodrich grounds or, where necessity required, borrowed from local clubs; matches against other evacuated schools, such as Westminster and Radley, took their place on a fixtures card which included Cheltenham College, Monmouth School, Wrekin, Malvern, Shrewsbury and Christs College, Brecon. It is fair to say that the reduced numbers and straitened circumstances of exile did nothing to diminish the competitive edge of Felstedian teams, whose daunting reputation in the Eastern Counties was soon resounding among the hills and vales of the far West, too.

When the Axis forces were all but defeated, it was time for the return to Essex to be contemplated. The School was in fine fettle, having survived a change of Headmaster in mid-term of its exile. It seemed clear that far from suffering paralysis as a result of its upheavals, Felsted was very much the better for the change. The following sentiment expressed editorially in an early wartime edition of *The Felstedian* exemplifies the profound effects on the community, purged perhaps and revivified by enforced removal to the far pavilions of Ross-on-Wye: 'Already the Hereford atmosphere has had an effect on the School traditions, and much that is inconvenient and absurd has been ousted … we of the Goodrich Era of School history must see that the traditions we hand on are as fine as those which we have inherited.'

After ten years in post, Revd Bickersteth could look back with considerable satisfaction on the achievements of the School under his command, both before and during the wartime exile. When the call came from the Archbishop of Canterbury, Dr Temple, to resume a more public ecclesiastical role, he could not refuse. The County of Kent and its chief towns were in the thick of the defensive campaign against the Luftwaffe, which Churchill had dubbed the Battle of Britain. Bickersteth's previous war service, and his brilliance as a preacher and leader of men, made him a perfect candidate to be Archdeacon of Maidstone and Canon Residentiary at Canterbury Cathedral. In the midst of the School's greatest challenge in well over 400 years, he had to relinquish his hold on the reins and heed the higher call. Thus it was that in April 1943, Canon Bickersteth left Ross-on-Wye and Felsted School to their relative tranquillity and went back to the war.

This time the Governors did not have to look very far to find a new Headmaster: in A.H. Andrew, a Felsted Master appointed by Stephenson in 1932 to teach at the Junior House, who had resigned to take a commission in the RAF, where he was currently on active service, they believed they had the strongest of contenders for the vacant Headmastership.

ALISTAIR H. ANDREW (1943–7)

It can have been no easy task for the Felsted Governors to put together an extensive list of potential candidates in the white heat of wartime. Although the threatened invasion across the Channel had not materialised by the end of 1942, the outcome of the European theatre of war was by no means decided. Furthermore, Rommel was yet to be ousted from North Africa, the Japanese forces were threatening British India in the East, and the American involvement was still primarily confined to its own defensive campaigns against that same enemy in the Pacific. In such times of uncertainty, the chief instinct is to stay put; Andrew might well have felt flattered to be chosen, but at the same time he might have evinced a number of doubts as to the wisdom of accepting the appointment.

A month short of his 35th birthday, Alistair Hugh Andrew was relatively inexperienced as a schoolmaster, though he had been promoted to the Housemastership of

Windsor's after only three years' service in the main School. He had been educated at Marlborough and Trinity College, Cambridge, where he had graduated with a Second Class History degree. After several years pursuing a business career, he had sought employment in education, and had in the first instance been taken on by Revd Stephenson, in 1932, as Assistant to Jacob at the Junior House. He had made a considerable mark in a short time, and had a proven record for all-round schoolmasterly involvement in a busy boarding school schedule of activities and sports: Master in Charge of swimming, Librarian, Bury societies enthusiast; above all, the *sine qua non* for peer approval, he had shown himself to be a gifted teacher. He had also recently made a highly suitable marriage; his wife, Mary (née Wordsworth and great-great-granddaughter of William Wordsworth, the Poet Laureate), was well versed in the social expectations of boarding school communities, so would prove a decided asset to a prospective Headmaster. Perhaps most tellingly at a critical stage for the School, Alistair Andrew had experienced at first hand what Felsted was, both at home in Essex and in exile at Ross; such familiarity would be invaluable in the event of the return journey, once hostilities had ceased. All to the good; but on the debit side were two salient detractions: more than half of the Felsted Common Room he would be expected to lead would deem him to be their junior by length of service; more likely to count against his candidature was the fact that if appointed he would be the first Head in the School's 380-year history not to be a clergyman. The Governors were sure, nevertheless, that he was their man, and Andrew accepted. He would have to win over the gainsayers of the traditionalist cadre by rapid and decisive leadership.

As a wartime leader, Andrew was to prove every bit as effective as his predecessor: his resourceful approach to the necessary privations of a 'make do and mend' culture reassured the Common Room sceptics almost at once. Refreshing, too, perhaps, was the layman's eye which Andrew brought to the scene: a clerical Headmaster, notwithstanding the engagement and brilliance of his sermons in Chapel, can appear somewhat remote and other-worldly to a schoolboy, whereas a man of action who had served his country in the RAF, albeit in a backroom 'cloak-and-dagger' role, would have radiated an aura of dash quite irresistible to the putative young warriors in his

charge. For the first time in the School's long history, the title of Chaplain (reserved by ancient statute in the Foundation Deeds as the appellation of the original chantry chaplain, and, from 1564, of the Schoolmaster) would be revived: the senior clerical Master, Revd G.E. Ingle, took on the role in the first instance, to be succeeded a short time later by Revd L.S.K. Ford, the first specialist School Chaplain to be appointed. The majority of Andrew's other staff appointments were to prove short-term covers for permanent incumbents on war service, but two names deserve special mention: P. Gant and J.H. Lee both joined the Common Room shortly after the return to Essex and gave long and distinguished service to the School.

In most other respects, Andrew persevered in nurturing the time-honoured Felsted traditions, and by the autumn of his second year in post was able to begin planning for the homecoming, as the Army would be relinquishing its tenure in the early spring of 1945. But in one decision he made were sown seeds of future controversy, which could never have been foreseen at the time: when Ingle resigned, much as Bickersteth had before him, to play his part in post-war reconstruction, the Housemastership of his House fell vacant and Andrew himself took on the role. At the time, it must have seemed the simplest and most convenient solution: the Headmaster and his family were billeted in Old Hill Court, just a few steps from Hill Court, the temporary home of Follyfield-in-Exile; co-tenants there were Windsor's, with their Housemaster, E.H. Lockwood, living in and able to provide the necessary overnight supervision. Doubtless, Andrew also believed himself well-qualified for the post, in view of his previous (albeit brief) experience as Housemaster of Windsor's before the war. He relished the closer engagement with his pupils that a Housemaster could achieve, though perhaps in making such a decision he was treading a risky path, since focusing too closely on a particular 'county' might well draw the sovereign's gaze away from the demands of his 'realm' as a whole.

Upon the return to Essex, Andrew moved into the private side of Ingle's (as Follyfield had been redubbed in honour of its founding Housemaster), relinquishing the Headmaster's official residence adjacent to School House. There the Masters' Common Room was afforded spacious ground-floor communal space, and two bachelor Masters were accommodated upstairs. Pupils, too, were included in the redistribution of the generous top floor. This was perhaps the most striking of Andrew's reforms, once the tedious business had been accomplished of reversing Bickersteth's mighty exodus, to bring the School back to Felsted lock, stock and barrel.

Andrew was fully appraised of the depredations of four and a half years of military occupation of the buildings and grounds, where the Army authorities had paid scant thought to what long-term damage their incursions were inflicting on the premises they had so precipitately commandeered. Concrete bases for Nissen huts and timber-framed structures were everywhere to be seen, ringing the perimeters of the playing fields and even encroaching upon the hallowed turf of the Front. Asphalt pathways criss-crossed the greensward, and fields of half-ripened barley swayed gently in the breeze where the rugby and hockey pitches had previously been marked out. Within the buildings themselves, chaos reigned: the Army had left everything much as it had been under its occupation, save that a coat of Army-issue grey distemper had been slapped on any surface that could be reached by paintbrush. With the valuable expert assistance of local firm J.S. Alderton and Sons, Andrew and his valiant staff, both teaching and domestic, set about the reconstruction, much as the rest of their countrymen were doing in every corner of the war-torn land. The boys, too, were eager to lend a hand, but it took the best part of an entire academic year to restore order and dignity to the ravaged campus.

But the life of a school must go on; numbers had necessarily dropped over the period in exile, and Andrew's first priority was to get his roll back to pre-war levels. A possible source of extra pupils had only recently come into the reckoning: following R.A. Butler's Education Act of 1944, the Fleming Report had predicated the view that the independent and direct-grant schools might be co-opted into partnership with Local Education Authorities (LEAs) in mutually beneficial arrangements. Funding secondary schooling at fee-paying institutions for individual pupils was certainly a cheaper

option than having to raise the huge capital sums required to build sufficient new schools in the austerity times of post-war reconstruction. Many urban institutions had suffered bomb damage, and the repairs and reconstruction works were likely to stretch government coffers to the limit.

The Labour Party's General Election victory in June 1945 had returned a government likely to view such a state – private alliance with mistrust; but many LEAs were all too keen to have the educational needs of their youngsters quickly and efficiently supplied. Andrew saw the benefit of opening discussions with Education Departments in Essex, and struck a deal with Southend-on-Sea to receive up to six boys per year in the first instance. The Governors agreed to a provisional period for such an agreement, concurring with the Headmaster's view that, in the fullness of time, Felsted might grow to be a school of 500 boys, were the Southend-on-Sea partnership to develop as planned and other LEAs be minded to join the scheme (enquiries had been received from East Ham and Croydon Education Authorities).

The first four Southend boys joined the School in September 1946, and settled into boarding life very well. They had barely started their second Felsted term when catastrophe struck the School community: in the early evening of 14 February 1947, on their way to the East Essex Hunt Ball in Chelmsford, Alistair Andrew and his two passengers were killed in a head-on collision with a double-decker bus. The undoubted cause of the accident was the atrocious road conditions, brought about by the worst winter weather in recorded history: snow had piled many feet high on the verges, narrowing the roadway, and the surface was glazed with

inches-thick packed ice. Perhaps Andrew had swerved to make way for the bus and been catapulted back into its direct path; it will never be known exactly how the tragedy unfolded.

Alistair Andrew, two days past his 39th birthday, was dead. To lose its Headmaster in such circumstances is undoubtedly the very worst of disasters for a school: no provision for a smooth succession is possible, and the outpourings of shock and grief can paralyse a tight-knit boarding school community. In this case, there was a remarkable response from pupils and staff: inured, perhaps, by their recent wartime vicissitudes to upsets and upheaval, the community rallied its collective forces; as in the best of human societies, the worst inflictions of fate can bring out the very best in its members.

The funeral was attended with stoicism and resolve on the part of boys and staff alike; the end-of-term play, *Hamlet* with Philip Latham, the future West-End star, in the title role, was performed in the most poignant of circumstances; the Senior Master, Thomas Cooper, took over as Acting Headmaster, until such time as the Governors could instigate the process, at short notice, to appoint a permanent replacement. The School soldiered on manfully to the term's end, encouraged no doubt by the fortitude of Mrs Mary Andrew, the late Headmaster's widow, who continued, despite her terrible bereavement, to manage the domestic affairs of Ingle's House, and rendered support to bachelor Cooper in his social and entertainment duties as locum tenens Headmaster. But the stuffing had well and truly been knocked out of the community; the long-term ramifications of the fateful encounter of a bus and a car on the Broomfield Road would only emerge during the ensuing dozen years or so.

The cast of *Hamlet*, 1947; Philip Latham (fe 1939–47) seated centre.

10 | Keeping Calm and Carrying On 1947–68

The untimely demise of Alistair Andrew brought for the Governors an intriguing opportunity, albeit not one they would voluntarily have chosen to face within two short years of the School's return to Essex: the chance to set Felsted's future course on a different heading. While Bickersteth and Andrew had steered the School through the most treacherous of wartime seas, they had essentially maintained the traditions and ethos of the rural Edwardian public school that Dalton and Stephenson had between them fashioned in the previous 50 years or so.

Even more so than the Great War, the Second World War had convulsed the old order of British society to the very marrow. A Labour Government had introduced the National Health Service as one of its first far-reaching post-war social reforms, and it was bidding fair to realise its dream for a state-funded provision of compulsory secondary education too. The private sector must look to its laurels; in particular, the public schools must carve for themselves an unassailable niche, lest they be sidelined and eventually superseded by the new tripartite system, which Mr R.A. Butler, MP and Conservative Education Secretary (and Governor of Felsted School since 1929), had predicated in 1944. The public schools would certainly position themselves as the academic competitors of the newly established grammar schools; but the rivalry might prove terminally damaging to the fee-charging sector in the long run. Very nearly a century after the previous serious crisis of identity for the School, when Wratislaw and Grignon had reinvigorated a tired institution, it was again a critical time in the School's fortunes; the Governors must act decisively to safeguard the future.

CECIL M. HARRISON (1947–51)

Acting Head Cooper was to prove himself a most able inter-rex. His service to Felsted had begun as far back as 1910, and he had been Housemaster of Stocks's since 1920. No one knew the School better, and he had been right-hand man to both Bickersteth and Andrew, before, during and after the Herefordshire exile. His interregnum was spectacularly successful, not least because he enjoyed the full confidence and (somewhat fearful) respect of staff and boys alike; the loss of Alistair Andrew was most keenly felt by the entire community, and Cooper was a figurehead of calm stability personified, at a time of deep disturbance in the School's collective psyche.

Meanwhile, the Governors had found a new Headmaster who seemed to fulfil all their demanding criteria.

Cecil M. Harrison, Headmaster (1947–51).

Far left: T. Cooper (Master 1910–49) and (left) O.I. Simpson (Master 1936–69).

Cecil Marriott Harrison was Senior Classical Master at Charterhouse, a school which had forged a stellar reputation for its academic prowess, without notable deterioration in its all-round sporting and cultural performances. His own accomplishments in academic realms were also impressive: a King's Scholar at Westminster School, he had proceeded to Trinity College, Cambridge, where he had taken a First in both parts of the Classical Tripos. His early teaching career saw service in two notably academic establishments, Nottingham High and Dulwich College. A strong academic, then, but no stronger than many, if not most, of his predecessors at Felsted; in his favour, too, was his wartime service as a captain in the Royal Signals. Counting against him, no doubt, was his age (he was just 36 on appointment), and the fact that he would appear not to have had any direct pastoral or organisational experience as boarding school housemaster; neither, on the face of things, did he care very much for athletic pursuits. In short, in choosing Cecil Harrison as Andrew's successor, the Governors were

taking a significant risk; if they realised this at the time, then the later unravelling of their gamble must have weighed the heavier on their collective consciences.

The new Headmaster and Mrs Harrison moved into the private side of Ingle's House, where the Andrews had preceded them. The House was now run by O.I. Simpson, House Tutor under Andrew, who had been appointed Housemaster by Cooper in the wake of Andrew's tragic demise; so there was from the start a problematic division of responsibilities relating to the domestic arrangements: Mrs Harrison had assumed the role of housekeeper from Mrs Andrew, but was answerable to Simpson rather than her husband in the in-House pecking order. Although Harrison reported to the Governors that the relationships were cordial, he nevertheless complained that the situation was not tenable in the long term, and expressed his intention of moving back to Stephenson's as soon as a married Housemaster could be found for Follyfield (as Ingle's was again to be known, by Harrison's decree after consultation with the boys in the House). The Housemaster Simpson, only

The 'nips' hard at work in the Dutch Block.

recently 'promoted' from the Junior House, was a bachelor, so his tenure was precarious, to say the least. After the death in February 1949, of T. Cooper, the serving Stocks's Housemaster, Harrison saw his chance to move Simpson into School House, believing this to be a satisfactory resolution of the difficult situation; he assumed the Housemastership of Follyfield himself, asserting that no suitable married candidate was available for the post.

In the light of later developments, it must be surmised that these decisions, among others, were not accorded universal approval by the more senior ranks of the Masters' Common Room, where resentments had begun to fulminate quite early in Harrison's tenure, in response to the new Headmaster's occasionally peremptory style of management and apparent disdain for the Felsted way of doing things. The unbiased observer might well conjecture that Harrison's inexperience as a leader of men, allied to his heady past associations with three of the so-called 'great' public schools, as pupil and master, may have given a misleading impression of his true sentiments as he assumed his appointment at Felsted School, an establishment disinclined to give best to any other in the

land, much less to schools they had confronted victoriously on the games field in times gone by.

In general terms, however, Harrison's reign began favourably enough, though his propensity for direct and pejorative criticism of much that Felsted held dear won him few immediate supporters within the teaching body and associated adult community, though his readiness to consult with his Prefects did begin to establish his credentials as a consultative rather than the more usual imperative authority figure. Harrison had construed that his mandate was primarily to raise the academic standards of Felsted, which had slipped during the exile: as numbers dropped, entry standards at Common Entrance of necessity had had to be lowered. The immediate aftermath of the return to Essex had been a scramble to fill the School once more, and in Harrison's view this had given the impression to preparatory school heads that Felsted would be happy to accept their less gifted boys. He was at pains to reassure the Governors of his full confidence in the teaching competence of the staff, but it is clear from later developments that Harrison's robust criticisms of the academic performances of the boys were taken much amiss by the Common Room in general.

On the credit side, however, Harrison did take it upon himself to tackle the shortcomings he had discerned: he introduced Latin as a compulsory subject in the Fourth Form, and brought Greek back into the curriculum for the top performers. The extra-curricular intellectual stimulation of the boys had for some time been the preserve of the Bury societies, and Harrison sought to consolidate this important feature of the School. As a means of applying some judicious pressure on the Governors to see things his way, he invited a Ministry of Education inspection team to review the School's academic performance.

The General Inspection took place during the Spring Term of 1949: the report was overwhelmingly positive, in particular praising the Headmaster's wise organisation of the curriculum, and heaping encomiums upon the teaching of the Assistant Masters they had observed in action. It was not an entirely positive review of the School's academic provision, however, as the Inspectors had noted that the somewhat rigid structure of the School Certificate programme in the lower forms was demonstrably impeding the wider-ranging acquisition of knowledge that the top scholars would need to experience if the success rate at the Open Scholarship examinations for Oxford and Cambridge colleges was to be enhanced. A note of warning was also sounded in the light of the impending major overhaul in the public examinations system, due to be implemented in early 1951. Following the raising of the school leaving age from 14 to 15, in 1947, the Ministry of Education had predicated that the School Certificate would be replaced by a new General Certificate of Education, at 'Ordinary', 'Advanced' and 'Scholarship' levels; in the opinion of HM Inspectors, Felsted did not seem to be making ready for the significant changes that this innovation would require.

In responding to the criticisms detailed in the Inspection Report, which drew particular attention to the absence of formalised leadership within the academic departments and the fact that Heads of Department received no specific emoluments relating to their status, Harrison wrote: 'I should however make it clear that in my opinion, as little interference as possible should be made with Masters' methods of teaching. One man finds he gets his results in one way, and one in another, and provided the results are got there is nothing to be said for imposing a stereotyped system.' One senses here the nub of the Headmaster's underlying reluctance to tackle the entrenched attitudes of some of the longest-serving senior members of staff, whose adherence to the long-established Felsted 'way' was proving intransigent in the new light of the new regime. In all probability, Harrison was perceived as an outsider, whose unassuming, sympathetic and accessible approach to his high office, attested to by numerous Felstedians of that era, did not chime with dyed-in-the-wool Felstedian traditions. That the Governors had probably selected their new man for just those reforming qualities was to prove no balm, once the festering resentments found their voice.

On the surface, Harrison paid little heed to the undercurrents of opposition within the Common Room. He threw his support behind the activities of the newly instigated Andrew Society (the elite Upper Sixth forum for intellectual debate, proposed by Alistair Andrew, but inaugurated in his memory during Cooper's interregnum) and the recently revived Concert Club; took his place in the orchestra and on the stage; and directed several major dramatic productions,

including *Henry IV, Part I* and *Twelfth Night*. In the course of a comparatively brief reign, Cecil Harrison did all he could reasonably have been expected to do in a wide range of key activities: his support for the Cadet Corps and for the Bury was unflagging, and he laboured hard to renew the long-standing but war-interrupted links with the School's Mission in London's Docklands, through staunch endeavours to re-establish regular visits and fund-raising occasions. In this last area of dedicated concern, Mrs Harrison was enthusiastically involved, too. Perhaps only in the matter of athletic sports and games was his interest less than fully engaged.

The Church of the Ascension, Docklands (top) and a scene from *Twelfth Night*, 1950.

Even so, it is difficult to discern the causes of the breakdown in relations between so devoted a Headmaster and the Governors who had appointed him with such wholehearted optimism just three and a half years before. Without doubt, Harrison felt himself undermined by some of his senior staff; there may have been unconscionable and surreptitious 'briefing' against their Headmaster that found its mark. In an uncanny replaying of the unfortunate events which led to Grignon's dismissal in 1875, Harrison found his position untenable. Lacking the full and unequivocal backing of the Felsted Governors, Harrison sought alternative employment. He applied for and was appointed to the Headship of the King's School, Peterborough, an establishment very different from Felsted in its city location and mainly day-boy student body.

Cecil Harrison left to take up his new post at the conclusion of the Summer Term 1951. His departure was acrimonious, to say the least, since Harrison himself could fathom no clear notion why he had been summarily forced from office. For the second time in the School's history, Felsted's name was mud in the corridors of influence of the HMC; one particularly potent potential ally of Harrison's was the redoubtable Robert Birley, Head Master of Eton and formerly Headmaster of Charterhouse, under whom Harrison had served as Senior Classical Master. If Harrison's dismissal were to appear to have been unjustly wrought, then his successor as Felsted's new Headmaster might find his election to the HMC brotherhood somewhat problematical; to be denied membership of this association of the 50 or so leading public schools was a consummation devoutly to be evaded, however justly deserved the sanction might be.

Cecil Harrison's appointment at King's, Peterborough, was clearly a success: his period in charge lasted fully 18 years. Having latterly taken holy orders, he relinquished his headship in 1969 to take up parish work as Vicar of Aislaby, north Yorkshire. He retired from public life in 1979 and died on 15 August 1986. In dispassionate retrospect, it might be concluded that Felsted was not ready for Harrison, nor was Harrison equipped for the task he had been assigned: it was a clear-cut case of 'Dr Fell' on the Common Room side, which, despite a facility for winning the trust and even the affection of the boys, Cecil Harrison's relative inexperience had been unable to mitigate.

HENRY E. REEKIE (1951–68)

With the impending departure of Cecil Harrison, the Governors of Felsted School were faced with a decidedly awkward situation. Their ill-fated attempt to inject into the School a reforming new ethos had failed in most spectacular and unfortunate circumstances. If Felsted's reputation were to survive the scandal likely to be fuelled by the rumours and counter-rumours surrounding the sacking of the Headmaster, then the successor to be sought must be a most exceptional individual, to be sure, and someone who would be prepared to trust a Governing Body that had proved less than reliable in its support for the previous incumbent. In the event, the Governors achieved a veritable masterstroke of political perception: they invited back a long-serving and well-regarded former Felsted Housemaster, Henry Reekie, to take on the direction of the School he had left in 1945. If the intention had been to steady a distinctly rocky ship, their choice could not have fallen upon a better candidate: the recent uncertainties within the School would be assuaged, and in due course, too, might the desired reforms be masterminded.

Henry Enfield Reekie had joined the Felsted Common Room as Engineering Master in 1929, a post requiring him to oversee not only the Workshops, but also to take responsibility for the School's water supply, the electricity generation plant and the boilers and drainage systems. In short, his role corresponded in modern parlance to that of the present

Clerk of Works, with some Mathematics, Physics and Biology teaching thrown in for good measure. Joining the slavishly hierarchical Common Room under these terms might well have daunted many a lesser mortal: for Reekie, the challenge was readily taken up. His own educational provenance was impeccable: schooling at Oundle and a Natural Sciences degree from Clare College, Cambridge, gave him the requisite cachet to overcome the 'practical' as opposed to 'academic' nature of the work he had undertaken at Felsted.

It was not long before his conspicuous talents as a schoolmaster were seen to good effect: he was appointed House Tutor in Follyfield under its founding Housemaster, Revd George Ingle; took on the organisation of the Scout Troop; and played centre forward for Felsted Rovers, the local football team. Only five years into his service at Felsted he was given charge of Windsor's House; but in 1936, after just two years, he had had to relinquish that post upon his marriage to Miss Pauline Seeman. Reekie's conspicuous gifts for a leading pastoral role were far too valuable to be kept in abeyance for long; Headmaster Bickersteth soon brought him back into the house-magisterial fold by appointing him Housemaster of Elwyn's in 1938. Reekie shepherded that House through the war years and exile at Pencraig, Ross-on-Wye. Alongside his onerous duties he somehow found time to obtain a pilot's licence, and subsequently took on the wartime role as Officer Commanding the Felsted School Air Training Corps (ATC), which had been awarded the unit designation No. 501, in recognition of its being the very first such contingent to be established at a public school.

When Reekie accepted the appointment as Headmaster of St Bees School in 1945, the selection panel must have been delighted to secure the services of such a talented and widely experienced candidate. After a six-year stint directing the affairs of an establishment broadly similar in size and ethos to Felsted, Reekie was ideally qualified to fill the vacancy left by Harrison's departure; besides, he was already an elected member of the Headmaster's Conference, an accolade not easily rescinded. The Felsted Governors had nimbly sidestepped any embarrassing kerfuffle arising from such residual ill will that might be levelled at them at the HMC; besides, they had secured the services of the 'safe pair of hands' the School so badly needed in the circumstances.

Henry and Pauline Reekie were welcomed back to Felsted with great warmth by the entire community. Despite having to pull rank over erstwhile colleagues of longer service in the School, Henry Reekie's calm, avuncular self-assurance, allied to a tall-framed poise and dignity, meant that his reign began in the most auspicious circumstances. He soon won over the Common Room and boys alike, with his firm but kindly style of man-management. That he might have been at his core a reformer did not at first manifest itself: for a year or two the School reverted to its pre-war mindset: rigid discipline, cold baths and games-obsessed hierarchies. But Reekie was a canny operator; he realised the need for change, but saw the wisdom of planned evolution rather than rapidly imposed revolution: first improve the environment, then tackle the underlying ethos would seem to have been his governing principle.

Within the first five years, Reekie had brought about several notable developments in the School's infrastructure, which would pave the way for more fundamental reforms in the fullness of time. Like Harrison before him, Reekie understood that the Head must preside over his School from a central location, and he insisted from the outset that Stephenson's be restored to the Headmaster's use as lodging and administrative hub of the School. By mid-1952, he was

The School House dining hall, *c.*1968.

able to move from Follyfield to Stephenson's, thus bringing to a close the unhappy experiment begun by Andrew during the Ross-on-Wye sojourn, and prolonged upon the School's return to Essex.

The perennial problem of overcrowding in the School House had been addressed once again by Harrison, but his solution, to build another out-House, had been shelved by the Governors, on the grounds of expense. Now action must be undertaken, since fashions were rapidly changing in terms of what were deemed suitable standards of accommodation in a modern boarding establishment. Felsted must modernise or be left behind.

In the first instance, the dingy interior of the School House, which retained much of its 1860s hostel-style

Right: Junior Room and (below) Gepp's junior dormitory.

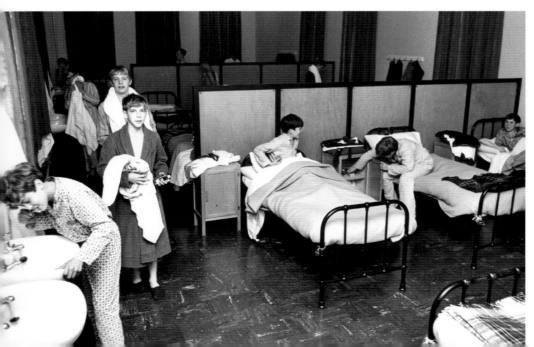

ambiance, was subjected to a much-needed overhaul: House rooms and studies were remodelled and dormitories and washing facilities reorganised. The vast and underused Sanatorium building was earmarked for development into overflow boarding accommodation, and two of the larger wards were immediately commandeered for dormitory use; thus began the migration of Gepp's House from darkness into light, as it were. An extension to the existing building was begun, to provide a private side for a Housemaster and his family, alongside living and working accommodation for the boys. The work was completed with commendable alacrity and Gepp's completed the transfer into its independent quarters in time for the Autumn Term of 1956.

Reekie's building spree continued apace: he drew up plans for a new boarding House, to inherit the remaining former Sanatorium accommodation, to which further extensions would have to be added. In order for this development to be possible, a new Sanatorium must first see the light of day. Again, once the green light had been shown, building works were swiftly accomplished: by the Autumn Term of 1960, the prefabricated structure of the new San had been completed, it was sited on the edge of New Prysties field, to the north of the building it was replacing. J.A. Cockett and 20 of the youngest boys in the School took possession of their new domain, termed initially the Waiting House (later to be named after the Chairman of Governors, Lieut. Col. E.H. Deacon, JP, DL). It is no great wonder that space was becoming a critical issue: when Reekie arrived there were 311 boys in the School; by 1961, numbers had increased to 436. The Governors saw the wisdom of the Headmaster's plans, and gave their approval for Deacon's House to be completed. Once the extensions were ready, volunteers wishing to move to Deacon's were sought from other Houses; by the start of the Autumn Term of 1965, Cockett had a full complement, and Felsted had its seventh boarding House.

Three further projects undertaken during the early phase of Reekie's building programme were a new block of studies for Elwyn House, overlooking the Front; a specialist Geography room (to be named Ruggles-Brise), skilfully positioned in the angle between the Grignon Hall and the main 'Memorial' classroom block, giving weatherproof access all the way from School House to the Library for the first time; and the

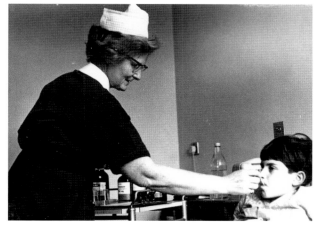

recommissioning of the Old Pavilion by the Elwyn's path as the J.F. Taylor Memorial Tuck Shop.

The rapid expansion in numbers brought further headaches in the academic spheres, too. Very close to Henry Reekie's heart, for reasons not too hard to discern, was the provision of first-rate science-teaching facilities, and perhaps nearest of all was the desire to enable the technically minded boys to further their skills and knowledge in workshops fully equipped for the modern world of design and manufacture. Of course, Felsted had fostered a pioneering tradition in this field; its existing workshops, brainchild of Headmaster Dalton, and where Reekie, in his former incarnation, had plied his pedagogic trade, had been in use since 1906. If these had been avant-garde at the outset, it would take more than a lick of paint now to turn the clock forward to Reekie's satisfaction; after all, he was himself a product of Oundle School, where the great F.W. Sanderson had introduced, around the turn of the twentieth century, an Engineering side to rival the technical colleges of the day. Reekie had seen at first hand what could be done: he had himself laboured in the original Felsted workshops, and now had acquired the prestige and influence to bring about the much-needed modernisations. In truth, the old workshops were no longer fit for purpose, so plans were drawn up, under the knowledgeable eyes of the Headmaster, for a completely new building, to be sited a

dozen yards to the south-east of the existing workshop area, and continuing the line of the Science Block overlooking the Colts cricket ground. The project was designed and overseen by Old Felstedian architect R.O. Foster, FRIBA. The single-storey construction would provide a woodwork shop, a metalwork shop and forge, as well as a drawing office and storerooms; once commissioned, all technical activities, including the popular boat-building activity, could be housed under one roof. The redundant building, in the fullness of time, would be surrendered for use by the expanding Works Department, whose task was the general maintenance of the School's facilities, under the aegis of the Bursar's department. As a centrepiece of the Whitsun celebrations in 1964, the Quatercentenary Year, the New Workshops were formally opened by Mr J. Crittall, Chairman and Managing Director of the Crittall Manufacturing Company and Vice-Chairman of the Felsted School Governors.

Clockwise from top left: Tuck Shop; J.F. Crittall opening the New Workshops, 1964; Metalwork lathes in operation; old-fashioned TLC in the New San, 1956.

Quatercentenary celebrations (clockwise from top): Whitsun ball rock band; military tattoo; summer fete revelry.

Henry Reekie's early years had not been wholly untrammelled by unsteadying incident, however. In his second term in office, on 29 February 1952, there was an outbreak of fire in the Grignon Hall, which bid fair to repeat the disastrous conflagration of 1930; happily, this time round, the flames were extinguished before they had taken hold. This might well have been an omen, since the very next day British Rail withdrew the passenger service to Felsted via Dunmow and Braintree, which had been ferrying Felstedians to and from the School since the 1870s; the age of road transport was 'hurrying near', and the Beeching cuts were still a decade in the future, but the line was no longer profitable, so that was the end of the matter. The final 'fly-past' of the ironically named 'Felsted Flyer' was cheered to the echo as it lumbered away uphill towards Little Dunmow and into history; the smoky haze generated by the sugar beet 'campaign' brought a discreet veil down upon the scene.

A strong believer in educating the whole man, Henry Reekie lobbied the Governors for permission to appoint a specialist Art Master: History of Art (and, to a lesser extent, practical work) had been ably supported by non-specialists for a good many years. However, just before the war, purpose-built studios had been provided on the upper floor of the newly enlarged science laboratories, and the creative arts were proving more and more popular as leisure pursuits among the boys. With unerring judgement, Reekie found the right man for the post: T.W. Goodman joined the staff in 1957; his influence was immediate and very positive indeed. Very quickly, Goodman established a tradition of Speech Day exhibitions of pupils' work, and inaugurated the practice of exchanging works with Rugby and other public schools, for 'home and away' exhibitions.

Having seen his new Art Master so satisfactorily ensconced, Reekie found himself having to disrupt the happy situation very shortly thereafter: he had found the provision of teaching space for biological sciences particularly unsatisfactory when he was Senior Science Master, overseeing the extensions to the Science Block undertaken just before the outbreak of the war. Now he saw the possibilities for redeveloping the designated Art Room into well-appointed and airy Biology laboratories. Although the consolidation of the sciences under one roof made perfect sense in all respects, the removal of Goodman's Art Department to the Old Schoolroom in the centre of the village, in time for the

Autumn Term of 1960, must have felt like banishment to the outer darkness, and Goodman's initial response was not conciliatory. However, the new abode became a veritable mecca for the artistically minded boys, and was soon rivalling the Bury as a venue for out-of-school aesthetic pursuits. By this time, Goodman had taken on the Wardenship of the Bury, too, so he was in a pivotal position of influence over the broader cultural education of a good many Felstedians of the period. The many first-rate artists and art historians who came under Goodman's aegis during his 30 years of service to the School will have great cause for gratitude; certainly, he was instrumental in winning recognition for the creative arts at a time when the ethos of athleticism still held strong.

As time went on, Reekie's calm influence was to begin to bear fruits in terms of a steady improvement in the academic achievements of his pupils; an outcome arrived at by careful adjustment of the curriculum, and the inculcation of a powerful *esprit de corps* among the Assistant Masters. A good many of Reekie's reforms would be taken as read by present-day educators, such as his early insistence that science subjects must be made available to all students, at whatever stage in their school career, and that all below the Sixth Form should study at least one science to certificate level.

It goes without saying that present-day parents expect regular written reports from their son's or daughter's teachers, and these were indeed furnished in some form or another in Reekie's day and before that. Nevertheless, face-to-face

meetings with those Masters, arranged for the specific purpose of discussing a boy's progress and achievement, were virtually unheard of in the majority of public schools. An individual Housemaster might arrange a cocktail party to which a selection of parents and schoolmasters might be invited for ad hoc consultations, but regular official meetings had not been thought necessary, by either party in the contract. Henry Reekie thought otherwise: in the Summer Term of 1964, the first

FELSTED SCHOOL CCF ARMOURY RAIDED BY THE IRA

An incident of potentially disastrous consequences to Felsted's reputation was the raid on the Armoury, carried out in the early hours of 25 July 1953. John Stephenson (alias Sean MacStiofain), Cathal Goulding and Manus Canning, three enterprising but ill-informed would-be IRA guerrillas, broke into the premises and loaded their down-at-heel panel van with a substantial panoply of Corps weapons: the haul included 108 Lee-Enfield .303 rifles, ten Brens, eight Stens, two trench mortars and a supply of dummy mortar rounds. Under the impression that they had netted the arsenal of a bona fide regular Army depot, they made off towards London at a leisurely pace. They had contrived to get as far as Bishop's Stortford before the ever-vigilant arm of the law brought to an end their foolish exploit: the van's overloaded condition and newspaper-blinded windows alerted the attention of a patrolling constable, who investigated and made the arrest. It can have been little consolation to the culprits as they began their eight-year prison sentences to discover that not one of the weapons had a serviceable firing pin, since all were used exclusively for parade-ground drills and weapons-training exercises, and had been neutered to that end.

of consultations between Tutor and pupil. Thus was the relationship between teachers and taught subtly mitigated: the student learns to take more personal responsibility for his academic progress; the Master realises that friendly exchanges with his pupils involves no loss of dignity or discipline. Reekie's thoughtful reforms were beginning to undermine the ossified Edwardian 'Fortress Felsted', which had repulsed his predecessor's less well-disguised assaults.

As Henry Reekie's term of office moved into a second decade, the School was approaching the significant celebration of the Quatercentenary of its Foundation. The Governors agreed to the Headmaster's suggestion that the occasion should be made the opportunity for a number of major development projects – some to improve the existing public buildings, and others to provide such new facilities as might be required to meet the demands of a widening curriculum and the sharply increasing competition between boarding schools, instigated by the coming-of-age of the highly selective state grammar schools (ironically, the brainchild of Felsted Governor Butler's 1944 Education Act). How best to attract fee-paying clients away from top-performing day schools was to become the defining and perennial issue for the public schools in the next 20 years at least.

Long-range development plans had been drawn up as early as 1960, with a view to approaching the 400th anniversary celebrations on the wings of a significant capital reserve, and fund-raising events were the first item on the lengthy agenda. Reekie had presided over an unprecedented increase in boy numbers, and public spaces like the Grignon Hall and the Chapel, designed to accommodate a school population of 350, were now being expected to house nearly 450. The Chapel, in particular, needed to be extended for a second time. Besides 'housekeeping' improvements, any headmaster likes to propose at least one eye-catching building project, and Reekie was no exception to this trait: his plan for the construction of a Music School, where general musical activities as well as individual tuition and practice could be centralised, was greeted most warmly by all. It was thought that to cover all the building costs of the various projects, great and small, a budget of some £140,000 must be envisaged. With the help of the Old Felstedian Association, the Quatercentenary Fund was launched, with a five-year lead-in time to the 1964 deadline.

invitations to such a meeting were received by parents of the boys in the Fourth Form; by the following year, the parents of the Fifth Form and Lower Sixth boys had been similarly bidden to attend and hear for themselves the judgements of the wise.

Reekie also introduced system of personal tutoring for the Sixth-Form boys, which endures, little altered, to the present time: in essence, each pupil's work and progress would be closely overseen by a designated Master, who would be attached to a particular House and mentor half a dozen of its boys. Every three weeks, 'chits' with progress reports would be collected from all the subject teachers, to form the basis

That the fund-raising effort was able to meet the target, with something to spare, says a great deal about the popularity of Reekie's projects and the high regard in which the Headmaster himself was held by Old Felstedians and parents alike.

The extensive remodelling of the Chapel, masterminded by architect S.F. Dykes Bower, FRIBA, Surveyor to the Fabric of Westminster Abbey, would take the best part of two and a half years to complete. Between the Summer Term of 1962 and the Autumn Term of 1964, Felsted School held its corporate worship in the parish church, just as it had during the first three centuries of its existence. In spite of a spate of unfortunate delays and unforeseen hitches (which included the bankruptcy of the firm engaged to install the heating system and a fire at the factory where the organ was being rebuilt), the reopening of the building was perfectly timed for the first phase of Quatercentenary celebrations at Whitsun 1964: the Foundation service in Holy Cross Church was relayed to the Chapel, where a second congregation was able to participate by proxy, so to speak. The Chapel was formally rededicated by the Bishop of Chelmsford, on Saturday, 25 July, in the presence of Her Majesty Queen Elizabeth The Queen Mother. The laying of the foundation stone for the Music School, to be sited between Ingram's Close and the Chapel, on land bordering the Stebbing Road, was carried out on the same day by Her Majesty The Queen Mother. No one who witnessed the day could deny that Her Majesty was the epitome of poise and friendly grace, as she chatted with the Prefects and took time to speak with village folk who thronged the Front to greet the most serene of royal visitors.

Felsted School was indeed fortunate to have secured the attendance of such a high-ranking and popular royal figure; but it probably came as no surprise to those in the know, since Reekie had already proved himself something of a specialist in securing high-profile guests for the great School occasions of his era: HRH Princess Alexandra of Kent had attended Speech Day, 1957; Speech Day 1959 saw the prizes distributed by Admiral of the Fleet, Sir George Creasy, GCB, CBE, DSO, MVO, DL; in November 1960, Lord Montgomery of Alamein came for the day: he addressed the boys after morning Chapel and was entertained by the Prefects at luncheon in School House; and Sir Dermot Boyle, Marshal of the Royal Air Force, was the Guest of Honour at Speech Day, 1961.

HRH Queen Elizabeth The Queen Mother meeting the School Prefects, 1964.

The construction of the Music School was completed by the Summer Term of 1965, and was officially opened on Speech Day, 19 June, by Rt Hon. the Lord Butler of Saffron Walden, who was by this time Master of Trinity College, Cambridge, and still, after 35 years on the Board, an active Governor of the School. The building, with its distinctive 1960s flat roof, central auditorium and surrounding teaching and practice facilities, was destined to play an important part in the broadening and liberalising of the curriculum over the next four decades; in 2009, Dr Michael Walker's first year as Headmaster, it would be replaced by the present-day Music School, adjacent to the Lord Riche Hall, and the vacated site redeveloped for private housing. A further laurel bestowed upon the School in honour of the Quatercentenary of the Foundation was the grant by the College of Arms of the Riche arms, authorised for use henceforth as the School's official badge. Baron Riche's device, 'Gules, a chevron between three crosses botonny or', had long been in use unofficially

Headmaster Reekie with the Common Room, 1964.
Back row (l to r): C.J. Throndsen; D.C.M. Waddell; H.K. Maitland; M.F. Walker; J.B. Cameron; G.D.C. Tytler; Revd A.L. Martin (Chaplain); J.H. Bottomley; W.J. Oram; CSM L. Watson (PT Instructor); A. White. Middle row: J.E. Reeves; C.A.H. Lanzer; N.W. Allison; F.M. Craven; C.H. Gregory; J.A. Cockett; R.J. Lewis; P.L. Hawthorn; E.A. Beaulah; T.L. Rowland Jones; J. B. Hall; B.H. Impey. Front row: Revd H.W. Last; P. Gant; J.H. Lee; A.S.M. Ronaldson; F.G. Macrae; M.R. Craze; J.F. Alston; H.E. Reekie (Headmaster); A.U. Payne; O.I. Simpson; G.A. Mason; D.R. Millard (Bursar); M.W. Mann; R.S. Stephens; D.A. Sturdy

at Felsted, adorning many a building and honours board; but after the receipt of the sumptuous parchment scroll, bearing the signatures of the three principal Heralds, Garter Principal King of Arms, Clarenceaux King of Arms and Norroy and Ulster King of Arms, and trailing three heavy gilded seals, Felsted School's right to display the Riche arms as its own was now enshrined in law.

In extolling the achievements of any particular Headmaster, it is all too easy to forget that even the best of leaders must rely heavily upon the support of a talented and tireless Common Room, to say nothing of the numerous band of bursarial and domestic staff labouring in the wings. Reekie was indeed fortunate in having a good many first-rate Masters; his own appointments almost without exception proved their mettle once entrusted with their roles in the School.

Several of these were men of outstanding merit, who would leave an indelible mark on the School community and are remembered with respect and affection by those they

tutored, taught or coached. It is always invidious to select individuals for special mention, but headmasters, however successful, should not be permitted to claim all the credit for a school's success. Of Reekie's earlier appointments, C.A.H. Lanzer, J.A. Cockett, E.A. Beulah, R.S. Stephens, F.M. Craven, D.C.M. Waddell (OF) and H.K. Maitland were all destined to serve significant terms as Housemasters, while P.L. Hawthorn, T.W. Goodman and Revd H.W. Last, along with the aforementioned Lanzer, Beulah, Waddell, Maitland and Craven, would lead their academic departments and spearhead the many curriculum reforms of the 1960s, 1970s and 1980s. Stephens, Beulah, Craven and Maitland would in due course serve terms as Second Master, too.

In those times, virtually to a man, all Masters helped with sports coaching and other out-of-class activities; under Cockett (GB hockey Olympian and Cambridge double-blue), with Beulah, Waddell (Scotland trialist) and Maitland (Cambridge blue and Scotland international) to the fore,

Felsted's hockey fortunes reached heights of success not seen since the 1920s and early 1930s. Others of slightly later vintage to serve the School with distinction for 20 years or more include M.F. Walker (Head of Science and Elwyn's Housemaster), R.C. Down (Head of Classics and Librarian), J. High, T.G. Pockley and N.S. Hinde (Housemasters all, and the latter serving a spell as Director of Studies, too), W.J. Oram (Engineering Master) and R.G. Hodgson (Head of German and Warden of the Bury).

In 1968, after a notably successful 17 years' service, Henry Reekie's reign came to an end with his resignation, having attained 60 years of age. He and Pauline retired to Marlborough in Wiltshire, where they lived contentedly until Henry's death in 2000, aged 92. An 'old-guard' traditionalist he certainly was by nature, but his legacy of strategic and well-crafted though modest reforms can be said to underpin much of what the School was to become in subsequent years, under the next three Headmasters.

Scroll from the College of Arms, granting the Riche coat-of-arms to Felsted School.

SECTION V | THE MAKING OF MODERN FELSTED

Reform and Renewal 1968–2008

Henry Reekie's impending departure from the scene after nearly 17 years brought up for the Governors once again the momentous opportunity to set the School's course on a path of radical modernisation. The traumas of Andrew's tragic death and of Harrison's dismissal had to a large extent been cauterised by Reekie's unflappable stewardship. There had been substantial developments in buildings, in particular, and gentle tinkering with the curriculum, the timetable and the general ethos, but in many fundamental respects, the Felstedian of the mid-to-late 1960s would not in all probability have found his School much different, had he found himself transported back in time to a House JR or to the Chapel or Grignon Hall of pre-war times. But the world beyond the confines of the School's narrow margins had most definitely altered: the Swinging Sixties were well advanced; hair length (and *Hair*) had become a political issue; and the Labour Party's ill-starred Circular 10/65 had signed the death warrant for Local Education Authority grammar schools across the land. There might be troubles ahead for a new incumbent Headmaster, but also distinct opportunities to forge a new place in the academic pecking order for a leader of proven bold and visionary outlook. This time, the Governors chose well: a second successive scientist, who was also a serving headmaster; and a man whose wide-ranging and well-travelled educational experience could bring a much-needed global perspective to this quiet Essex enclave.

Anthony F. Eggleston (1968–82)

Anthony Francis Eggleston, MA, OBE, came to Felsted with impeccable academic credentials: he had been a Scholar at Merchant Taylors' School, Northwood and had proceeded to St John's College, Oxford, as the Sir Thomas White Scholar of his year, to read Chemistry. After taking a second-class Honours degree, he spent two years as a subaltern in the Royal Artillery, seeing active service in the Suez Canal zone.

Anthony F. Eggleston, Headmaster (1968–82).

Upon demobilisation, Eggleston began a teaching career at Cheltenham College. After two years in post, his yen for foreign climes had clearly returned, since he was appointed Senior Science Master at the English High School in Istanbul, Turkey. A recurring career pattern was emerging: after a two-year stint, he returned and stayed rather longer at his old school, Merchant Taylors'. In 1962, aged 34, he became Principal of the English School in Nicosia, Cyprus. His leadership and diplomacy during the increasingly disturbed early years of the newly independent but still deeply divided

Cypriot state earned him the accolade of an OBE. Thus were the qualities forged which would be brought to bear in less violent, but nonetheless combative, circumstances as he and his wife, Jane, arrived to take up residence in Stephenson's, in time for the start of the Autumn Term 1968.

From the very first, it was apparent that the Egglestons were an inspired selection to fill the void left by the departing Reekies. On the surface at least, Eggleston bore a physical resemblance to his predecessor: both were tall men, poised and patrician in bearing, and measured of speech. Both commanded attention in public situations, and both exuded calm authority in their exchanges with Common Room, pupils and parents alike. Jane Eggleston, too, had the assured touch of an accomplished Head's wife, stepping at once easily into the role of organiser and shaper of the wider School and village community, so tactfully consolidated by Pauline Reekie over many years' residence in Felsted. But if the traditionalists among the staff and Governors, perhaps lulled by Henry Reekie's avuncular conservatism, thought they were in for an easy ride under his successor, it would not be long before Eggleston's radical plans for the reshaping of the School's future began to emerge to unsettle the comfortable status quo; within two short years of his arrival, Eggleston had persuaded the Governors to embark upon a ground-breaking and unprecedented reform: the proposed admission of girls into the Sixth Form. It would be fair to assert that this proposal met with dismay in many quarters, though its very revolutionary boldness also won substantial support, too. It would take all the force of argument that Eggleston could bring to bear, and a good deal of luck: an innovation such as this was fraught with danger, and a Head who gambled and lost would not remain long in his post.

Contrary to the received wisdom of the time, the decision to introduce co-education at Felsted was taken for educational rather than financial considerations: Eggleston's analysis of the future boys' registrations had convinced him that numbers were extremely healthy; the downside being that among preparatory school heads the notion was spreading that Felsted was a very good school for the weaker candidate. The Governors had agreed that such a reputation must be rapidly and emphatically dispelled. Tony and Jane Eggleston had plenty of experience dealing with the teething problems

of a new dispensation; bringing co-education to Felsted probably held fewer terrors for them than for others of less sanguine dispositions. But Eggleston knew what he was doing: almost the first major development he had overseen during his stint as Principal of the English School in Nicosia was the amalgamation under one roof of the two separate boys' and girls' sections. Thus, in 1962, was born the very first co-educational boarding establishment in the eastern Mediterranean area. Besides, Eggleston's experience, as well as his careful sounding of the experiences of other heads of co-educational establishments (mostly day schools at that time), had convinced him of the wisdom of introducing academically able and ambitious girls into the Sixth Form mix: he was able to demonstrate within three years of the girls' arrival that

Top: 'Heading towards the 21st century' (left to right) Stephen Roberts (1993–2008); Tony Eggleston (1968–82); Edward Gould (1983–93) and Mike Walker (since 2008) and (above) Mrs Elsie Thorne with Manor House girls, 1973.

the overall standards of attainment at A level had improved markedly. As Eggleston had predicted, boys whose competitive instincts had formerly been directed towards athletic rather than intellectual strivings were seen to stir their academic stumps, rather than allow their female counterparts to challenge their dominance on the academic frontline.

Eggleston's assured liberalising touch was manifest in other early innovations, aimed at moving forward the School's social ethos: in sanctioning the establishment of a Sixth Form Club, in September 1969, he was courting further controversy. The groundbreaking new venture, to be housed in the redundant Masters' billiard room behind Ingram's Close, known locally as the Rabbit Hutches, proposed that at the weekend there would be opportunities for socialising, at which the consumption of wine and beer by pupils over the age of 17 years would be permitted, always under the strictest of supervision by the responsible Common Room authorities present. This was to prove a significant step for an institution still hesitant about placing unwarranted levels of trust in its inmates. Eggleston was also quick to review the disciplinary practices, in particular the infliction of corporal punishment by School Prefects, which tended to hamper the progressive aura he wished to bring to the School. Though the cane was in diminishing use under Reekie, there were still a number of Masters whose reliance upon physical correction as a first (and only) resort was a source of some embarrassment to a Headmaster and Governing Body contemplating the admission of girls into the School. Eggleston sought a path of sensible evolution, and the Prefects of their own choice very soon relinquished their prerogative, once and for all. It was intimated to Common Room, too, that disciplinary standards need not necessarily decline were the stick to give way to the carrot wherever possible.

From the first, Eggleston's brief had been to shepherd the fortunes of a school still substantially trapped in an Edwardian mindset; the rapidly changing Britain of Carnaby Street, Beatlemania and the 'would-be Woodstock' generation must be acknowledged, and sooner rather than later. If the introduction of girls came to be seen as perhaps the most eye-catching of Eggleston's early reforms, it was by no means the only one to polarise opinion in the School. As for so many heads of independent schools before and since, the need to

acquire and then sustain an appropriate level of academic respectability bulks largest in the list of desirable goals to be sought. While Felsted had always produced a steady crop of Oxford and Cambridge entrants, the easy passage from public school to the ancient universities could no longer be relied upon. For countless generations, admissions had been effected through long-established personal contacts between schools and colleges (often allied to certain closed awards to be held by the alumni of specific institutions at a particular College); but now the emerging baby boomer generation, so many of whom were products of the new state-run grammar schools, were casting their caps into the Oxbridge ring. The Colleges perceived that the competition was likely to raise the academic standards all round; unless the best candidates were admitted, a College's standing in the Norrington or Tompkins league tables might suffer serious decline. Similarly, to ensure its reputation in the increasingly competitive market place, a school must ensure that the vast majority of its leavers be fitted for entry into higher education. With the emergence of a dozen or more new 'plate-glass' universities, as well as a proliferation of polytechnics and training colleges, during the 1960s, acceptance on a university degree course was becoming almost the only accepted outcome for the sons and daughters of fee-paying families.

Eggleston set about some quiet but insistent reforms to the curriculum and timetable, which he knew would initiate the improvement in standards he had been enlisted to bring about. His teaching staff appointments reflected his priorities, too: to the dissatisfaction of the sporting fraternity, a man's prowess on the games field (and they were mostly men to start with) cut less and less ice; the sole criterion to be entertained was the quality of the academic input to be expected from the candidate in question. Happily, in most cases, intellectual rigour and athletic ability were not necessarily mutually exclusive: Felsted's enviable reputation for sporting excellence did not suffer unduly in the light of the Headmaster's avowed insistence upon first-rate academic credentials in those he brought into Common Room. Among the earliest of his appointments was the introduction of a Director of Instrumental Music (R.A. Lawrence) and of the first Economics specialist (P.R.H. Soper). Strong academics who arrived at this time and whose contributions

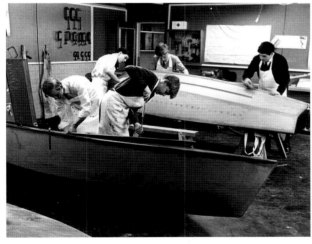

For good measure, Eggleston also instituted the post of Director of Studies: it fell to Peter Gant, Master since 1946 and long-serving Head of Mathematics, to be the first to take on this vital coordinating role in the reformed hierarchy of 1974. At the same time, the post of Second Master was accorded official status, when R.S. Stephens was promoted half a dozen places up the ladder of seniority and, in effect, appointed as deputy to the Headmaster. For the time being, both posts would be filled from within the existing Common Room ranks; another 20 years would pass before newly appointed Headmaster Stephen Roberts would appoint from outside Felsted Mark Allbrook of Hurstpierpoint College to be the first designated Deputy Head. By then, however, the majority of independent schools had adopted the practices of the maintained sector in separating, to all intents and purposes, the roles of teaching staff from the leadership cadres: heads and deputy heads were increasingly required to be trained administrators, not simply successful schoolmasters and mistresses whose long service had fitted them for high office by dint of their past service and experience in their own school.

By the end of his third year in post, Eggleston had overseen some considerable changes to the landscape and ethos of Felsted: girls were here to stay; cafeteria service had come to the main School House dining hall; enlistment in the CCF had become voluntary (with community service

Above: the last days of physical jerks on the Front.

Out-of-class pursuits c.1971: (top left) School glider taking to the skies; (bottom left) getting the sailing dinghies ship-shape.

would include noteworthy stints as Masters in Charge of major sports included C.H. Tongue, Dr T.P. Woods and long-term incumbent as Head of Science, R.P. Ballingall. Later, Eggleston brought British Olympic long-jumper A.L. Lerwill to Felsted as its first 'professional' Director of Physical Education; in partnership with A.W.S. Thomson, appointed at the same time and also a trained teacher of PE and experienced exponent of a range of sports, Lerwill would galvanise many aspects of curricular and extra-curricular PE. No longer would the entire School parade fully changed along the Front under the beady eye of the 'Arge (the last incumbent to oversee this time-hallowed but almost universally reviled institution was RSM John Davey) for 20 minutes of physical jerks during morning break.

FELSTED SCHOOL
1978

HOCKEY		CRICKET		RUGBY FOOTBALL	
ALDENHAM	WON 4-0	KINGSWOOD, S.AFRICA	LOST 4 WKTS.	HAILEYBURY	WON 20-3
FRAMLINGHAM	WON 7-0	ALDENHAM	WON 127 RUNS	ST. PAUL'S	WON 12-4
THE LEYS	WON 4-0	IPSWICH	DRAWN	FRAMLINGHAM	WON 76-0
ST. LAWRENCE	WON 8-0	BISHOP'S STORTFORD	DRAWN	R.G.S. COLCHESTER	WON 46-6
MILL HILL	WON 3-0	ST. PAULS	WON 4 WKTS.	BISHOPS STORTFORD	WON 26-9
GRESHAMS	WON 6-1	THE LEYS	WON 8 WKTS.	IPSWICH	WON 42-0
SOUTHEND H.S.	WON 2-0	BEDFORD	DRAWN	R.G.S. NEWCASTLE	DRAWN 7-7
CHELTENHAM	WON 3-2	HAILEYBURY	WON 6 WKTS.	TRINITY, GLENALMOND	WON 14-0
ENGLISH INSTITUTE,		MILL HILL	DRAWN	MILL HILL	WON 57-0
HEIDELBERG	WON 6-0	HIGHGATE	WON 145 RUNS	KING'S CANTERBURY	WON 11-0
UPPINGHAM	WON 9-0	WINCHESTER	WON 9 WKTS.	GRESHAM'S	WON 39-6
SHERBORNE	WON 2-1	EASTBOURNE	DRAWN	THE LEYS	WON 52-3
REPTON	WON 5-1	TONBRIDGE	DRAWN	WOOLVERSTONE HALL	WON 31-3
		CLIFTON	DRAWN		

M.J.R.French
T.J.Wheaton
C.P.S.Hall
R.M.Mitchell
G.C.Stephenson
M.Eldred
K.J.Baynes
N.T.Gadsby
A.G.Mathie
A.J.Macklin
J.W.Bright

G.C.Stephenson M.G.Baker
M.J.R.French R.N.R.Vartan
N.T.Gadsby J.L.I.Balch
M.A.Rigby A.J.Macklin
R.M.Mitchell E.J.Fairhead
R.T.Griffiths

A.J.Macklin R.S.Cherry
M.J.R.French C.F.Ewbank
K.J.Baynes M.King-Davies
S.I.Shipton N.C.E.Speakman
R.M.Mitchell O.W.Trevelyan
G.C.Stephenson P.D.Gray
A.D.Banks M.A.Rigby
R.T.St.C.Brown D.A.Ross Russell

Above: *annus mirabilis* honours board and (right, top to bottom) the undefeated School Firsts of 1978: hockey XI, cricket XI and rugby football XV.

available as an alternative activity); soccer and fencing were officially recognised as minor sports; and a 'Dri-pla' all-weather hockey surface, largely subsidised by the Philipps Old Felstedian Fund, was in use by the summer of 1971. The Philipps Old Felstedian Fund was set up in 1948 by Lord Milford (L.R. Philipps, d 1889–92), in memory of his two elder brothers, J.W. Philipps (Viscount St Davids, r 1873–8) and Major General Sir Ivor Philipps, KCB, DSO (r 1873–6). The Philipps Fund exists principally to provide large loans to enable capital projects to be started. An ambitious programme of building proposals was now placed before the Governors: even-handed consideration was given to academic, domestic and sporting facilities. Eggleston and his Common Room advisers had displayed commendable vision in their deliberations; could the necessary funding now be found?

The new Howard-Clarke Craft Centre was opened in June 1975, in memory of J.F.M. Howard-Clarke (d 1934–9); killed in action at El Alamein, 1942. Next, an extension was begun to Manor House to be called the Thorne Wing (1976); and construction of a new building to accommodate Stocks's House on a separate site between the Chapel and the Bury was initiated, thus facilitating subsequent further remodelling of School House, where Mont's and Windsor's would spread their wings more comfortably (1978). At the same time, a

Friends of Felsted proposal for the provision of a sports hall (to be sited on the existing asphalt parade ground and hard tennis courts alongside the Stebbing Road) was rejected on grounds of cost (estimated at some £140,000). Two years later, a revised plan was approved and the Palmer Sports Hall took shape. The official opening, on Speech Day 1979, was carried out by Mr Dickie Jeeps, Chairman of the Sports Council, who also unveiled an honours board in the lobby, commemorating the unbeaten (in all but one match) seasons of the hockey and cricket XIs and the rugby football XV of the calendar year 1978.

Eggleston had also turned his mind to renewing his initial assault on the undercurrents of academic lethargy he had diagnosed upon first arrival; his approach included addressing matters of policy as well as the provision of improved teaching facilities. A new Biology laboratory, financed by a grant from the Augustine Courtauld Fund and named Courtauld in honour of the former School Governor, was added to the upper floor of the Science Block; later a new chemistry laboratory, named Chittock, to honour the memory of long-serving Science Master, Crawford Chittock, was also added. To counter any accusations of a science-oriented bias on the Headmaster's part, planning was instigated for the construction of a new classroom block, though the Reekie Building would not become a reality until its opening by former Headmaster Henry Reekie in person, on Old Felstedians' Day, 4 July 1981. A further important benefit of this development, which united English and Classics teaching in a suite of six full-size classrooms and two seminar rooms, was the possibility to group Modern Languages and Geography along the Memorial Block corridor, and to unite Mathematics and Economics/Business Studies in the Dutch Block; until this rationalisation into subject areas, classrooms were allocated to Masters in turn by seniority, some new arrivals having had to spend a number of peripatetic years before achieving the nirvana of a room of their very own!

Just one such was C.C.H Dawkins, first Head of Computing at Felsted, under whose innovative direction a specialist computing centre was inaugurated, in Old Fives Court, by the Stephenson Gate, where a tractor shed and gardeners' store had long been in occupation. The venerable building saw the installation in 1975 of a two-ton Elliott 803 machine; by 1982, Pitteway (as the teaching area came to be named) had been equipped with 26 new BBC computers. As the computer age dawned upon the Felsted scene, the Computer Centre was soon developed further, becoming the epicentre of a vast and rapidly proliferating web of cables, known to the *cognoscenti* as the Felsted Econet. With typical perspicacity, Eggleston had

The Wallis Computer Centre, 1986.

brought a cutting-edge technological era into being: Felsted School's computing expertise has remained at the forefront of evolution and innovation in this field ever since.

More fundamentally, Eggleston sought to promote in the School a greater general regard for the scholarly priorities of its students – by no means an unusual desire in a headmaster, but one that had often fallen upon unresponsive hearts and minds. Eggleston's renewed campaign was launched with the promulgation throughout the School of a document entitled 'Academic Ginger': there would be a designated Upper Upper Sixth Scholars' room (named Coulton and situated upstairs in the Douglas Pavilion, to be used by the School Prefects once the Oxbridge examinations were over); a distinctive tie was introduced to be worn by Scholars; and a more rigorous programme for the Sixth-Form tutorial provision inaugurated. Pupils in the Sixth would henceforth choose their own Tutor and there would be regular, timetabled opportunities for tutorial meetings; a greater emphasis would also be accorded to the fortnightly written reports. For the Lower School, a complex grading system was introduced, designed to record the precise level of a pupil's attainment in each subject, as measured against the year norms. Of all pedagogic preoccupations, the designing and implementation of a satisfactory grading system has surely consumed more man-hours and provoked more controversy than any other: the ensuing decades have seen several root-and-branch reviews, but Eggleston's proviso that effort as well as attainment be taken into account has remained at the core of each successive remodelling of the Felsted grading system to the present day. Two further fundamental institutions were the introduction of Senior Scholarships and the establishment of

The Felsted School Bookshop.

the post of Master of the Scholars. The Senior Scholarship awards were to be made once pupils had completed the first year of their A level studies, to be held for the remainder of the student's Felsted career: the principal criterion for citation was the potential for Oxbridge entry in one or more subjects. In addition to the kudos of the title Senior Scholar, there would be a tangible reward in the form of a substantial book allowance at the School bookshop. The Master of the Scholars' brief would be to oversee the enhancement of the intellectual experiences of all the Scholars, and to act as super-Tutor where a student appeared to be struggling to fulfil his or her promise. With only minor modifications over time, these last two institutions remain in force to this day, and continue to play an integral role in encouraging scholarly ambition and excellence in the brightest Felstedians.

By the end of the 1970s, Tony Eggleston no doubt felt that he had achieved as much as he could to begin the rebranding of Felsted School for the modern, egalitarian age. The School was demonstrably successful in a wide range of activities, and, above all, the academic outcomes were showing signs of distinct improvement. In Eggleston's last three years, the pass rate for A levels rose beyond 87 per cent, and more than 30 places were achieved at Oxford and Cambridge Universities (this in a period when the top-performing state grammar schools and direct-grant day schools were making determined and increasingly successful assaults upon those hallowed portals). The Sixth-Form girls were fully integrated and accepted at Felsted; gaining pace, too, was the trend for other boys' boarding schools to follow suit. Tony and Jane Eggleston quite rightly

felt they had imprinted a lasting mark on the landscape of School and village, and that it was time to seek sunnier climes once more, where new challenges might be faced and both could renew their former close acquaintance with the classical antiquities so dear to their hearts: Eggleston accepted the post of Principal of the Campion School, Athens, for January 1983.

Of the many enduring legacies of the Eggleston period, perhaps one which deserves public acknowledgement is the fact that the School became a more humane and happier environment for the middle-of-the-road Felstedian: the one-size-fits-all hegemony of major sports, the divisive brutality of physical punishment and the insularity of general outlook no longer held uncompromising sway. The admission of girls had naturally altered and broadened the canvas of activities and softened the rigidity of compulsion in other traditional areas of endeavour. There had emerged a renewed enthusiasm for the cultural extra-curricular pursuits, and outreach activities such as community service and the annual PHAB (a nationwide charity dedicated to bringing together groups of people with differing physical abilities for shared social and educational activities) course were firmly embedded in the Felsted programme. The Eggleston era had wrought substantial and deep-rooted change; it would fall to his successors to maintain the momentum of progressive reforms.

Tony and Jane Eggleston.

Edward J.H. Gould (1983–93)

Edward John Humphrey Gould, MA, FRGS, arrived to take up his post as Headmaster in time for the start of the Summer Term 1983. The Spring Term interregnum had brought for Second Master, Tony Beulah, the opportunity to crown his lengthy and all-encompassing career with a stint at the very top of the Felsted hierarchy, as Acting Headmaster; whence he was able to oversee the smoothest of transitions for the new regime. From the first, despite his inexperience in the hottest of schoolmasterly hot seats, Gould was to prove himself a consummate leader, who honed his managerial and directorial skills to perfection over the ten years his reign was destined to cover. There would be plenty of surprises in store: there was a great deal more about the new Headmaster to belie any presumptions made on first acquaintance, which the rugged (not to say pugnacious) physical appearance of a rugby blue and international oarsman might have intimated.

In contrast to his immediate predecessor, Gould's background was impeccably boarding school: he had been a boy at St Edward's School, Oxford; after taking an honours degree in Geography and a Diploma in Education at St Edmund Hall, Oxford, he had joined the teaching staff at Harrow School. While at Oxford, Gould had found time to gain four rugby football blues, a half-blue for swimming, and had progressed so well in rowing as to earn his seat in a representative Great Britain eight. Once ensconced at Harrow, he served a 16-year academic and pastoral apprenticeship, rising rapidly up the conventional ladder of internal promotion: he was soon appointed Head of the Geography Department, subsequently

relinquishing that post to take on the Housemastership of the Headmaster's House. Edward and Jane Gould had found their true métier: they were a couple whose genuine and complementary gifts for organisation and hospitality would in due course be seen to better and better effect, first at Felsted, and in due course at Marlborough College, too.

The earlier years of the Gould era coincided with the boom times for the independent schools, ushered in by Margaret Thatcher's second and third overwhelming General Election victories; the Labour Party's avowed animosity towards the sector was, for the time being at least, consigned to the Opposition backbenches. With the blessing of the Governing Body, Edward Gould set about realising his vision to promote Felsted as the premier boarding institution in East Anglia. Where boarding numbers had begun gradually falling in the country at large, and most especially in the leading rivals locally, Felsted's popularity continued to buck the trend: thus it was with considerable confidence that Gould instituted the first professional marketing programme at the School, which included the production of a video film prospectus, narrated by the well-known television personality Kenneth Kendall (OF), advancing at the same time his first major building proposal: the provision of a second girls' boarding House. The two-block extension to Garnetts farmhouse, designed to accommodate 34 Sixth-Form girls in single or double bedsitters, was ready for occupation by the first cohort in the Autumn Term of 1984. With Dennis Hawxwell, a more than competent project manager, in charge, the School's Works Department was taking on more and more adventurous projects: a good instance being the complete renovation of the Victorian swimming bath, which was fully relined and retiled, gained a new entrance suite of changing facilities and a securely rebuilt roof, all carried out by the School's own workforce. At the same time, refurbishments were carried out in the Chemistry and Electronics areas of the Science Block.

Gould was not finished building yet – not by some distance: by December 1985, plans were afoot to transform the Old Gymnasium (by this time, a dilapidated Victorian structure, consigned since the opening of the Sports Hall to the ignominious role of scenery store) into a workshop theatre, with an attached rondavel to act as pavilion for the Colts cricket pitch, as well as reception area during

Edward J. H. Gould, Headmaster (1983–93).

theatrical performances. The Friends of Felsted, aided by a legacy from the William Hunt Trust, were instrumental in getting this project off the ground; at the same time, serious structural weaknesses were discovered in the Chapel spire and bell chamber, which necessitated its removal for urgent restoration in the Spring Term of 1986. By the summer of that year, the coffers had been lowered considerably, yet there was a good deal of unfinished business on the development front: a handsome grant from the Wallis family permitted the provision of a state-of-the-art Information and Computing Technology building, to be sited in the copse of chestnut trees between the War Memorial (Library) Block and the recently extended Science Block. The Wallis ICT Centre was completed in record time, and was in full use by March 1986. With the Felsted computer interconnection network now radiating from a more central hub, it would not be long before all buildings on the campus could be linked by the extending tentacles of the Econet. Was it perhaps more than mere coincidence that several electronic noticeboards had appeared unannounced at key crossing points around the School during the course of that fateful year, 1984? Pupils and staff were now electronically apprised of the latest administrative and sports information and could see in advance what delights the luncheon menu had in store. More than one Common Room wag was heard to comment acidly that Big Brother had lost little time in bringing his omniscient powers to bear upon Felsted's quiet groves of academe.

The vacancy left behind in the Old Fives Court site was quickly put to good use: convenient for access to the Chapel, and sufficiently remote from the major thoroughfares of the

Top right: storm damage to Stephenson's, 1987 and (below) the new Hunt Pavilion, with Hunt Theatre behind to the left (formerly the old gym) to which it has been added.

School for privacy and confidentiality to be maintained, Gould thought it a perfect venue for the establishment of Felsted's first ever Chaplaincy Centre. The pastoral care furnished by the House staff could now be supplemented effectively by the Chaplain; Religious Studies teaching, too, had found a permanent home. Somewhat ironic, though, was the fact that this secondary use of the building soon usurped the primary purpose, and it was deemed necessary, some two decades later, to re-establish a separate Chaplaincy Centre in the Old Pavilion, once the Tuck Shop had been removed to the more central location of the Cromwell Centre.

As always, new plans often involve subsidiary arrangements, and the Hunt Theatre project was delayed until such time as the Craft, Design and Technology (CDT) Block had acquired its second storey. This project was progressing well until the great storm of October 1987 wreaked its devastation on the campus: the partially constructed roof of the new top floor was lifted and shifted several feet laterally, with the result that the work had to begin again. Though no casualties were sustained, the School suffered considerable damage, not least of which was the comprehensive annihilation of the Headmaster's motor car, which received the full weight of a Victorian chimney, crashing down within inches of the front steps of Stephenson's; by the greatest of good fortune none of the top-floor rooms, also badly mauled by the falling brickwork, was occupied at the time of the disaster. Once the damaged upper floor of the CDT Block had been reinstated, the Craft Centre could be moved into its new

Far left: Headmaster Edward Gould and Head of School, Simon Walker, greet HRH The Princess Royal upon arrival at Felsted and (left) HRH The Princess Royal meets the Housemasters and their wives in the newly opened Lord Riche Hall, 1989.

abode, the scenery store could be relocated to the vacated space in the Old Laundry, and the conversion of the Old Gym and the construction of the attached pavilion could proceed. The opening ceremony for the delayed Hunt Theatre and Pavilion facility eventually took place on 10 September 1988. Meanwhile, a new study block for Elwyn House had appeared to the right of the Old Pavilion, masking the less attractive rear view of the main House as seen from the Front.

The years 1986 and 1987 had seen considerable building work, and there was a good deal more to follow. Gould's defining building project, launched in early 1987 with a major Friends of Felsted appeal, was for the provision of a new dining hall and Common Room complex: the plans involved the construction of a purpose-built refectory, where all catering could be centralised (a considerable economic saving here) and where all pupils might benefit from the House-based family luncheon service he was importing from his former stamping ground. At Harrow, Gould had observed the pastoral benefits associated with 'family service' catering, which of course had been the established practice in Elwyn's and Follyfield from their foundation; in the new dining arrangements would be nurtured the sense of corporate Felsted School identity that Gould was most keen to promote.

The chosen site, which initially failed to meet with the Uttlesford District planning department's approval, would require the relocation of the existing 'Dri-pla' hockey pitch, a factor that would add considerable expense to the £800,000 budgeted for the project. Happily, the Philipps Old Felstedian

Fund was able to make a substantial donation towards the cost of a new AstroTurf pitch, to be located on Prysties beyond the Sanatorium hedge. The Philipps hockey pitch was ready for use by the spring of 1988; the official opening took place in October of the same year, the centrepiece of which was an exhibition match between an all-stars Old Felstedian side and a team of former internationals. This splendid occasion celebrated the immense debt owed to John Cockett, who had recently relinquished the reins after 25 years' peerless service as Master in Charge of hockey and cricket at Felsted.

The Lord Riche Hall was indeed the most ambitious of the many building projects of the late twentieth century: the building was conceived on the grand scale, to include a lofty and commodious dining hall, the ancillary preparation, cooking and storage facilities, and roomy upstairs accommodation for an extended Masters' Common Room suite. The design by architects Nicholas Hare allowed for each House to occupy a separate bay of the main dining area; the food was to be served from electrically heated serving trolleys, positioned along a central aisle. The breakfast and evening meals for the boarders would continue to be cafeteria service, but the midday meal would become a formal affair, with an opening and closing Grace and waiter service supplied by members of each House. The construction was carried out by local firm C.G. Franklin Ltd of Chelmsford, and the completed Lord Riche Hall was opened formally on 18 May 1989 by HRH The Princess Royal, who arrived on the Front in a helicopter of the Queen's Flight.

John Cockett.

Three views of the Lord Riche Hall.

The Lord Riche Hall won several accolades for its innovative features, including the Uttlesford District Council's Design Award for 1989 and the Civic Trust Commendation for 1990. However, the formal luncheon service proved impracticable in the light of an increasingly time-strapped daily timetable, where lunchtime orchestra rehearsals, tutorial meetings and early-departing away fixtures began almost immediately to disrupt the formality that Gould's intention had predicated. After an experimental period of two full terms, it was agreed that the cafeteria model should be reprised, though there were attendant headaches for the catering staff, whose existing facilities were not ideally suited to a continuous flow of customers. Over the ensuing two decades there have been further additions to the service areas of the Lord Riche Hall, which have improved the logistics, though the fundamental awkwardness of access and egress at the business end of the Hall remains a design flaw that has proved impossible to resolve. In other respects, the Hall has proved itself to be a significant asset: indubitably, it is an excellent venue for large-scale concerts, festival dinner dances and Speech Day extravaganzas. Nonetheless, the final building costs of close to £2m outstripped the original budget, and there were to be far-reaching consequences of this serious

with a view to establishing for non-sporting activities a fair allocation of the available out-of-lessons hours. Concepts such as 'Protected Time' and 'Priority Time' were pressed into current Felsted parlance, and the community at large benefited from a more balanced approach to the question of how the students' time was spent. No appreciable deterioration was noted in the success rates of the main sporting teams, yet there was a surge in popularity and a concomitant improvement in the standards achieved by those whose chief interests lay in the musical, artistic or dramatic fields of endeavour. Nevertheless, Gould thought it sensible not to meddle with the time-honoured format of three whole school days (with early evening lessons after games time in the winter months) and three half-holidays (Thursday afternoon being the CCF and Community Service priority time). Thus were preserved the essential rhythms of the boarding school week, to which all conformed, including the small number of Home Boarders, who stayed each day until 9pm, when evening prep was done.

On the academic front, Edward Gould's time in office saw the introduction in 1986 of the new GCSE examination to replace O levels, and the inauguration of academic league tables. In a drive to continue to promote Felsted's credentials as a creditable alternative to the local grammars, Lord Riche Scholarships were introduced at the Preparatory School, to entice talented 11-year-old boys from maintained primary schools to join Felsted. Within the School, Gould quickly introduced a system of 'commendations' and 'rewrites', believing that industry and excellence of achievement relative to ability must be rewarded on a regular basis throughout the working week. Substandard performance, too, must reap the whirlwind of redress: unsatisfactory written work must be resubmitted, with the imprimatur of the Housemaster's signature appended. From now on, pupils had good reason to bring their triumphs and setbacks to the personal attention of Tutor and Housemaster, and this routine contact gave greater emphasis to the primacy of the School's academic focus; for the assiduous and well-motivated student, there was the added incentive of tangible reward in the form of book tokens to be won.

During this period, the national Assisted Places Scheme was in full swing, but the recipients of bursaries joining Felsted were overwhelmingly from independent school backgrounds, something Gould was determined to counterbalance in

overspend, the crippling financial ramifications of which would return to haunt the Governors during the latter half of the next decade.

Despite all that Eggleston had attempted to do to mitigate the stubborn resistance of the 'flannelled fools and muddied oafs' partisans, Gould found a weekly timetable disproportionately favouring the 'major' sport of any given term. So denominated 'minor' sports had little status, and clubs and societies, not to mention music, drama and the creative arts, were accorded only peripheral acknowledgement in the weekly round of activity. It was Gould's firm belief that to attract a wider clientele, who were voicing increasingly negative attitudes to compulsion of any sort where leisure activities were concerned, Felsted must make room for a much wider range of extra-curricular pursuits. He set up the much-parodied WeTCo (Weekly Timetable Review Committee),

Edward and Jane Gould.

the fall was 13.3 per cent; the figures for the Independent Association of Prep Schools was a staggering collapse in boarding numbers of 47.5 per cent, and for Felsted Preparatory School the 36.8 per cent fall held alarming implications for future admissions to the Senior School of boys wishing to board. For nearly ten years, Senior School numbers had been sustained at just under 500 pupils, a figure reached in Eggleston's latter years, but by 1992 the roll had fallen to 426, and the annual fee for a boarding place had topped the £10,000 mark for the first time: with an economic slump showing little sign of abatement, the bleakest of scenarios was becoming a very real prospect. To make matters worse, the Children Act of 1989 had vested responsibility in local councils for the regulation of all residential institutions catering for youngsters. Boarding schools, too, were to fall under their jurisdiction; this would undoubtedly impact further upon the worsening situation. The new statutory regulations would bring inspectors trained to judge standards of care in children's homes into boarding schools, where traditional pastoral practices might be found wanting; more specifically the level of supervisory responsibility vested in the senior pupils would raise some fundamental objections on the part of the inspecting team. Radical remedies to the menacing problems of falling numbers and the changing regulatory climate must be sought, and quickly, too.

Headmaster Gould began wide-ranging consultations with Governors and Common Room, with a view to consolidating a planned introduction of full co-education throughout the Felsted Schools. The proposal had already been put forward for a pre-preparatory section, which could easily be conceived as an entry point for girls as well as boys at the youngest age group. M.P. Pomphrey, until recently Housemaster of Gepp's, had been appointed Headmaster of the Preparatory School, and his wholehearted support gave considerable impetus to the groundbreaking decision to admit girls throughout the age range. The outline proposal was duly endorsed by the Governing Body in February 1992, and the first difficult steps were undertaken immediately.

The Preparatory School would prepare for the admission of girls as well as boys in September 1993. A pre-preparatory department would also be opened at the same date. Given a year's lead time, the requisite alterations to the

the admissions policy of the School. In the event, it was demographic and macroeconomic factors that were to determine the principal decisions of the last three years of Edward Gould's ten-year reign. By this stage, a serious and far-reaching recession was taking hold in Europe, which undermined the stability of the British financial and business community. Inevitably, the uncertainty began to affect the confidence of parents whose children were being educated outside the maintained system. The flight from boarding to day was the first symptom of the dangerous malaise that was to threaten the independent schools' very existence; what the doctrinaire hostilities of the liberal left had failed to bring about was now a very real possibility.

The A level results remained impressive, and the new GCSE was proving equally productive of pleasing outcomes, yet the numbers of future registrations were drying up. Where Felsted's boarding numbers had been holding up throughout the late 1980s, in defiance of the national trends, by early 1990 a steady decline was beginning to make itself felt. Between 1987 and 1992, HMC schools generally saw a drop in boarding admissions of 32.7 per cent, whereas at Felsted

accommodation and facilities could be completed. At the Senior School, the innovations would be more problematic: it had been agreed that Stocks's House would be most easily converted to accommodate the first junior girls, given its modular internal design. Therefore, arrangements must be put in place for the reallocation of those boys in the House who would be remaining at the School in the next academic year. Stocks's closed at the end of the Summer Term of 1992, and would remain unoccupied for a full academic year, while alterations and refurbishments were carried out. Meanwhile plans were drawn up for the requisite extensions to the Manor and Garnetts, which would enable those existing Sixth-Form girls' Houses to open their doors to younger entrants when the expected demand for Third Form places began to pick up. Mrs J.M. Burrett was appointed Housemistress designate and took up residence with her family; it was an advantage that she was *in situ* to oversee the conversion works as they progressed throughout the untenanted year. But still the overall numbers in the School continued to decline: to 388 in the autumn of 1992; this depressing trend only partially alleviated by the admission of 44 children into the pre-prep department, and the consolidation of the Preparatory School numbers at 125. An all-encompassing review of the process by which Felsted's journey to full co-education was to be effected was published for the community's general edification in February 1993; therein in uncompromising terms was clarified the carefully mapped way ahead. The Governors, the Common Room, the students and their parents seemed united in their approval of the plans, and in their desire to see the successful management of the various stages of the development.

In the event, there was even more significant upheaval to be faced. At the end of the Summer Term 1993, after ten years in post, Edward Gould would be leaving, albeit with considerable reluctance, to take up his appointment as Master of Marlborough College. Gould had served Felsted well for the best part of a decade, and his reputation for firm and decisive leadership was fully established in the higher echelons of British independent education; it came as no surprise, then, to learn that he would be moving on to further challenges elsewhere. Edward and Jane had become so very much a part of the fabric of Felsted that it was quite clearly as much of a wrench for them to move on as it was for Felsted to see them go.

Stephen C. Roberts, Headmaster (1993–2008).

STEPHEN C. ROBERTS (1993–2008)

On the face of things, the Governors were hopeful of attracting for the Headmastership of Felsted a strong list of contenders; the School was increasingly gaining press coverage for its continuing excellence on the sporting scene, while the move to full co-education might prove a powerful draw to the widest constituency of applicants. In the event, the appointment of Edward Gould's successor was by no means a straightforward process, since the recent steep drop in numbers and the true nature of the underlying financial insecurity of the School, once disclosed to shortlisted candidates, had daunted all but the most courageous. Nonetheless, in appointing Stephen Cheveley Roberts, MA, PGCE, a serving housemaster at Oundle School, the Governors were confident that they had found for Felsted a new Headmaster who possessed not only the requisite academic and pastoral leadership experience, but also the business acumen and determination to confront successfully the difficulties threatening to engulf the School. Felsted was not alone in facing the very real possibility of functional insolvency: the 1990s saw the disappearance of well over 100 private schools, of which a score or more were HMC or Girls' Schools Association establishments.

Stephen Roberts had been educated at Mill Hill School and University College, Oxford, where he had taken a degree in Physics, stayed for a Postgraduate Certificate in Education, and played hockey at University level. His previous teaching experience had included stints teaching Physics at Christ's Hospital School, and as Head of Physics and subsequently

The advent of fully co-educational teaching at Felsted School.

swingeing economies had become a paramount necessity. By far the largest cost area in any school's budget is the wages and salaries bill. Falling numbers quickly translates into smaller classes, and amalgamating classes and cutting down on options can allow teaching-staff redundancies to be contemplated – and unpopularity courted as a result. The Works Department and ancillary staffs, too, were vigorously pruned, with voluntary redundancies and early retirements given first priority. All this had to be managed while the positive public face of the School continued to be sedulously promoted.

At the same time as the parlous financial situation was being rectified, the new Headmaster addressed himself to the other great task before him: the advancement of full co-education at Felsted. The conversion of Stocks's House had already been completed, and the first girls took up their places in September 1993, Roberts's first term in office, to a considerable fanfare of publicity. Within weeks, Mrs Burrett's pioneering flock of boarding junior girls had grown from four to six, as word spread that co-education was up and running at the Senior School. However, the next phase of the original plan, the proposed extensions to Garnetts and the Manor, could not be contemplated in the prevailing straitened financial circumstances: the Governors needed to realise cash liquidity, not indulge in further capital expenditure. Along with the sale of a significant proportion of the existing staff housing stock held in the village, it was decided that certain parcels of development land within the Mile might also be relinquished – 'needs must when the Devil drives', as they say; the School's bankers were insistent that the deficit be radically reduced, and the looming threat of insolvency was a powerful spur for the Governors' reluctant decision-making at this juncture. Thus began a ruthless shedding of assets deemed surplus to absolute requirement; and small housing developments began to appear on the periphery of the School's playing fields: on the old hard tennis courts on Stebbing Road and on the site of the old Scout hut, adjacent to Garnetts House on the Braintree Road. Of even greater significance was the decision taken to transfer the remaining Manor House Sixth Formers to Stocks's in time for the start of the 1994/95 academic year, and to sell off the valuable central village house, along with its attractive garden plot, where planning permission for further housing might be sought.

as boarding housemaster at Oundle. By coincidence, both of Roberts's previous schools had become fully co-educational during the time he was on the staff. His formative service had thus ideally prepared him for the task to be laid before him at Felsted, to mastermind the implementation of Gould's fledgling co-education reforms. Additionally, a year spent in the world of City banking after coming down from Oxford had inculcated a knowledge of accounting and credit analysis that would certainly stand him in good stead in the financial minefield he was about to enter. Perhaps if it had been more widely appreciated how serious was the financial situation he had inherited, Stephen Roberts's early years might have afforded him more public approbation for his management of the School's affairs, which for reasons of safeguarding morale he had felt reluctant to justify by detailed explanation or clarification.

In the early months of his administration, Stephen Roberts concentrated upon the pressing budgetary difficulties brought about by the catastrophic drop of very nearly a quarter in student numbers: with steadily diminishing income, the balancing of the books became ever more problematical, and

On Speech Day 1994, towards the end of his first year in post, Headmaster Roberts had nailed his colours firmly to the mast; in uncompromising terms, he laid out his overarching philosophy: 'It is essential that Felsted develops from being a boys' school with girls to a fully co-educational institution, where boys and girls have the same opportunities, and respect each other as equals.' He added, 'To achieve this it is essential that there are female members of staff in positions of authority.' This laudable principle proved less easy to bring into being, since the proportion of women on the staff at that date was a mere 10 per cent, of whom two were part-time teachers and another the Librarian. Almost at once, Roberts was able to show the sincerity of his pledge: in September of that year, he brought in Dr Kay Stephenson as Head of Chemistry (the first woman to be appointed as an academic Head of Department); she would become Head of Science, and in due course was promoted to be Director of Studies. In 1997, Mrs Jenny Burrett left Stocks's House to serve on the Senior Management Team (SMT) as the first Senior Mistress in the School's history. Gradually, the balance of the Common Room began to match that of the student population, and by the close of the 1990s, the figure for female teaching staff had risen to more than a third. By the end of Stephen Roberts's 15 years in post, the proportion of women on the staff had risen above 40 per cent, secure evidence that Felsted's co-educational credentials had been firmly cemented.

With boy numbers continuing to fall throughout the mid-1990s, however, Roberts was constrained to put before the Governors a different solution to the question of providing sufficient accommodation for the influx of younger girls expected in the coming years: with new buildings ruled out for the time being, the only possible way forward was for a second boys' House to follow where Stocks's had blazed the trail. Roberts had witnessed at Oundle the heartache associated with such a decision, so was well prepared for a backlash of protest when Follyfield was chosen for conversion. Since internal refurbishment had only recently been carried out, and many rooms and dormitories already converted to bedsitters, it was easy to see that in terms of practicality and cost, no other alternative could be contemplated. Once the boys had been allocated to other Houses, Follyfield's public areas received

some much-needed redecoration, in readiness for the arrival of the first cohort of 14 Third- and Fourth-Form girls who joined the House at the start of the Autumn Term 1995. Felsted's second girls' 13-to-18 House opened under the joint direction of Alastair and Moira Grierson Rickford, whose experience in charge of Garnetts was to prove invaluable in getting the new venture up and running successfully.

Top: 'new wine in old bottles': Stocks's House, 1994 and (above) Follyfield, 1996.

125

The new Sixth Form wing at Garnetts.

Happily, as the new millennium was being welcomed in, recovering pupil numbers were sufficiently buoyant to permit Headmaster and Governors alike the confidence to contemplate adding the Sixth Form wing at Garnetts. By the beginning of the academic year 2002, then, the School's new House structure had been established: Stocks's, Follyfield and Garnetts for girls, and Gepp's, Windsor's, Montgomery's, Elwyn's and Deacon's for the boys. But the continued decline in the proportion of full-time boarders in each House was proving as intractable a problem as ever; Stephen Roberts's second groundbreaking reform, the radical restructuring in 2007 of the House system as a whole, would go some way to address this fundamental concern.

The pressing priority of Roberts's early years had obviously been to tackle the financial crisis, yet he was also minded to introduce reforms of a fundamental nature within the academic staffing hierarchy, too. After only two terms in post, Roberts persuaded the Governors of the need to modernise the management structure by appointing from outside Felsted the School's first ever Deputy Head. From the outset, Mark Allbrook proved a most capable and composed incumbent, who brought a much-valued steadying influence to bear upon staff and students alike, during the more turbulent early terms of the Roberts era. However, it took time for the new dispensation to be fully assimilated, since the Deputy Head was indisputably the Head's man, and not, therefore, a Common Room colleague, as had been the case with the Second Masters of former times. Roberts did recognise the wisdom of reviving

the post of Senior Master, such that the conduit of Common Room opinion could be maintained, though the nexus of direction of the School's affairs had moved most assuredly away from a whole-staff consensus mode to that of an elite Senior Management Team formulating and executing policy decisions. In introducing this new arrangement, Roberts was following the example of the maintained sector, where management systems of this type were already well established. By the time of his departure, Roberts had worked closely with two further Deputy Heads: Allbrook was succeeded in 2002 by M.R. Christmas, who in turn was followed by D.M. Lauder, who arrived at Felsted in 2007.

Ironically, the Governors' decision to divest the School of its saleable property, vital as this policy might have been at the time, had an unintended but serious long-term effect: while trumpeting the boarding school ethos of the School, the essential supporting network of a close-knit community of locally resident staff could no longer be sustained. One of Roberts's fundamental reforms, namely, the requirement that all teaching staff be involved in evening supervision duties within the boarding Houses, was thus somewhat compromised by the dearth of affordable housing in the immediate vicinity of the School. By the mid-1990s, a growing contingent of the teaching staff was constrained to commute from considerable distances, since the cost of private housing in the village was often well beyond the means of newly appointed Common Room members. Once the School's financial position had been stabilised, it became a priority to replace some of the lost staff accommodation, and in particular the provision of married quarters for the Assistant Housemasters/mistresses was placed high on the list of proposed building developments. These would take some time to become a reality, however.

The decision taken in 1995 to launch a Friends of Felsted Appeal was a bold step: in showing such a positive and forward-looking public face, the School was signalling its optimism at a crucial time. The Cromwell Centre, built in the cloister court behind Backhouses, and the Art and Design Block at the Prep School gave tangible evidence of resilience and ambition. The refurbishment of the Willis organ in Chapel and the provision of floodlighting for the Philipps pitch, funded in part by individual donation, were further marks of an underlying determination to pull through the hard times.

A SPLASH OF HOUSE COLOURS ON THE FELSTED SPORTS FIELDS

In common with many boarding schools, Felsted's Houses had developed elaborate trappings to denote the sporting achievements of their inmates; but no identifying badge of affiliation for new entrants and for those as yet unblooded in House teams had ever been sanctioned. However, in 1994, Headmaster Roberts, in consultation with the Housemasters, sought ways to strengthen the boys' House identities: Felsted was famous for the plethora of sports club and colours ties, but the rank and file had for many years been constrained to wear a nondescript navy blue tie. Roberts welcomed the suggestion advanced by the Housemasters for the adoption of a new distinctive basic uniform tie, with each House to be designated by a different coloured stripe. In heraldic terminology the colours are: Gules (red) for Gepp's; Or (gold) for Windsor's; Azure (blue) for Mont's; Argent (silver) for Elwyn's; Vert (emerald green) for Follyfield; and Purpure (purple) for Deacon's. These colours remain in current use for the boys' House ties; nowadays they also find more vivid expression in the games shirts worn by students for House match engagements.

Not to be outdone, the girls, too, soon adopted distinctive sportswear, usually arranged in attractive quartered colours, for their House matches. Stocks's chose claret and dark blue; Follyfield kept its pre-conversion emerald green, paired now with sky blue; Manor quarters pink with dark green; Garnetts players sport an eye-catching combination of green and garnet red; and Thorne House has an elegant pairing of purple and cream.

The boys' Houses have followed suit, adding a second complimentary shade to the original House colour. House matches at Felsted are visually much enlivened by this innovation; one slow to take root in Felstedian iconography, but no less welcome for its latter-day appearance on the scene.

Sixth Form Centre
mezzanine working area.

fulfil a quasi-adult role in the community. Roberts's proposal, placed before the Governors in 2005, to introduce the International Baccalaureate (IB) Diploma programme in the Sixth Form would certainly also influence the changing nature of boarding-school life. The IB Diploma had been introduced with varying degrees of success in a number of HMC schools, and Headmaster Roberts felt there was a good case for its introduction at Felsted. Ostensibly, he surmised that offering the IB option alongside A levels would help to consolidate Felsted's popularity with a well-established market in Germany and central Europe, but influxes of greater numbers of foreign students would certainly also bring significant new influences to bear upon the School's social mix and general ethos.

By early in 2003, the Felsted Schools counted over 800 pupils on the roll, and confidence was beginning to revive: Roberts and the Governors again contemplated expansion and building projects. Plans for a second AstroTurf hockey pitch and for the redevelopment of the old School House dining hall into a Sixth Form Centre were approved. By January of 2004, the new Cockett pitch was in operation and the Sixth Form Centre opened its doors in time for the Autumn Term 2005. Another project which had been contemplated somewhat earlier, the replacement of the ailing and superannuated Music School of 1965, could now be revived. The valuable site between Ingram's and the Chapel had long figured on the Governors' list of possible saleable assets, and plans had been drawn up for its development for housing, always provided that the musicians could be found suitable alternative accommodation. Once the planning authorities had authorised the proposal to extend the Lord Riche Hall complex to the west, towards Deacon's corner, the cost-effective project could move forward. During Roberts's final year, the building works were instituted, and though the official opening did not take place until his successor had been in post for some time, nevertheless, the new Music School, with its impressive suite of teaching rooms and the fine Barbara Karan Auditorium, will stand as Headmaster Stephen Roberts's most visible legacy.

The Board of Governors and their enterprising Headmaster must take great credit for the ultimate success achieved by this courageous strategy.

Despite the changing demographic of his staff, Roberts pressed ahead with his review of the tutorial and pastoral arrangements. The model he intended to introduce predicated a House-based deployment of tutor teams, the majority of the Common Room being contractually obliged to undertake evening duties once a week. Inevitably, the prefectorial system, so long a training ground for the leadership skills of the older students, would require overhauling, too. With the introduction of adult oversight within all aspects of boarding House life, some older pupils quite naturally began to conceive of themselves as no longer regarded in the former light as potential leaders of their Houses and of the School at large. While it is recognised that the time-honoured system was by no means a perfect one, potentially there could be serious teething troubles associated with the introduction of the local council Social Services Department's recommendations, as those reaching the top of the School sought the traditional emancipation from the petty regulations of their junior years, but were not in return empowered to

By the time he had accepted the offer from the governing body of the Stamford Endowed Schools to become the next Principal, Stephen Roberts had instituted his last and perhaps most enduring reform: the further restructuring of the

The Barbara Karan
Auditorium (BKA) in the
new Music School.

House system. Essentially, Headmaster Dalton's institution of the conventional 13-to-18 age range boarding houses was proving less and less appealing to parents and prospective students alike. Changes in society generally, especially in the expectations of young adults for greater freedom and self-government, meant that the established hierarchical structures no longer held sufficient attraction. Roberts put his proposal to the Governors: Garnetts and Windsor's would become Upper Sixth Houses; Montgomery's (boys) and a revived Manor House (girls) would cater for day pupils in the ground floor of School House; and the remaining Houses would accept only boarding students for the first four years of their Felsted career. A new category of admission, the 'occasional' boarder was instituted; these students were contracted to sleep in House a minimum of three nights per week. The proposal was carefully designed to consolidate the boarding ethos of Felsted, and to adapt the School's structure to take into account the paramount importance of academic focus in the final year of secondary schooling, when university applications and the need to prepare for the self-reliance of independent learning and living are key priorities. The introduction of

the IB Diploma cemented the underpinning wisdom of the restructuring plan; in due course, the examination results achieved by the first post-reform Upper Sixth constituted a further strong endorsement of the new dispensation.

Stephen Roberts left Felsted for Stamford at the end of the Summer Term 2008, having served a full 15 years in post. His substantial achievement in steering the School through the minefields of the financial crises of his early years, his consolidation of the boarding-school ethos, and the progress he ushered in during his later years must all be fully acknowledged; as too must be the wider community's debt of gratitude to Dr Joanna Roberts, who, despite being fully involved in her own professional pursuits outside the School, was a strong support to her husband throughout his time in office.

In 1993, Roberts had taken on a faltering establishment, with a rapidly collapsing roll of 358 pupils and a substantial black hole at the bank; he left to his successor, Dr M.J. Walker, a remodelled and vibrant community of 485 students, and a renewed confidence to forge its future on the national and international stage. Modern Felsted owes Stephen Roberts a very great deal.

12 | THE CO-EDUCATION STORY

AND NOW FOR SOMETHING COMPLETELY DIFFERENT … (1968–70)

The appointment of Tony Eggleston as Headmaster brought to Felsted a convinced proponent of the co-educational principle: he had recently masterminded the amalgamation of two single-sex schools in Cyprus, and his reforming credentials had strongly recommended his candidature to the School's Governing Body. It can have come as little surprise when early in his tenure Eggleston placed before the Governors his radical proposal to introduce girls into the Felsted Sixth Form. This is not to say that all were supportive of the idea of establishing co-education at Felsted School; after all, there were five Old Felstedian Governors, whose instincts might in certain cases have been of a conservative hue. Nevertheless, Eggleston's carefully presented arguments for reform prevailed, and his plans to expand the School's numbers towards the 500 mark were given a wholehearted nod of approval, the condition being that a two-year trial period be explored, in the first instance. Felsted would become only the second HMC school to take this groundbreaking decision.

Characteristically, Eggleston had done his homework well: the first HMC school of note to embark upon the admission of girls was Marlborough College, in 1968. The experiment had been a cautiously approved success for the Master, John Dancy, who had undertaken the introduction of girls 'to consolidate the liberal position' in contemporary independent education; in a school of significantly larger numbers of boys, the influx of a dozen or so girls was met with little overt opposition, though the pioneering cohort of girls at Marlborough certainly faced significant covert resistance from their male counterparts. Numbers there grew steadily over the next two years (from 15 to 27, then 41), as parents with children at girls-only boarding schools cottoned on to the perceived academic and social advantages of moving their daughters to a boys' school Sixth Form.

Eggleston had noted the growing popularity of this market, at the same time seeing the wider possibilities for moving Felsted forward in a new educational climate; he knew that co-education in the Sixth Form could work to Felsted's benefit just as well; the intervening years have proved how right he was, with virtually all HMC boys' schools of comparable status having followed this lead. Thus it came to pass that, in the Autumn Term of 1970, the first 11 girls were admitted to the hallowed portals of an exclusively masculine domain.

Mrs Elsie Thorne, the first Manor Housemistress, with husband George (Music Master, 1922–61).

One feature of the Marlborough experiment that Eggleston wisely did not replicate was the allocation of small numbers of girls to the existing boys' houses, where accommodation was found on the upper floors (areas perhaps formerly occupied by the matrons and housemaids). At Felsted, girls were housed from the outset in separate quarters; even as numbers rose, their accommodation was never compromised by the difficulties experienced at Marlborough, where the cheek-by-jowl propinquity with the boys caused considerable friction and tribulation for the authorities, to put it politely. The Manor House, a large property on Station Road just past the village stores and garage, was acquired for the purpose, and Mrs Elsie Thorne, wife of long-serving Music Master, George Thorne, was given charge of the girls in the newly established boarding House.

EARLY BIRDS (1970–5)

The researcher who searches in the annals of the Felsted archives will find little evidence that Eggleston's 'great leap forward' had an immediate impact on the deeply entrenched status quo. The Blue Book of the first few years does not list the Housemistress by name (this may well have been a simple printers' omission, of course); and though a couple of House Prefects appear in the listings from the second term onwards, no girl appears to have been appointed as a School Prefect

until the Autumn Term of 1976 (Caroline M. Mason), by which time numbers had risen to 38. It was clearly a slow evolutionary process at the time, and the first cohorts must have felt that they were here 'on approval' and had to shout very loudly for their collective voice to be heard.

Numbers remained at around two dozen girls for several years, and the practice of 'boarding out' a few of the Upper Sixth (in smaller private houses, with resident staff acting as house parents) became the established norm from 1971 onwards. It is clear to see that this was an expedient resolution, but the dislocating influence on the individuals may not have been immediately apparent; or, if it was, then financial constraints had proved uncompromising. This situation continued, despite the establishment of the Thorne Wing extension (which allowed overall girl numbers to reach 40), until the opening of Garnetts in 1984. Many an Upper Sixth Manorite of that period may well recall with nostalgia her year of emancipation in digs above Headman's or in Garnetts (pre-redevelopment), despite the fact that a semi-detached school lifestyle probably had its disadvantages, too.

STEPPING UP TO THE MARK (1975–83)

For the first 20 years or so, the girls admitted to the Felsted Sixth Form were members of an elite corps: demand from parents (no doubt prompted by their daughters, tiring of the perceived restrictions of their girls-only educational experience) grew apace in the mid-to-late 1970s. Applications began to outstrip places by three to one. Felsted could choose its girls from a wider pool of able and talented students, and competition for places became fierce. This situation prevailed well into the 1980s, and many excellent candidates had to be turned away. Who does one select in such circumstances? The Marlborough blueprint of 1968 stated that they should admit 'girls who could fit in' and 'girls who would be able to cope'. These precepts were certainly high on the selection panel's mind (the Headmaster and Mrs Jane Eggleston) when interviewing prospective Felsted girls. Those who passed muster were indeed a resilient and energetic band of pioneers. Truth to say, the Sixth-Form girl entrants in the early years played an increasingly central role in the academic, cultural, musical and athletic life of the School. To leaf through the pages of *The Felstedian* magazines of the 1980s and 1990s is to come across incontrovertible evidence that the advent of girls at Felsted has been wholly beneficial to the ethos and ambiance of the School.

In the early years, it was to drama and music, in particular, that the girls' talents were drawn; but as numbers grew, it was the sporting dimension which began to assert itself. Felsted had for generations seen itself (and been perceived by those

beyond its purlieus) as a formidable production line for international, national and county sportsmen, and the new arrivals were expected to make their mark in this sphere, too. Perhaps it is of greatest significance in the acceptance and assimilation of the girls at Felsted that under the coaching and guidance of Marion (Oxford blue) and Henry Maitland (Cambridge blue and Scotland international), the girls' hockey teams began to compete effectively against their opponents on the circuit. Over the years, Felsted's girls have owed a considerable debt of gratitude to the dedication and efforts of Marion (in whose memory is dedicated the annual Speech Day prize for the outstanding girl's sporting achievement) and to Henry; their contribution to the long-term establishment of the co-educational sporting credentials of Felsted School is outstanding. In subsequent years, as numbers have increased, the School's standing as a major competitor in girls' sport has grown exponentially. Results in the last few years have shown that few of our regular competitors these days are confident in anticipating their clashes with Felsted's girls' teams without a qualm or two of trepidation.

CONSOLIDATING SIXTH FORM CO-EDUCATION (1983–93)

With the arrival of Edward Gould as Headmaster in 1983, the co-education path was further explored and expanded. Within a short time, Gould realised that the space in Manor, despite the relatively recently opened Thorne Wing extension, was not coping effectively with the 40 girls in the School; he resolved to rationalise the accommodation and pastoral oversight of all the girls in the School, and so bring to an end the dislocation of boarding out a proportion of the Upper-Sixth girls, a legacy of the Eggleston expansion in numbers. The Governors were persuaded that Garnetts (already accustomed to housing four Manor seniors within the existing private accommodation) should be the site to be developed.

The annexe building at Garnetts was completed in good time for the first enlarged intake of Sixth-Form girls in the Autumn Term of 1984; with a complement of 60 altogether, the numbers were beginning to approach a quarter of the post-O level cohort in the School. Most classes were co-educational, music and drama were well supplied with female talent, and the Sixth-Form dances began to have an in-House

Marion and Henry Maitland with the girls' hockey team, 1987.

feel about them. On visiting nights, the Garnetts and Manor common rooms were thronged by hopeful male postulants, who had the choice between a trek down the 'vill' or a hike across the playing fields in furtherance of their social life. Headmaster Gould continued the practice of appointing a married Housemaster when vacancies arose in the two girls' Houses, and in many cases the incumbent would expect to be moved up to take charge of a boys' House when a vacancy occurred. One should beware of reading too much into this practice; no slight was intended to the girls themselves, it was simply the accepted pathway of promotion deemed appropriate at the time.

A NATURAL PROGRESSION (1993 TO THE PRESENT)

When the Governors' choice fell upon Stephen Roberts to succeed Gould, they had found the architect they needed to press forward towards establishing a fully co-educational School. The Preparatory School was admitting girls in the younger years, and it could not be denied that the wider economic situation was placing pressure on the Senior School to fill the empty spaces that were beginning to gape in the overall numbers of pupils on the roll. This is not to say that the process was merely a financial expedient, though no one can deny that with boy boarders in East Anglia becoming ever scarcer it would certainly help the Bursar to balance the books if sufficient girls could be admitted to the Third Form. One serious issue has always arisen at this juncture: namely, the mismatch between the traditional independent education systems for boys and for girls. Prep schools keep their boys until 13, while many senior schools for girls recruit at 11, in accordance with the practice in the maintained sector of British secondary schooling. Thus Felsted needed to bring girls to its own prep school, as well as try to recruit from co-ed preps in the area.

At the same time, competition was growing ever fiercer: Oundle, Oakham, Greshams, and The Leys had already made the move to full co-education; Rugby and Uppingham were also mooting a similar evolution. Above all, the next step had to be accomplished without compromising the finances in the short term: thus conversion of existing boys' Houses was the only expedient way forward. Edward Gould had taken the initial decision to close Manor and to convert Stocks's into a

girls' 13-to-18 House. The layout and internal accommodation here was more suited to this adaptation than any other of the houses, and so it came to pass that one of the four original 1890s School Houses (albeit long departed from its original accommodation in the main buildings) began a new life, with Mrs Jenny Burrett as the first Housemistress appointed at Felsted since Elsie Thorne, 25 years before.

Headmaster Roberts took the evolutionary process a stage further by dispersing Follyfield's boys to the other remaining boys' Houses and opening the House to girls in the Autumn Term of 1995. Within the next five years, the proportion of girls in the School rose to roughly a third; a respectable ratio of 1:2. Overall numbers have climbed back towards the 500 mark, and there has been a need to accommodate a greater number of girls throughout the age range. Headmaster Mike Walker's contribution to the co-ed story is the creation of the newest girls' House, named fittingly in memory of the pioneering first girls' Housemistress, Mrs Elsie Thorne.

Manor House bedsitter 1985 (above) and (below) Thorne House (formerly the Sanatorium).

SECTION VI | FELSTED SCHOOL AT 450

13 | FAITH, PHILOSOPHY AND THE WIDER HORIZONS

CHAPEL AND CHRISTIAN WITNESS AT FELSTED SCHOOL

The Chapel stands very much at the centre of Felsted School life, as it has ever since its first services were conducted by Revd Grignon, Head Master (and Chaplain) at the time of its first opening. Times change, and with societal evolution the modes and practices of organised religion have to evolve and adapt: Christianity finds itself very much at the edge of modern-day British culture, and for many students the notion of church and personal engagement with religion is far from familiar territory. Successive School Chaplains, here as everywhere else, have sought to develop the appropriate medium through which a spiritual dimension may be presented, in the context of a modern, largely secular and consumerist lifestyle. It is safe to assert that Felsted still has a Christian heart, and the heartbeats are strong and insistent, even now.

Alistair Andrew was the first lay Headmaster to preside at Felsted, and since his appointment in 1943 the School has relied upon the services of a Chaplain to orchestrate its religious life. The Chapel itself began life as long ago as 1873, was extended with the addition of two transepts in 1926, and was thoroughly remodelled and substantially extended as part of the Quatercentenary celebrations of 1964. The interior is airy and spacious, allowing for a congregation well in excess of 600, when the need arises on high days and holy days.

The Bickersteth Chapel, within the extended south transept, was established in memory of Felsted's last clerical Headmaster, Archdeacon Bickersteth, MC, whose service as a First World War military chaplain had won him such renown. Above the altar in this side chapel can be seen one of the Chapel's iconic curiosities: the shrapnel-shattered bronze head and upper torso of a wayside *calvaire* figure, retrieved near

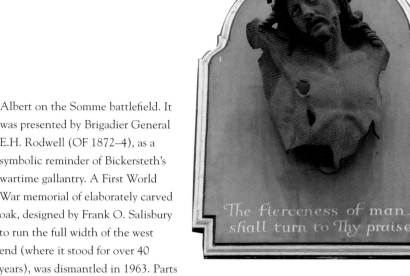

The fierceness of man shall turn to Thy praise

Albert on the Somme battlefield. It was presented by Brigadier General E.H. Rodwell (OF 1872–4), as a symbolic reminder of Bickersteth's wartime gallantry. A First World War memorial of elaborately carved oak, designed by Frank O. Salisbury to run the full width of the west end (where it stood for over 40 years), was dismantled in 1963. Parts of that memorial, in particular the panels bearing the names of the fallen, were retained and incorporated in the screen at the rear entrance lobby; the names of those Felstedians who gave their lives in the Second World War were added at the same time.

Nearby is the tablet recalling the two Old Felstedian holders of the Victoria Cross, Lieut. Walter Hamilton, The Guides, and Capt. John Green, RAMC. Much of the Victorian stained glass was removed, but the enlarged transepts have windows commemorating Second World War Old Felstedian losses. The broken marble headstone in the porch was originally set up in a cemetery in Ostend, Belgium, where, in 1915, Flight Lieutenant David Keith-Johnston (OF 1909–12), Royal Naval Air Service, was buried by his German foes, having been shot down during a raid on the dockyards. The inscription, *Ehre dem Tapferen* (Honour to the brave), reflects sentiments of a different age.

The churchmanship in Chapel has tended in recent times to move towards the evangelical wing of the Church of England, with a succession of ecumenically minded clergymen appointed to the Chaplaincy, since the incumbencies of Revd Alex Martin (1964–73), who left Felsted to become Director of the Bloxham Project, and Revd John Pinner (1974–81). Pinner's successor was Revd Robert Clarke, whose ministry combined an innovatory approach with an energetic desire to promote an inclusive and accessible ethos in the School's worship and witness.

Clarke was soon to be appointed Housemaster of Manor (and subsequently of Deacon's), thus crucially dividing his professional focus. His incumbency was much enlivened by the supporting roles played by his youthful Assistant Chaplains, one of whom caused much merriment (but rammed

home his homily effectively) while preaching a St David's Day sermon, by attempting to eat a daffodil. A feature of this period was the growing involvement of pupils in the planning and presentation of daily Chapel services. It could be said that, as with the daffodil incident, the 'medium' occasionally proved more memorable than the 'message', though the underlying principle, a desire to promote relevance, remained a constant thread through the 1980s and 1990s. Under Revd Christopher Jervis (1985–7) and Revd Christopher Griffin (1988–98), the pastoral outreach begun by Clarke was further developed, and in-House services, including Holy Communions, were a regular feature.

The incumbency of Revd James Hart (2000–6) ushered in the new millennium; his contribution was to bring into sharper focus the community aspects of the Chaplain's work, with the Chaplaincy Centre, established in Bob Clarke's time in the Old Fives Court by the Stephenson Gate, seeing increasing numbers of visitors. Revd Jonathan Brice (2006–11) introduced a style of ministry in sharp contrast to that of his predecessor: he had served more than a decade as Missioner at the Ascension Church, Custom House, and brought to his very different role at Felsted a rugged, 'muscular' directness of vision. Contacts with the Docklands Mission were strengthened, especially with the continued

Opposite: Speech Day Chapel service; (above) the shrapnel-damaged bronze of Christ, and (left) the headstone of David Keith-Johnston.

involvement of Mrs Shara Brice with the Ascension Eagles, the cheerleader group she had established in that community. Felsted is proud to remain one of the few schools whose Victorian Christian philanthropy in setting up missions in deprived areas of London's East End has been sustained and developed into the twenty-first century.

Among other innovations during his ministry, Revd Brice introduced high-spec audio-visual technology into Chapel, a feature still proving its worth in the modern teaching and learning context; but a fundamental drawback (in Chapel as in the classroom) is that there is a real risk that the medium can very quickly become the message. Brice was careful to mitigate that danger through thoughtful and engaging preaching and wholehearted participation in the extra-curricular and sporting life of the School. He left Felsted after the Summer Term 2011, to take up the post of rector of Christ Episcopal Church, in Aspen, Colorado, US.

After an interregnum of over a year, during which the Vicar of Holy Cross, Revd Colin Taylor, helped to hold the fort, Revd Nigel Little arrived to start his Chaplaincy. His Christian witness and vision were honed in parish work, first in Highgate, North London, and latterly in Willerby, a village in the suburban sprawl of Kingston-upon-Hull, East Yorkshire. Revd Little believes fervently in proactive Christian ministry, supporting all sections of the School community; he has revived a more traditional Anglican style of regular worship, while continuing to welcome the involvement of staff and pupils in services. His first characteristic innovation was to re-establish a separate Chaplaincy Centre in the Old Pavilion, the original office by the Stephenson Gate having been subsumed for teaching space by the Religious Studies Department. The management of Felsted's Christian life remains in very good hands indeed.

THE FELSTED PHILOSOPHY OF LEARNING

The appointment of Dr Mike Walker as Headmaster in succession to Stephen Roberts in 2008 would usher in the introduction of many new ideas for refocusing the educational experience offered to the School's students. The departure of Deputy Headmaster Mark Lauder to the headship of Ashville College provided the opportunity for a reshaping of the Senior Management Team (SMT). Building upon the Roberts developments in this vital area, Walker introduced a further reorganisation: academic and pastoral issues would henceforth become the separate fiefdoms of two dedicated Deputy Heads; the post of Director of Studies thus summarily being abolished. At the same time, two new posts were created: Deputy Head Welfare and Deputy Head Co-curricular; in addition an Assistant Headship was also inaugurated. Thus was constituted a Senior Leadership Team (SLT) fit for purpose in the hard-wired contemporary world of school management.

A new wide-ranging Felsted Philosophy of Learning, introduced in 2011, underpins all teaching practice throughout the entire age-range and across all academic departments. Students and staff alike are comprehensively involved in the processes of learning, with careful evaluation of aims, tasks and outcomes at frequent intervals, thus ensuring continuity and development of the Felsted educational experience.

Felstedians at all levels are enjoined to be 'Ready', 'Resourceful', 'Resilient', 'Responsible' and 'Reflective'; prized qualities such as intellectual curiosity, taking the initiative in developing one's knowledge, persistence under pressure, taking ownership of one's own learning and working effectively with others as a team are foregrounded. The five 'Rs' for students are balanced by the five 'Cs', which help to define the teachers' role: 'Communicating', 'Connecting', 'Challenging', 'Creating' and 'Clarifying'. There is certainly no intention to standardise teaching styles or lesson content, but a new focus on the students' role in the classroom partnership is very much to the fore in the new dispensation. However, in keeping with modern theories concerning methodology, Felsted's academic aims are placed uppermost in all respects, whilst a holistic overview of the students' experiences is never far from the evaluation process. As has always been the case, Felsted prides itself on its pre-eminence as an establishment where its value-added indexes, both in the academic and all-round character-building aspects of education, are impressive. The accolade of 'outstanding in all respects', accorded by Ofsted in 2011, bears witness to the School's continuing progress on all fronts.

Felsted School now defines itself as an establishment dedicated to the provision of a broadly based education for life, within a supportive and caring community. Fundamental to the School's ethos is the international dimension: the students are drawn from a diversity of national and ethnic backgrounds, and are encouraged to adopt a global outlook wherever possible in the course of their learning experience.

The introduction of the Felsted Diploma, a unique innovation in British independent education, further underpins the values and visions of Felsted School in the modern context, focusing the attentions of teachers and students alike upon the centrality of their partnership in the educative process.

Above: IB students in national dress and (above left) Dr Walker addresses the Speech Day audience.

INTERNATIONALISM AT THE FOREFRONT OF THE FELSTED VISION

The year 2010 will long be remembered as the dawn of Felsted School's new incarnation as an English independent school with an international vision. For very many years, the student body has included a fair proportion of foreign nationals, as well as expatriate Britons from lands afar, which has leant the School a cosmopolitan flavour and prompted not infrequent celebrations, such as Chinese New Year and Australia Day. The Lord Riche Hall has often been decked with the flags of many nations, and the luncheon menu deftly tweaked to waft the scents and tastes of exotic fare to the waiting hungry hordes. It goes without saying that many trips and sporting tours to the Continent and beyond have also found regular inclusion in the calendar of events. At no time since the exile in Herefordshire brought a sense of adventure to Felstedians of that era could the School have been accused of narrow-mindedness or insularity.

Above: Felsted Round Square visit to Thailand and (right) King Constantine of the Hellenes arriving to address the 2012 Round Square Conference at Felsted.

However, the arrival of Dr Mike Walker in 2008 was to usher in a truly revolutionary phase in Felsted's international vision. A number of happily coinciding factors were to force the pace considerably over the ensuing years, but it was Walker's ambitious vision and the energetic involvement of key staff and students which served to consolidate the rapid progress made in the initial months of the project.

By the end of 2010, Felsted had been admitted to the Round Square organisation as a global member, played host to its third Model United Nations (MUN) conference and adopted Magic Bus as a designated charity. In addition, the British Council had bestowed upon the School its prestigious International School Award, for 'outstanding development of the international dimension in the curriculum'; the Namibia Expedition in the 2009 summer holidays had by that time already earned the coveted World Challenge accolade for the skills development programme realised during the trip to southern Africa.

ROUND SQUARE SCHOOL

Headmaster Walker's conviction that Felsted has a role to fulfil on the wider stage has underpinned a good deal of his vision for moving the School forward in the twenty-first century; membership of the Round Square movement was therefore always a dearly held aspiration. Building upon contacts established by the earlier MUN activities, Modern Languages teacher David Lucius-Clarke fostered Felsted's candidacy sedulously through 2009 and 2010, achieving recognition for the School and acceptance into the Round Square family at the conference held in Thailand in October 2010. Speech Day 2010 proved to be an especially important occasion, since the Guest of Honour was the former European Regional Round Square Director, Mr Christopher Hunter. His presence and encouraging words of welcome were well received by the assembled company. Henceforth, Felsted could take its place as a fully-fledged Round Square establishment, linked fraternally with a worldwide brother- and sisterhood comprising some 100 schools.

The School's Round Square credentials were accorded further attestation by the visit of King Constantine of the Hellenes to attend the European Regional Conference, held at Felsted over three days in November 2012. Without doubt, the Round Square adventure has much to offer Felstedians in the coming decades; the organisation of future contacts and involvement with the movement are always granted the highest priority.

MODEL UNITED NATIONS

T.J. Vignoles joined the staff as Head of English in 2006, bringing with him a strong aura of internationalism, if one can put it that way. He had pioneered the Model United Nations concept in several previous postings, including one at an international school abroad. Before long, MUN had found

a place among the many intellectual co-curricular activities on offer at Felsted. In particular, it was to the elite debaters and public speakers that the new option would appeal; trips to the UN headquarters in Geneva to witness the operations of the General Assembly and to attend debates at other MUN centres served to strengthen the popularity of this most worthwhile educational pursuit.

Felsted MUN has taken considerable strides forward in the wake of the acceptance of Felsted into the Round Square family; playing host on several occasions to the worldwide MUN organisation, for the first time in February 2010. A two-year cycle has been established, so that MUN conferences were held in 2012 and again in 2014. Students participating in these high-profile get-togethers profit significantly from opportunities to interact on the international stage; Felstedians have certainly valued their experiences, both home and away, and the MUN activity has become a central pillar of the School's internationalist agenda.

MAGIC BUS, MUMBAI

Felsted School's charitable activity has gained a specifically internationalist perspective of late: Magic Bus (a charity concerned with helping the street children of Mumbai in India) has presented a worthy focus.

Matthew Spacie, MBE (OF 1983–5) is the CEO of Magic Bus, an organisation he founded in 1999, as a result of his observation of the appalling poverty and deprivation to be seen in the streets of Mumbai. He formulated the notion that through sporting endeavours, the lives and horizons of many destitute youngsters might be irrevocably changed for the better. Magic Bus provides opportunities for training and match-play in a range of sporting activities, sweeping the children away from their lives of grinding poverty and onto the field of athletic challenges and achievement. Spacie's success in developing this work over the years earned him the award of an MBE in 2007.

It was at Speech Day 2009 that Matthew Spacie made his thrilling and emotionally charged appeal to the Felsted community. He brought before his audience the wrenching poverty he was engaged in combating, and presented some of the many heart-warming outcomes achieved for those fortunate enough to be welcomed on board the Magic Bus. No

one present that day could fail to be moved by Spacie's deeply held conviction that what his charity was doing was of the utmost significance in the context of humanitarian endeavours. Felsted warmed to him and to his concerns forthwith.

The happy outcome has been that specific fund-raising efforts have been undertaken with Magic Bus as the beneficiary, and an annual trip has been instituted, where Felstedian volunteers are given opportunities to join the project, working with the children and seeing for themselves the range of help given and the success rates achieved by Spacie's staff of helpers. The Magic Bus Mumbai Expedition has become a highlight of the autumn half-term break each year; this is a worthy cause, likely to feature long in the calendar of Felsted's outreach activities.

Top: Felsted MUN at the Geneva UN General Assembly Hall and (above) Felstedians working with Magic Bus youngsters in Mumbai, India.

14 STARTING BLOCKS: FELSTED PREPARATORY SCHOOL

Any Felsted Preparatory School alumnus setting foot upon the purlieus of his alma mater after an absence of 20 years or more would have a hard job finding his bearings. Such have been the changes and expansions since the latter days of its incarnation as the Junior School, Felsted (1956–83), and before that as the Preparatory House (1895–1903) and later as the Junior House (1903–56). Both the campus and the ethos have been altered so radically as to render irrelevant any comparison between then and now: the Felsted Preparatory School (FPS) of our time has placed itself at the very forefront of educational innovation; it is an institution whose management and leadership structures, philosophy and environment are wholly focused on the students' individual development, in an ambiance of concerned care and cooperation.

When Michael Pomphrey took over from Tim Andrews as Headmaster in 1992, the Prep could accommodate 150 boys aged 8 to 13, of whom roughly two-thirds could be boarders. The educational and social experience of the pupils was still recognisably the traditional mix of formal lessons and regular team sports, alleviated for some by drama, music and hobbies. The advent of co-education in 1993 ushered in a new era, though little really changed for some time thereafter. Clearly, the arrival of girls was a boost to numbers, but also raised many social and logistical conundrums to be faced. Essentially, FPS remained much as before, despite the avowed determination of all concerned that it should cease to be a boys' school with a few girls dotted about the place.

Fundamentally, the viability of the Senior School's co-educational future was wholly dependent upon the efficacy

full
Section VI: Felsted School at 450

of its successful introduction for the younger years. Under Pomphrey's leadership, progress was steady: there had been no major building development since the opening of the Ross Hall in 1971, but now substantial projects, including the establishment of the pre-prep teaching area and the building of the Evans Wing (opened in the Autumn Term of 1994 and comprising a number of airy classrooms, with additional space allocated to Art, CDT and ICT facilities), were evidence of the Governors' optimism that the expansion of FPS could be relied upon in the long run. Subsequent progress was to vindicate their confidence: upon arrival, Pomphrey had found 136 boys in the school; when he left, the co-ed roll stood at 332. It must not go unremarked at this juncture that Mrs Jennifer Pomphrey, like Mrs Chrissi Andrews before her, was a model of managerial efficiency and pastoral kindness in her conduct of the domestic side of FPS operations throughout her husband's eight-year tenure.

With Pomphrey's departure in 2000, to take over the bursarship of Harrow International School, Thailand, the Governors' choice of successor fell upon Eddy Newton, an experienced preparatory schoolmaster in the traditional mould. Despite promising growth in pupil numbers, Newton's time in office was not one of unalloyed contentment: the preparatory school world, at least so far as the East Anglian region was concerned, was undergoing a serious reshaping. The virtual disappearance of boarding at FPS meant that parents requiring a traditional style of pre-senior school experience for their sons were increasingly looking elsewhere, and, in consequence, the demographic of the clientele was changing. Nevertheless, Newton set about developing

the concept of a transitional 'phase' for the top two years, where the prospective move onward to the Senior School was anticipated by the establishment of a separate 'upper' section, to be housed in a new building, sited to the east of the main boarding house and Head's residence. Thus, one highly significant legacy of his relatively short incumbency would be the Courtauld Centre; this substantial project was completed in 2003, just before Newton's departure to take on the headship of Chafyn Grove, Salisbury. Years 7 and 8 were now masters of their own enclave, the new block furnishing both a physical separation from the more junior years, and a symbolic sense of the impending transition to the Senior School. Modern science teaching facilities were included as an important feature of the provisions of the new block. Eddy Newton's successor, Mrs Jenny Burrett, would in time make a good deal more of this feature, as we shall see.

Mrs Burrett's association with Felsted began as far back as 1983, when, as a newly qualified Modern Languages teacher, she joined the Senior School staff. After a two-year stint, during which she served as Tutor in the Manor House, she left for pastures new, returning in 1992, at the instigation of Headmaster Stephen Roberts, to serve as the inaugural

Opposite: second prep in 1905, from 9 to 9:45 p.m.

Above: the Courtauld Centre at FPS and (above left) the Junior House 1895.

Felsted Preparatory School in action (clockwise from right): story-time with Headmistress Mrs Jenny Burrett; scampering between lessons, and Mrs Jane West, Stewart House Phase leader, in the classroom.

Housemistress of Stocks's House, which opened its doors to lower school girls in 1993. Soon she was elevated to the newly designated position of Senior Mistress. Not long thereafter, she accepted a return to housemistress duties, this time in Follyfield. The Governors found themselves in wholehearted agreement with Headmaster Roberts when he proposed the appointment of Jenny Burrett as the first Headmistress in the long history of the Prep; no one had been more fully involved in the process of co-educational development at the Senior School. To add lustre to her credentials, she had also done sterling service as a teacher of French and Spanish on 'both sides of the Braintree Road'. She knew Felsted very well, and, what is more, Felsted knew her pretty well, too, and liked very much what they had seen thus far.

Jenny Burrett took up the reins in September 2004. She quickly set about remodelling the fundamental structure of the Prep, adapting the existing pupil career path in a new and innovative way; at the same time, she sought to reconstitute the pastoral and management structures, to accord with her overarching vision for the School. Over the longer term, Mrs Burrett's reforms are addressing fundamental educational issues regarding the improvement and modernisation of the School's curriculum and teaching styles. All staff members of FPS are wholly committed to their Headmistress's watchword: 'Every child matters.'

With Courtauld House, as we have seen, already in place for the top two years, and the pre-prep (later to be known as Stewart House) accommodating the first three years

(Reception, along with Years 1 and 2), Headmistress Burrett instituted two corresponding middle Phases: Ffrome Court (comprising Years 3 and 4) and Cloisters (for Years 5 and 6). Each Phase would be overseen by a senior teacher with Assistant Head status and responsibility, with a designated pastoral team in support. Thus a pupil's passage through the four Phases of the Prep would allow for learning experiences and development processes within a defined parameter, and for promotion to the next phase to become a goal to focus an individual's motivation.

Assisted in her work by Deputy Head, Mr Tristan Searle, and the Heads of Phase, Mrs Burrett moved the process forward without noticeable disruption to the established rhythms of FPS life. The sense of a family community was considerably enhanced by the simple application of the Phase system: pupils found their feet in a defined peer group, with leadership and service opportunities to be experienced at every stage of the educational process, not just in the final year of the preparatory school journey, as had been the case under the old dispensation.

Mrs Burrett's vision was greatly assisted by the completion of two further building projects of considerable scope and ambition, financed by the munificence of two generous benefactors. As total numbers grew apace and the age range expanded to encompass a full nine-year spread, the main public space, the Ross Hall, was proving inadequate to contend with an ever-widening range of uses. The construction of the Roed Sports Hall, opened officially on 15 November 2008, made viable by the funding offered by the Roed family, long-term benefactors of Felsted, allowed the Ross Hall to be developed as a centre for the performing arts; drama, dance and choral music could thereafter continue to thrive in a dedicated space at the heart of the School. The Philipps Music Centre furnished further useful practice space for budding instrumentalists and singers.

The pre-preparatory phase, located since its inception in 1993 in prefab buildings bordering the Cloister Field at the western extremity of the FPS campus, was in sore need of relocation to purpose-built accommodation, with an ambiance better equipped for the reception and formative education of Felsted's youngest pupils. Stewart House, a splendid, self-contained development designed by Cowper Griffiths Architects, the funding helped in part by a substantial donation from Old Felstedian Mr Andy Stewart (fe 1960–7), took shape on a site between the Courtauld Centre and Follyfield House, on Braintree Road. Stewart House was formally opened by Mrs Judy Stewart on 21 January 2012. Meanwhile, the former home of the pre-prep has undergone a thorough makeover and expansion, providing for Ffrome Court an impressive, tailor-made learning environment in which Young Felstedians can thrive during the second phase of their FPS adventure.

Felsted Preparatory School goes from strength to strength; rated 'Outstanding' in all categories by recent Independent Schools Inspectorate (ISI) and Ofsted inspections, its place as a leading independent junior school in the region is confirmed. Nowadays, total numbers stand at some 470 pupils, and the range of academic, technological, cultural and sporting activities continues to be developed and expanded. In

tandem with the Senior School, FPS has embraced the World School ethos of the Round Square organisation, and focuses on the Round Square motto, *Plus est en vous* ('Make the most of what you could be'), without losing sight of the Felsted Schools' overarching invocation: *Garde Ta Foy*.

Top: Stewart House from the playing field and (above) the Roed Hall.

15 | Corps Values and Community Service

When Headmaster W.S. Grignon got wind of the Secretary for War's circular of 12 May 1859, addressed to all County Sheriffs, he realised that he was already ahead of the game, something for which he was to become rather famous as his term of office at Felsted wore on: he it was who later developed a viable cricket bowling 'catapult', which the School team made use of in the early 1870s. In a nutshell, the government 'powers that be' were becoming increasingly concerned that the latest Napoleon on the French throne was again promulgating anti-British policies. In response to this all-too familiar scenario, it was deemed sensible to inaugurate a countrywide system of home guard units, to be fully trained and ready to rush to the defence of our vulnerable shores at a moment's notice. The local Defence Volunteer Corps of the 1790s, disbanded after Waterloo, were to be revived, but on an official and national footing.

From the outset, Grignon set out his stall to make the Corps one of the best in the land; no easy task, since the lines of communication between this Essex rural outpost and the centres of power were somewhat rudimentary. The railway had yet to arrive, and the ancient Roman roads hereabouts were hardly better than drove-ways and single-track footpaths. The village itself was off the beaten path between Colchester and Dunmow, and Chelmsford was a slow dozen miles distant. Nevertheless, an energetic start was made: an eye-catching grey uniform with scarlet facings was procured for the recruits, and old-style muzzle-loading rifles were pressed into service for drills and firing. The Felsted contingent joined with other local Rifle Volunteers (RV) contingents for exercises and collaborative parades and field days. An incident reported by one of his pupils attests to the resemblance one might adduce between the fanatical Grignon and Captain Mainwaring of *Dad's Army* fame. Grignon ran his cadet corps himself, overseeing all

its activities. On one public occasion, when reviewing his troops, Grignon very nearly paid the ultimate price for his amateur status as a military commander: it appears that some unwary and culpably lax boy had left the ram-rod lodged in the barrel of his rifle, which was then accidentally discharged during the drills. The aforesaid rogue ram-rod flew forth and all but decapitated the commander as he passed in front of his troops; the narrow miss is said to have conveyed the Head Master's best silk top hat precipitously into a nearby hedge. Admittedly, certain aspects of the tale have an apocryphal savour; but in essence the elements of gentlemanly muddling-through so typical of the period do ring true.

Another important innovation was to be introduced, just as the first contingent commander's hold on the reins was loosening: what every self-respecting Corps needs is a good band to add the cachet of military style to any route march or parade; and Felsted was not to be found wanting of this vital ingredient. In May 1876, the Fife and Drum Band made its first appearance: by all accounts the Felsted Band was a palpable hit from the first, applauded by all who heard it, be they Braintree locals or the denizens of rival schools on field days up and down the Eastern Counties.

The chief *raison d'être* of a Rifle Corps is the instruction of its cadets in the arts of contemporary warfare, so the major part of every term's activity was given over to drilling, rifle shooting and war games. One reads in *The Felstedian* magazine reports of collaborations with Haileybury, Bedford, The Perse and the Oxford and Cambridge Universities RV Corps in the Hatfield Forest; of battles with Forest, Harrow, Dulwich, Highgate and Merchant Taylors' in the Epping Forest area; and of skirmishes with the Braintree and Chelmsford Town RV battalions in and around Great Baddow heath. Victories and (very occasional) defeats are all detailed with appropriate military exactitude. By this time, too, an Old Felstedian had won the first of our two Victoria Crosses.

The Corps of Drums (clockwise from left): band parade in Felsted village (1905 etching); beating retreat, Stebbing Road, 1972 and piled drums, 2005.

Marksmanship was tested by order of the War Office, whose intentions were clear: to foster the highest standards in all cadets. Simultaneous postal matches were held, and opponents all across the country were engaged. The stage was now set for the greatest challenge ever to face the youth of the country; a few short years later would bring the ravages of

Shooting VIII of 1907 (above) and Victoria Cross commemorative plaque in Chapel (below).

the Great War; its insatiable jaws would grind over a thousand Felstedians, a quarter of whom would be swallowed up for ever.

As war clouds loomed once more after the Munich crisis of 1938, there came a new development in the Felsted Cadet Corps: the establishment of an Air Training Section in the OTC. Soon after the great migration to Ross-on-Wye, the War Office, keen to increase recruitment to the RAF, gave its blessing to the establishment of school-based Air Training Corps (ATC), no longer to be subordinate to the OTC. H.E. Reekie, Housemaster of Elwyn's at the time (later to return as Headmaster), took a commission in the Royal Air Force Volunteer Reserve and was the first commander of the Felsted

ATC, which dates its official inception from 1 February 1941, the very date upon which the countrywide ATC began; once again, Felsted was there from the very first day, proof of precedence being amply proclaimed in the Felsted ATC's designation as Flight No. 501, the first school RAF cadet contingent to be numerically identified.

At about the same time, the OTC changed its name (not for the last time!) to Junior Training Corps (JTC; the term OTC now being applied to the grown-up version, responsible for turning out the many thousands of officers that a new worldwide conflict required). Throughout the School's exile to Herefordshire (1940–5), the JTC and ATC continued to train its young adherents, and, as in the Great War, Felstedians young and old flocked to join the colours in their many hundreds, which for a relatively small school speaks volumes for the sense of duty and service inculcated by their hours on the parade grounds and games fields of Felsted and Ross-on-Wye. Not long after the School's return to its Essex home, the War Office decrees once again prevailed: in 1949, the Combined Cadet Force (CCF) was born of the amalgamation of the JTC and ATC.

Contingent Commander, Lieut. Col. M.W. Mann M.C., instituted a Naval Section, in Spring Term 1958, to cater for the sea-going instincts of the 'coastal Essex' lads. At the same time, a Royal Engineers troop was started, giving opportunities to the mathematically and scientifically minded recruits. The Ministry of Defence had not finished its dealings with schools cadet forces: in 1963, a New Model CCF was instituted. Felsted School, of course, was no newcomer to 'New Model' military innovations: a former parent, one Oliver Cromwell by name, had made a considerable name for himself by inventing the term in the 1640s! The Department of Defence cut the funding to CCF contingents; so the Corps became voluntary thereafter, and the rise of The Duke of Edinburgh's Award introduced strong alternative employment for active souls.

LIEUT. W.R.P. HAMILTON, THE GUIDES, VC (OF 1870–3)

Lieut. Walter Hamilton's gallantry at the Battle of Futtehabad (April 1879), during the Second Afghan War, was thus described in the medal citation: 'He courageously took over command of the Queen's Own Guides when his senior officer was mortally hit, pressed home the successful attack, and also rescued a fallen comrade from the hands of the enemy tribesmen.' Sadly, before the ink was dry on the citation, Hamilton was dead, killed a mere six months later in the desperate defence of the Kabul Residency against hordes of enraged local tribesmen. It is not clear whether Hamilton had been a member of the Felsted Corps, though his joining the Army directly from School suggests that it is likely that he had been one of Grignon's cadets.

VICTORIA CROSS FOR VALOUR

LIEUT· W·R·P HAMILTON
Queen Victoria's Own Corps of Guides
FUTTEHABAD · SECOND AFGHAN WAR
1879
· · ·
CAPT· J·L GREEN
Royal Army Medical Corps
THE SOMME · FIRST WORLD WAR
1916

Cadets enjoy the adventurous activities of the 21st century Corps.

SEND FOR THE 'ARGE

Throughout the interwar years, the Officer Training Corps (OTC) continued to occupy a good proportion of the boys; reports of excellent performances by the cadets and by the Corps of Drums band at Aldershot camps through the 1920s and 1930s may be seen in the pages of *The Felstedian* magazines of the time. By this time, the traditional role of the 'Arge (School Staff Instructor) had been well and truly established: as a matter of course, the School now engaged a thoroughly sound ex-soldier of Warrant Officer rank to oversee the activities of the OTC, as the nomenclature now required; the weapons drilling, warfare craft, shooting skills and physical 'jerks' (PT) were all subsumed under the Corps's aegis. Felsted's 'Arges continued to preside over whole-School break-time PT into the 1960s. Boxing, too, was the preserve of the 'Arge; the process of 'milling', where all new boys were required to don a pair of gloves and trade fisticuffs with all comers, was a typical importation from the military world. The travel writer, Douglas Goldring (OF), mentions the Felsted of his day as having 'a militaristic tone', and he does not seem to have been suggesting that this was in any way detrimental to the good education he had received there.
'Arges Ebert and Davey ruled the roost successively for 30 years and more, well into the 1980s; but it was during the incumbency of Staff Sergeant Instructor Paul Bartlett, who arrived in 1985, that a shift away from the warlike weapons drilling and skirmishing of yesteryear towards an emphasis upon self-reliance and adventurous training was instigated. In 1990, Major Bartlett became the first of this iconic clan to hold a Territorial commission and take over as Contingent Commander. The Bartlett Blade, given in his memory since 2004, is awarded annually to the cadet deemed to have made the most outstanding contribution to the Corps. But the 'Arge of old has had his day.

The quintessential Felsted 'Arge *c.*1885: Sgt-Major G. Wright, appointed by Headmaster Grignon, served well over 20 years as the School's drill and weapons instructor.

By the 2010s, Felsted's CCF had evolved even further, with recruitment taking place in the second year of the Senior School, with girls as well as boys welcomed to the ranks. Secondments to The Duke of Edinburgh's Award scheme were added to the more traditional military training, and gliding and flying offered to the RAF section adherents. Although an entirely voluntary option, the Felsted cadet corps has never been more popular. At Felsted, The Duke of Edinburgh's Award groups have for many years undertaken outward-bound activities, including testing hikes in the rugged North York Moors and among the tors of craggy Dartmoor; all the advantages of CCF self-reliance acquisition without the square-bashing, some might say.

Voluntary Service in the Community

During her husband's time as Headmaster, in the 1970s, Mrs Jane Eggleston was instrumental in instituting at Felsted a vibrant and energetic Community Service activity, which still endures in a much expanded form at the present time. Mrs Eggleston's primary purpose was to provide opportunities for service to the newly admitted Sixth-Form girls: initially the volunteers were deployed to visit and befriend elderly inmates of the Felsted Almshouses and residents in the Abbeyfield care home near Garnetts. Soon after, as numbers of girls in the School grew, the project was expanded to include regular visits to two other care homes for the elderly in the village.

Mrs Jane Gould continued her predecessor's work in organising the girls' voluntary service in this field; it was in Headmaster Gould's time in office that The Duke of Edinburgh's Award scheme and the Phab course were fully developed. The Community Service section was extended to include boys, and the range of activities diversified to include working parties deployed on projects in nearby conservation areas, and individual volunteers taking on visiting duties in special schools in Braintree and Chelmsford; a strong link was also developed with the Tabor Centre in Braintree. The work of A.D.G. Widdowson and Mrs Moira Grierson Rickford in broadening the range and diversity of the Community Service provision through the 1990s and into the new century must be acknowledged, too.

The introduction of the International Baccalaureate Diploma programme in 2006, with its compulsory Creativity,

Action and Service (CAS) component, alongside the similar service obligation required for the award of the recently developed Felsted Diploma, have significantly broadened the range and scale of service in the community undertaken by present-day Felstedians. Environmentalism has become a special feature of late, so working parties have been involved in helping with horticulture in the gardens of Easton Lodge and at the Phyllis Currie (Great Leighs) and Onslow Green conservation areas, and the grounds and environs of the School have come under special scrutiny, for the maintenance and propagation of the local flora and fauna.

The Felsted Diploma, in particular, gives opportunities for service in leadership roles, in many spheres of School life (including sports coaching), as well as in charity fund-raising and the long-established local visiting and Phab volunteering, as of old.

Opposite: Remembrance Sunday parade at the village war memorial.

Top: Duke of Edinburgh Silver Award group tackle the North York Moors and (above) community service volunteers at the Braintree Tabor Centre.

16 CREATING AND PERFORMING

MUSIC

Felsted School's strong traditions of choral and instrumental music continue undiminished; indeed, in recent times, the range and variety of attainment in this field might be said to excel those of many a previous era.

Prior to the opening in 1965 of the original Music School, music had endured something of a nomadic and hand-to-mouth existence at Felsted. Though from the earliest days of Grignon's reign various forms of musical performance had been encouraged, concerts and glees were a relatively sporadic occurrence in the termly round of activities. Only the choir seems to have held its own particular sway in the calendar; spontaneous evenings of song, where staff as well as pupils raised the roof, were a popular but intermittent feature of life, too. The pattern would appear to have remained much the same through both world wars and beyond – that is, that the School's musical fare tended to consist of a diet of small-group instrumental performance and much song, both sacred and secular.

G.H. Thorne, appointed Music Master in 1922 by Frank Stephenson, served very nearly 40 years on the Felsted staff, achieving a good deal in promoting individual and collective musical endeavour, but the range and scope of activity remained, in modern terms, rather narrow and understated. Professional choral performers and chamber instrumentalists were imported from time to time, and the long-established Concert Club continued to be well patronised throughout his time in post. With the arrival of Revd H.W. Last (Master 1957–73), initially to serve as Chaplain, the emphasis on developing musical performances of 'professional' quality began to take root, though in the main the major occasions tended to revolve around the vocal rather than instrumental virtuosity of Felstedians of that era. The great leap forward in the course of Last's stewardship was the opening of a purpose-built Music School in 1965; henceforth, practice and performances could be united under one roof, and collective musical endeavours could be centralised.

When R.A. Lawrence joined the Common Room in 1970, having been appointed Director of Instrumental Music, a significant new era was initiated: the story of Felsted's musical renaissance stems from that decision of Headmaster Eggleston's, early in his reign, demonstrating here, as elsewhere, his acumen in addressing the need to balance the athleticism of an outworn creed. Within his first three years in post, Lawrence had developed a viable concert orchestra comprising upwards of 60 competent players; then, as now, the expertise of instrumental teachers was pressed into service to support the performance of those whose talents they were nurturing. In 1973, Revd Harold Last retired, leaving Roger Lawrence in full possession of the musical fortunes of the School.

Over the course of the next 14 years, ably supported by L.R. Baker, appointed Assistant Director of Music that same year, the new Director's ambition and drive saw the orchestral playing honed to a level of skill and teamwork capable of performing such demanding works as Beethoven's *Choral Symphony* (1983). Choral music, too, flourished under the Lawrence baton: the Chapel Choir maintained the traditional high standards achieved under Revd Last; at the same time, a vocal group was developed to accompany the well-established and popular instrumental jazz band. During this period a number of outstanding solo performers emerged, including Stephen Panchaud (1977–82), a quartet of Stainer siblings (Dickon, Simon, Giselle and Benjamin), who scintillated successively (and occasionally ensemble) in the strings section throughout the 1980s, and Sarah-Jane Jimenez, whose electrifying voice graced many performances, not least

the acclaimed production of *Guys and Dolls* of 1986. The long-established Concert Club, which brought a regular diet of well-known professional performers to School and village, continued to thrive throughout this period.

The Lawrence–Baker partnership ended in 1986, when both left Felsted for new challenges elsewhere. Succeeding Directors Denny Lyster (1987–90), John Heritage (1990–3) and Jasper Thorogood (1993–8) strove to maintain the Department's momentum through increasingly fraught times, as student numbers were falling and budgets were radically trimmed. In particular, large-scale orchestral enterprises

Opposite: Music Master G.H. Thorne, seated centre, with the Choir of 1926.

Top: Schola Cantorum in fine voice and (above) strings ensemble entertain.

Orchestral concert in the Barbara Karan Auditorium.

became increasingly difficult, as manpower and talent grew ever thinner on the ground. The appointment of the current Director, James Lowry, in 1998, at a time when the financial position was improving, allowed for progress in the musical domain to be contemplated once more.

The opening of the new Music School, incorporating the Barbara Karan Auditorium, in the Autumn Term 2008, gave potent substance to the consolidation of music's key place in the Felsted pantheon. Academic music, composition and performance all reclaimed their place in the new dispensation,

with a state-of-the-art recording studio now providing laboratory-like facilities, where A level music technologists, among others, might weave their digital spells. The Lowry years have witnessed a steady renewal of the previous range and quality of musical activity; in particular, chamber recitals and festival occasions have held centre stage. Concerts for St Cecelia's Day, and gala affairs such as 'Music for a Summer's Evening', have found a starring role in the busy calendar of events. Collaborations with the Dramatic Society have also become an important feature, since the ever-encroaching

hegemony of public examinations has squeezed even further the time for co-curricular engagement by the students. Felsted Music School has the privilege of counting renowned cellist Julian Lloyd-Webber as its Patron, and the future seems bright indeed. Of particular note has been the development of opportunities for composing, using the music technology facilities on offer at the Music School.

A fine example of the high standards achieved by Felsted's musicians can be judged by the contribution of recent leaver Gus Nicholson (fcd 2007–12). He composed and acted as the principal director of his own stunning project, in association with the Round Square organisation: his composition, 'We Walk Together', was specially arranged for performance by a virtual choir, comprising singers from a range of partner schools from near and far, using the internet connections made possible by the world wide web. Felsted's share of the performance by our elite choir, Schola Cantorum, was recorded at Abbey Road studios and reprised on Speech Day 2012. Memorable, too, was the performance of Sixth Former Esme Smith, whose solo singing featured in the Opening Ceremony of the London Olympic Games of 2012. Ample evidence, if any were needed, that creativity and performance are very much alive in present-day Felsted.

Clockwise from top left: drummers Peter and Richard Rayner, BBC Young Musician finalists 2012; Music Technology suite and Gus Nicholson, Round Square virtual choir composer 2012.

ART

The provision and encouragement of practical creative art, sculpture and pottery have come a very long way from where things stood back in 1957, when Headmaster Reekie brought the first designated Art Master, T.W. Goodman, to Felsted, and opened a new Art School on the top floor of the new Courtauld Science Block. That area was soon requisitioned by the biologists, and Goodman moved his empire into the vacant Old Schoolroom in the village centre, where artists plied their trade for several happy decades. Goodman insisted upon developing in his pupils the disciplines of careful observation and secure draughtsmanship, also requiring all his A level students to take the Architecture paper. Not surprising, then, to find that several of his star pupils have found their métier in fields such as architecture, theatre design

Felstedians at their easels through the ages.

and commercial graphic design. Among the best known of Goodman's protégés, perhaps, are Tim Foster (fe 1958–67), designer of the Tricycle Theatre and other drama venues, and Michael Clarke (c 1965–70), Director of the National Galleries of Scotland.

In 2000, the Art Department's bags had to be packed up once more, when a move back into the main campus area was decreed, to occupy the space vacated some years previously in the former Craft Centre (sometime Victorian laundry) by the extension of the Craft, Design and Technology (CDT) building. Since then, the range and variety of artistic enterprises have been impressive, not to say expansive.

Bottom: '45 Trees' installation (2012) with Art Coordinator D.J. Smith and the IB students and (below) Follyfield Garden for the RHS Chelsea Flower Show 2013.

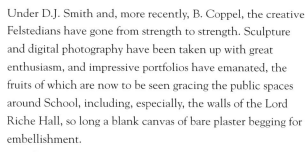

Under D.J. Smith and, more recently, B. Coppel, the creative Felstedians have gone from strength to strength. Sculpture and digital photography have been taken up with great enthusiasm, and impressive portfolios have emanated, the fruits of which are now to be seen gracing the public spaces around School, including, especially, the walls of the Lord Riche Hall, so long a blank canvas of bare plaster begging for embellishment.

This recent innovation is the brainchild of David Smith, who, having served a full term as Housemaster of Gepp's, was subsequently appointed to a new post, Arts Coordinator, with special responsibility for arranging the display of pupils' work in and around the campus. A special installation of living birch trees has been established to Smith's design, as a permanent memento of the 450th anniversary. Adjacent to the Cockett AstroTurf pitch have been planted 45 Himalayan birch trees, one tree for every decade of the School's history; further such installations are expected to follow, as the visual ambiance of the Felsted campus is further enhanced in the coming years. Not least of these developments is the garden installation for the new Follyfield site, by Paul King, RHS gold medallist and Felsted parent, first seen at the RHS Chelsea Flower Show of 2013. The continuing policy of siting canvases, sculptures and plantings in key locations around School continues to showcase the visual arts very much at the forefront of the Felsted scene.

DRAMA

Theatrical performances have long been a feature of Felsted's cultural scene. Certainly, a succession of future stars of stage and screen were to cut their thespian teeth under the Grignon Hall lights, among whom actors Richard Johnson (g 1941–3) and Philip Latham (fe 1939–47), and West-End theatre directors Sam Walters (fe 1948–58) and Max Stafford-Clark (fe 1950–9) are the best known of the immediate post-war generation. Even in the darkest days of wartime exile, plays and skits were regularly enacted. With the arrival on the staff, in 1947, of A.S.M. Ronaldson (OF e 1928–32) and his wife, Marion, a former professional actress, a considerable leap forward in the standard and ambition of the productions was noted. Shakespeare's comedies and tragedies, alongside Gilbert and Sullivan operettas, were grist to their mill; staff plays, too, were regularly presented, much to the delight of the School and village communities alike. The Ronaldson duo had set the dramatic bar at a dizzy height over a span of nearly three decades; theirs would indeed be a hard act to follow.

The second Grignon Hall fire, this time arrested by prompt action before terminal damage could be inflicted on the building, broke out on the evening of 29 February 1952; not the most auspicious leap-year day, assuredly. Again,

the cause of the conflagration, as with the fire of 1930 and the more recent destruction of old Follyfield, was traced to overheating electrical apparatus, in use earlier in the day for a rehearsal of *Hamlet*, which had to be postponed until the end of the Summer Term. This time, the firefighting by staff and boys was successful, even before the tardy arrival of the Dunmow and Braintree Fire Brigade. Happily, recent times have brought more stringent regulation of the equipment, along with professional standards of technical support for the productions of today.

Clockwise from top left: *Richard III* (1928); *Antony and Cleopatra* (1929) and Alan and Marion Ronaldson, mainstays of Felsted drama over three decades.

The long continuum of high-quality dramatic productions has been maintained and enhanced throughout the latter decades of the twentieth century and into the twenty-first. With the advent of Sixth-Form co-education and the appointment of a succession of able and resourceful schoolmasters as Director of Drama in the early 1970s, the Ronaldson tradition was maintained and enhanced. S.M. Manger introduced 'edgy' plays, such as John Arden's *Sergeant Musgrave's Dance* and Beckett's *Waiting for Godot*, while experimenting with 'youf culcha' offerings such as Peter Terson's *Zigger Zagger*. D.R. Graham-Young's preferences leant towards more challenging classical pieces: *Antigone* by Anouilh and Chekhov's *The Cherry Orchard* were early evidence of his belief that young actors can always rise to a challenge, if sensitively directed. *The Frogs* by Aristophanes was memorably realised in the Bury gardens; the Old Gym was put to use for 'workshop'-style small productions, thus promoting the notion that the building could find a new incarnation in the Sports Hall era. C.J. Clement specialised in rumbustious Gilbert and Sullivan operettas, including *The Pirates of Penzance* and *Ruddigore*, and energetic farces such as *Scapino*.

With Clement's successor, A.M. Homer, the production values and frequency of high-grade drama were assured; over a ten-year span, Homer produced a dazzling range of sparkling productions, including a spectacular rendition of *Guys and Dolls*, Brecht's *The Good Woman of Setzuan*, and

an unforgettable, punk-themed *A Midsummer Night's Dream*. Homer's penchant for small-scale, but gripping 'alternative' comedy brought to the Felsted stage such pieces as Stoppard's *After Magritte*, a double-bill of Pinter's *The Room* with Ionesco's *The Bald Prima Donna*, *After the Rain* by John Bowen, and Lorca's *The House of Bernarda Alba*. He continued the Graham-Young practice of affording to smaller groups of senior actors the challenging opportunity to ply their trade at the Edinburgh Festival Fringe. Homer also wrote and produced his own play, *Bacchus to Win*, an excoriating examination of the alcohol-fuelled teenage culture of our times. The drama horizons were thus considerably widened through the 1980s and 1990s, with significantly greater involvement by Felstedians of all levels of proficiency. House plays, directed and produced by the students themselves, continued to provide a potent proving ground throughout the last decades of the twentieth century.

The emphasis in more recent years has tended to be on large-scale musical theatre, where professional standards have been sought, in collaboration with the musicians, to put on family-style entertainments for the major showcase production

A Man for All Seasons performed by the Common Room, 1972.

each year. C.R.S. Lee (appointed Drama Director in 1993) combined forces with, first, Alex Keighley and, more recently, Hannah Grace (Theatre Designer and Technical Manager), to produce a succession of extravagant visual and vocal feasts to enliven the Grignon Hall stage; several of these productions would provide individual students with opportunities to taste the limelight of stardom.

Dr Lee's contribution over the past 20 years has been groundbreaking and far-reaching. He has introduced several particular elements which have greatly extended the scope of

school drama at Felsted. In particular, he began early on by establishing the Thespian Society, dedicated to developing in its members a deep love of the theatre and inculcating a wide-ranging experience of all that is best in British and transatlantic drama. Frequent group outings to attend the best of the West-End productions have continued unabated ever since. The Hunt Theatre has also been pressed into service as a venue for visits by touring professional productions; these performances have been made available to the wider public as well as to Felstedians large and small, generating useful revenue to be ploughed back into School productions. Lee also believes in the need for young actors to experience the 'feel' for their roles, and to get to know the settings and environments in which the dramas are set. Trips to relevant places across the British Isles and onto the Continent, to say nothing of the occasional jaunt across the pond to the US, are now a *sine qua non* of a Dr Lee production.

Another original innovation has been the practice of taking certain landmark productions on tour: the junior plays have regularly been played to audiences at various East Anglian preparatory schools, and, more ambitiously, exchange visits to US private schools, such as St George's School, Newport, Rhode Island, Emma Willard School, New York, and Taft School, Connecticut, are undertaken every two or three years. A regular venue on these trips has been the Bedford Hills Correctional Facility for Women, in New

Left: Felsted Drama tour to Bedford Hills.

FELSTED SCHOOL presents

Cabaret

Book by JOE MASTEROFF
Based on the play by JOHN VAN DRUTEN & stories by CHRISTOPHER ISHERWOOD
Music by JOHN KANDER   Lyrics by FRED EBB

ENGLAND 2003
26, 27, 28, 29 November GRIGNON HALL, FELSTED

USA 2004
3 April PHILLIPS ACADEMY, ANDOVER MA
5 April MIDDLESEX SCHOOL, CONCORD MA
8 April TAFT SCHOOL, WATERTOWN CT

Felsted School presents

EVITA

Lyrics by TIM RICE   Music by ANDREW LLOYD WEBBER

Originally directed by Harold Prince

17–20 November 2010

FELSTED SCHOOL
presents

OH WHAT A LOVELY WAR

Tuesday
28 November–
Friday
1 December 2000
in the Grignon Hall

York State, where Felstedians have performed on different occasions and always to rapturous acclaim. Blockbuster productions over this period have included *Joseph and the Amazing Technicolor Dreamcoat* (in 1995 and 2009), *Jesus Christ Superstar* (1997) and *Evita* (2010). *Oh! What a Lovely War*, first presented in 1985 and again in 2000, is due to be reprised as part of the School's 450th anniversary celebrations in 2014; and, more poignantly, as a centenary salute to the many Old Felstedians who served in the Great War.

There can be very few schools anywhere in the world with as rich a seam of creative talent, or with the quality of musical, artistic and dramatic direction to bring that talent to fruition; Felsted is certainly as MAD as they come.

A selection of blockbuster productions.

161

17 | SPORTING ENDEAVOURS

Team sports have long been the principal leisure activity in our schools, and the Victorian public schools were instrumental in developing the notion that to play games well was the highest ambition of the English gentleman. While academic endeavours were taken for granted, no shirker at sports was to be tolerated. In consequence, Felsted, like all its rivals, has courted the glory of athletic triumphs on the games field; for the most part, the School teams have met with more than a measure of success. Since the latter days of Head Master Grignon's time, Felsted has been forging a considerable sporting name, its cricket and hockey XIs, in particular, have gained a nationwide reputation as the ones to beat.

This is not to say that the School in the twenty-first century has stagnated in the outmoded creed of former times. Despite the passing into history's oblivion of boxing and fives, two mainstays of the Edwardian public-school athletic tradition, new fields of friendly strife have arisen to take their place on the Felsted sporting canvas. A Director of Sport has been in post for a number of years, and the range of available options has seen considerable growth of late. Students are encouraged to find athletic pursuits they enjoy, within the panoply of activities on offer; all will find sympathetic and specialist coaching to nurture that enjoyment. Felsted still lauds its successful sportsmen and sportswomen, of course, but nowadays all Felstedians are encouraged to find enjoyment in physical exercise, whatever their individual level of attainment might be.

Cricket has been played at Felsted since at least the early 1800s, when Head Master Carless secured for the School the lease of Little Field, behind Ingram's Close. The patron at that time, Lord Winchilsea, was a keen cricketer, and a founder member of the MCC to boot. Boys then played among themselves, and few reliable records remain of any official matches they may have undertaken, though certainly village cricket was growing in popularity in Essex, as elsewhere across the nation; it is believed that the School took on a Felsted village XI as early as 1865. By the time of the first edition of *The Felstedian* magazine in November 1873, it is clear that a fixture list was in existence, and regular engagements with local club sides were being enjoyed. Indeed, one of the accusations levelled by the Trustees (Governors) against Grignon himself was that he was reported to 'enjoy' his cricketing expeditions rather too well. Masters would be included in School teams in those days, of course, and not only in cricket. Since opponents were generally adults, there seemed no reason to restrict selection to boys.

Mont's winners of the Senior Fives competition, Spring 1973.

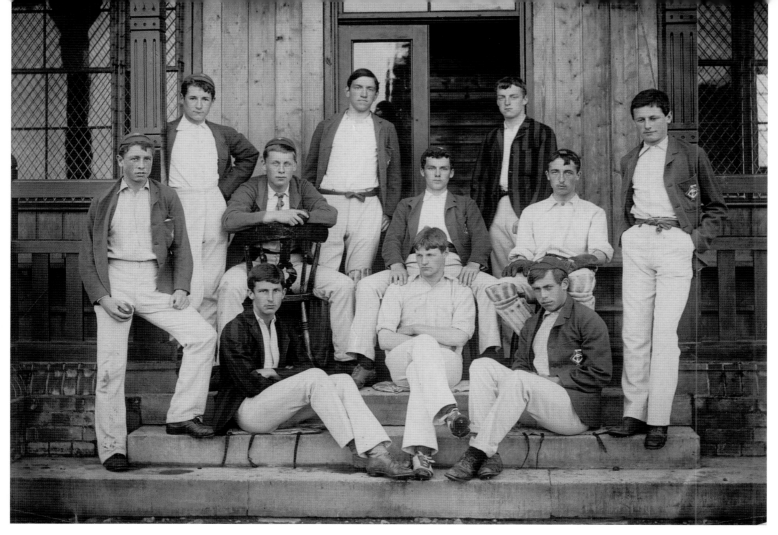

Felsted's first inter-school matches were against Forest School, Snaresbrook, and The Leys, Cambridge. By the mid-1880s, these matches were well established, though the majority of fixtures were against clubs. The School more than held its own against the newly formed Essex County Cricket Club, indeed beating them comfortably in 1876; but it was not until the 1920s that matches against school opponents predominated on the fixture list. However, by that time, Felsted had produced the first of its England caps: J.W.H.T. Douglas (a 1897–1901). After an interval of some 50 years, Felstedian cricketers again graced the national XI in rapid succession: D.R. Pringle (e 1974–7), J.P. Stephenson (fa 1974–83) and N.V. Knight (fb 1978–88). All three are now well known for their subsequent media careers, Pringle as cricket correspondent for the *Daily Telegraph*, Stephenson as MCC Cricket Secretary at Lord's, and Knight as a cricket commentator for Sky Sports. Other Felstedians to make their mark in schools and first-class cricket in recent times are M. Olley (fe 1972–82), Northants and Middlesex CCCs; E.J. Wilson (fa 1985–95), Worcs. CCC; T.J. Phillips (fh 1990–99), Essex CCC.

Much credit for Felsted's emergence as a cricketing powerhouse must go to a succession of excellent professionals,

whose expertise and understanding contributed so much to the process of bringing on the best talents of our players: C.M. Gough and R. Smith (Essex CCC 1934–56) in the 1950s and 1960s and G. Barker (Essex CCC 1954–71) in the 1970s, 1980s and well on into the 1990s. For an unprecedented 25 years (1971–96), Gordon Barker combined plying his trade in the nets with the post of Head of Grounds: the School's games fields profited enormously from his meticulous management; a goodly number of unbeaten sides were produced, and apart

Above: First XI on the Old Pavilion steps (1886) and (left) cricket coach Gordon Barker with his three crackerjacks: (l to r) N.V. Knight, D.R. Pringle and J.P. Stephenson.

163

from the three crackerjacks mentioned above, a dozen or more of his protégés would play at the top level in county cricket. A fitting tribute to his contribution was established with the opening of a set of state-of-the-art artificial surface nets alongside the Braintree Road. The key to the School's continuing pre-eminence at cricket lies in the excellence of the coaching regimes, allied to the strong tradition passed on from year to year.

Felsted's post-war cricketing pedigree was greatly enhanced by the careful nurturing of the Masters in Charge of cricket: J.A. Cockett (CUCC) held the post (coupled with running the hockey) for the best part of three decades, during which time the Felsted Robins Cricket Club, inaugurated in 1967, and the XI's participation in the Eastbourne end-of-term festival (first played in the summer of 1969) was well established. M. Surridge (also Master in Charge of Hockey), A.N. Grierson Rickford and F.C. Hayes (Lancs. CCC and England) successively maintained this enviable tradition and growing reputation throughout the 1980s and 1990s.

The advent of co-education in the mid-1990s brought difficulties in fulfilling block fixtures against the larger opponents, and the fixture list had to be adjusted accordingly; which is not to say that more recent Felsted XIs have lost that traditional competitive edge, or the skill and determination to punch above their weight.

By the time C.S. Knightley was Master in Charge in 2000, the emphasis on overs-limit cricket had pervaded the schools'

game, and Felsted XIs were quick to adapt to the shorter matches and different skills required, while always retaining a competitive edge in the more traditional declaration matches. The National Schools Twenty20 competition was won in successive years (2004 and 2005), and Felsted has reached at least the quarter-finals every year since. The Eastbourne Festival is no more, but Felsted hosts its own International Festival each summer, and undertakes tours of Australia roughly every four years (the first was in 1985 and the most recent in 2011). Felsted's cricket fortunes continue in good hands, with recently appointed Master in Charge J.E.R. Gallian (OUCC, Lancs., Notts. and Essex CCCs, and England) at the helm.

The earliest records of **football** at the School describe inter-dormitory (pseudo-House) matches in the first years of the 1870s. At that time, there was a plethora of different variants of football, and the rules later to emerge as soccer and rugger were in the process of codification; Felsted indeed played a local version of the Eton game. In this form, the round ball was forced forward towards a goal resembling rugby posts, and 'goals' scored for driving the ball between the posts. The 'rouge' was awarded for a ball driven over the line and touched down by an attacker. The 'rouge' was then offered for conversion at a 'bully', rather similar to a rugger scrum, but with the object of pressing the ball forwards through the opposition, rather than heeling back to your own players. Clearly, out-matches were nigh impossible, until such time as standardised rules of engagement had been formulated. Nevertheless, some success was recorded even then: a Cambridge University team were soundly defeated by 3 goals and 3 rouges to nil in 1873.

In 1874, the School games committee agreed to adopt the rules promulgated by the Football Association earlier that same year, and soccer thus became the main winter game at Felsted. From the first crop of Old Felstedian footballers, three are known to have won England international honours as amateurs: Clement Mitchell (1874–9), Henry Wood (d 1899–1902) and Jonnie 'Won't Hit Today' Douglas (a 1897–1901; of cricketing and boxing fame, too). The Old Felstedian FC played many fixtures in the north London Old Boys league, competing also in the FA Amateur Cup and the Arthur Dunn Cup for public-school Old Boys, even after the loss of major

Association football: (top) First XI 1899 and (left) today.

sport status at the School of their favoured 'footer' style.

The First World War brought many changes, not least of which was that soccer gave way to rugby football in 1917, and, as with so many superseded favourites, was accorded pariah status for many decades thereafter. Letters in *The Felstedian* magazine often plead eloquently, but in vain, for its restoration. Only after the return from Herefordshire do we find any relaxation of the prejudice, and soccer emerges from the shadows of opprobrium to be offered as an optional 'minor' sport, almost exclusively the preserve of the Sixth-Form over-16s.

After 1967, an official soccer team was reinstated, and a fixture list drawn up to include matches against local maintained schools and several of the traditional soccer-playing public schools, such as Brentwood and Westminster. By the mid-1990s, Felsted's soccer team had shaken off the

Cinderella status, and the 'no hands except for the goalie' football code was restored to official favour once more. In the present day, soccer has very much come back into its own: the School XI competes successfully in an East Anglian independent schools' football league.

The decision was taken at the height of the First World War hostilities to abandon the association game in favour of rugger. *The Felstedian* magazine cites the view that the new game was the manlier pursuit, and better suited to the inculcation of the moral fibre and courage required for the Front. Norman D. Mant (a 1914–19), among several other senior boys, is credited with having pressed for the adoption of rugby, and trial games were played in the Spring Term of 1917, when grounds were unfit for hockey. A letter from an anonymous Governor of the time attests to an 'in-House' rugby match having been played at the School as early as 1905, when the Prefects took on the rest of School House, so perhaps there had been a steady undercurrent of approval among the rank and file.

Rugby football: (top) an early rugger practice *c.*1917; (above) First XV of 1919 and (bottom right) Felsted forwards breaking through.

The first official out-match was against a Haileybury 'A' XV, a dyed-in-the-wool rugger school, in November 1917. Though the game ended in narrow defeat, the die was cast: rugby football was here to stay. The fixture versus Bishop's Stortford College also dates from that first season; with Haileybury, they are Felsted's oldest rivals in the 15-man game.

Rugby has continued to thrive at the School ever since. There have been a good many successful seasons, and rare is the rugger term when the XV, or indeed the other School teams, suffer more reverses than victories. The era of the dedicated schoolmaster coach has all but passed away: Felstedian rugger players over the past 50 seasons owe a great debt to the likes of R.F. Ballingall, C.H. Tongue, R.L. Feldman, A.W.S. Thomson and C.S. Knightley, all Masters in Charge who drew upon their own experience, aided by the support of willing colleagues and occasional professional coaches, to further the fortunes of Felsted rugby. Though rugger is the Autumn Term major sport, Felsted teams compete successfully in regional 'sevens' competitions, as well as taking part regularly in the Rosslyn Park National Tournament in the spring most years. During the October half-term, a 'fifteens' festival is held at Felsted, involving under-19 and under-15 teams from across the East Anglian region. The School's name is by no means unrecognised in its own hinterland.

Now in the capable professional hands of A. le Chevalier (Harlequins, London Wasps and Cardiff RFC), horizons are broadening. The 2012/13 season saw the appearance at Twickenham both of the First XV and the Under 15 XV in

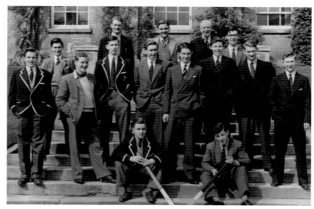

the Vase Final of the Daily Mail RBS Schools Cup for their age-groups, surely a sign that rugby is setting out its stall to rival hockey and cricket as Felsted's leading game.

For many, Felsted's prowess at **hockey** is the defining characteristic by which the School's reputation has been lauded throughout the nation and beyond. Hockey was first played as a scratch occupation as early as 1899, and adopted officially as the Spring Term game from 1901. From the first, it seems that the skills and tactical acumen required for success was something Felstedians developed with enormous avidity: Felsted was soon a force to be reckoned with; only The Leys could be relied upon to give as good as they got on the field of battle. For a period spanning several decades, Felsted ranked among the very best hockey nurseries in the land. In former times, it was problematic to discern just how good a particular XI might be, since fixture lists inevitably ranged more parochially than nowadays. Unbeaten Felsted sides, masters of the eastern counties circuit, could rarely test their mettle against the best of the rest. And whether Marlborough, Charterhouse or Kingston Grammar School could lower our colours was a matter of conjecture and (perhaps) conceited self-confidence.

During the Herefordshire exile, Felsted found its fixtures where it could, and doughty western opponents were invited to try occasions with us at hockey, as well as at the other team games, of course. This experience proved most salutary, and despite the restricted wartime numbers, the School almost invariably triumphed. The appetite for such contest was well and truly whetted. The inception of the Oxford Public Schools Hockey Festival would bring a welcome opportunity for schools to make new friends and test their skills against 'foreign' opposition. The management of this prestigious festival was in the capable hands of the Felsted hockey staff for over a decade, during the peerless period of the School's ascendency in the game, under its most influential commander-in-chief.

J.A. Cockett (CUHC, England and Great Britain) is often feted as the Master in Charge responsible for the long period of outstanding success for Felsted's hockey, and no one could deny the fruits of his long reign. For a quarter of a century and more, his influence pervaded all that was good and successful in the sport. He honed a very successful coaching team of schoolmaster coaches, including D.C.M

Felsted's hockey pedigree (top to bottom): First XI 1923, Public Schools Hockey Festival squad, Oxford, 1957 and Real Club Barcelona Tournament party, 1987.

Waddell (OF d 1944–9), H.K. Maitland (CUHC and Scotland) and Dr T.P. Woods (OUHC), each adding his own particular insights as the boys rose through the ranks, to arrive fully-fledged in the 'First Forty'. There, Cockett would weave the extra magic required to turn out the finished article. A measure of this coaching team's effectiveness: the Old Felstedian team carried off the Glenfarclas Old Boys Hockey Cup for the first two years of its existence. Among a veritable galaxy of Old Felstedian stars in the hockey firmament are to be numbered the following: F.H.V. Davis (e 1946–50), England and Great Britain (Captain); G.V.S. Nott (fb 1949–58), England; T.M. Lawson (fd 1954–61), Scotland and Great Britain; A.H. Ekins (d 1957–61), England and Great Britain (Captain); R.M. Oliver (fa 1953–63), England and Great Britain; T.J. Lowe (c 1958–63), England; and R.L. Cattrall (fh 1966–75), England and Great Britain (Captain).

Girls' sports to the fore (clockwise from above): hockey on the Astro; rounders in full flow and Malta Tour netballers 2009.

But there had been plenty to shout about before Cockett and before the Second World War. International caps for England had been won by J.L. Matthews (fe 1895–1903), also Great Britain; J.L. Beaumont (fe 1892–1904); J.S. Youle (c 1902–7); A.F.H. Wiggin (d 1902–7); C.E.N. (Bill) Wyatt (e 1927–31); and G.A. Baylis (fa 1929–35). C. Morley-Brown (fc 1915–22) played for Scotland.

By the 1980s, tours to Ireland and Holland had become a feature of the hockey calendar, and Felsted took part in the prestigious Los Reyes tournament hosted by the Real Club de Polo in Barcelona on several occasions, by special invitation. The girls' XI, too, has competed at the ladies' event at the same venue. Both boys' and girls' squads have also undertaken demanding tours to South Africa in the recent past.

The game of hockey underwent a major change with the arrival of the AstroTurf artificial surfaces of the 1990s. The School's immaculately manicured grass pitches had always been the envy of its opponents, and the installation of a 'red-gra' all-weather pitch in 1971 had provided alternative accommodation in wet conditions; but grass was king, so to speak. Once the Philipps and Cockett pitches were installed, no self-respecting exponent desired his stick-work to be upset by a bumpy or waterlogged playing surface, and skill levels

improved exponentially. In consequence, professional levels of coaching became de rigueur; Felsted employed a succession of South African international players, whose attentions could be applied to raising standard across the entire age range. With the appointment of D.J. Woods (Southgate, England and Great Britain) as Director of hockey, Felsted hockey embraced the professional age wholeheartedly. N.J. Lockhart, an accredited FIH (International Hockey Federation) hockey umpire, has added his not inconsiderable expertise to the mix since joining the staff as Head Groundsman and cricket coach in 1996.

When girls arrived in the Sixth Form, hockey and tennis were the first team games to be offered on a regular basis, once numbers had risen to levels conducive to competitive play. Mrs Marion Maitland (OULHC), supported by her husband, H.K. Maitland (CUHC and Scotland), began the process of developing a Felsted girls' hockey XI to take on regular matches. Steady progress was made, and the advent of full co-education proved a definite boost to the fortunes of girls' hockey at Felsted. Professional coaching, as with the boys, brought out the talents and nurtured teamwork and tactics.

In 1995, and again in 1998, enjoyable and successful tours to South Africa were organised. Experienced club players from Germany, in particular, joining the School for the IB programme, helped enormously to raise the general success rates for Felsted's teams. Felsted's girls are now every bit as competitive as their male counterparts, with championship success at Essex county level, as well as in regional and national tournaments. Unbeaten in 2005 and 2007, the girls' XI reached the national finals both years, and toured Germany successfully in 2008. Loren Sherer (fg 1996–2006) played for England under-21s, the School's first ladies' international 'cap'.

Introduced relatively early in the co-educational period as the Spring Term main girls' team sport, **netball** really came into its own in the later 1990s, once the junior girls were well embedded in the system. Specialist coaching and burgeoning success in inter-school encounters served to fire enthusiasm for the game. In 2005, the First VII recorded an unbeaten season for the first time; since then, Easter tours have been arranged in 2009 and 2011, to play in the international tournament in Malta. The School now fields ten teams, and the junior VIIs have also begun to register regular successes. The popularity of netball is assured, under the enthusiastic management of the mistress in charge, Miss S. Hookway, who is also Director of Girls' Sport at the School.

Rounders at Felsted started as a social game, often entertaining players of both sexes, but has now been adopted as a genuine girls' team sport for the Summer Term. Fixtures against other schools have been played in recent seasons, with Felsted's teams here proving hard to beat on the circuit. The future expansion of the fixture list is eagerly anticipated, as popularity waxes strongly among those for whom the tennis alternative holds less appeal.

Boys' **tennis** has flourished as an alternative to cricket since the 1960s. The Youll Cup (the Public Schools Championship) was won in 1972, perhaps the single greatest triumph: the School's teams have always performed steadily throughout the past 40 years, frequently winning through several rounds of the national competitions at Wimbledon and elsewhere. On the domestic circuit, the teams have always held their own.

Boys' tennis: Youll Cup winners in 1972.

The girls' teams, too, competed strongly from the start, in 1973. Initially coached by Mrs Diana Lawrence, and more recently by Mrs Jenny Burrett, a strong fixture list has been developed, and junior teams now take to the courts with success, too. Social tennis has also found its place in the calendar, and is much enjoyed by those whose specialisms lie elsewhere.

Squash has had its ups and downs in popularity. In former times, the game was taken extremely seriously by a talented band of players, encouraged by Common Room members of acknowledged expertise at the game. The addition, in 1978, of two new courts alongside the existing Gradidge courts gave an extra fillip to the game at Felsted. T.P. Woods (Oxford squash blue) led a particularly productive revival at that time, and demanding matches were played with opponents far and wide, both clubs and schools were entertained, and an annual West Country tour was undertaken.

Popularity waned after the departure of P.N. Keighley (Master in Charge of Squash 1990–5), also a keen promoter of squash as an inter-school sport; at Felsted, as almost everywhere else, fewer students took up the physical and mental challenges involved in this most taxing of individual sports. After a decade and more in the doldrums, there has been a revival of interest lately, and there are hopes that inter-school fixtures may again be entertained, before too long.

Badminton has grown in stature throughout the last two decades. Master in Charge C.J. Megahey may be credited with putting the game on the map at Felsted, and the lofty Sports Hall accommodation provides an ideal venue for the game.

Cross-country running and **athletics** have been a feature of the Felsted Summer Term since time immemorial, flourishing especially in the 1980s and 1990s, under the aegis of director of sport, A.L. Lerwill (GB Olympic athlete), and A.W.S. Thomson (Head of PE). The inter-House competitions, notably the Steeps race, the Road Relays and the Barker and Edmonson competitions, still draw the crowds, but inter-schools matches are few and far between. Dedicated athletes at Felsted still have opportunities to compete at local and regional meetings, however, and training and coaching is made available to those with a particular talent and interest.

Perennially popular, **basketball** has a long and generally successful history at the School, dating in the first instance from the opening of the present Sports Hall in 1978. Traditional rivalries are maintained in matches versus Haileybury and Brentwood, and links with local maintained schools have been especially valuable. Felsted's recent teams have continued to win many more engagements than are lost, it should be affirmed.

Felsted is the proud possessor of perhaps the oldest swimming pool in continuous use; for over a century, it has been the venue of competitive as well as leisure water sports. Inter-schools matches and participation in the Bath and Otter Cup competitions were features of the Felsted sporting scene. As with several other formerly popular sporting pursuits, **swimming** has lost its gloss, and now caters for an elite cadre of dedicated individuals. House galas for boys' and girls' teams are still held, and taken very seriously by those participating.

The Felsted Inter-schools Horse Show has taken its place in the calendar since 2007, and Felsted has entered showjumping and dressage teams in the national championships each year since then, too. Necessarily restricted to students who own their own mount and ride at home, the appeal of **equestrianism** is limited; nevertheless, in true Felstedian style, our riders have given a glowing account of themselves on every occasion.

Polo has also grown steadily in popularity, overseen by keen Common Room riders, Miss A.L.F. Simpson and T.J. Hietzker. Felsted fields two teams at the National Schools' Polo Tournament for Girls each year. Mixed teams have also participated at the National Senior Intermediate Polo Tournament, at the Rugby Polo Club; in 2011, both teams were placed in their division of the competition. Weekly training sessions are laid on, with trained mounts and specialist coaching supplied, at a nearby riding establishment.

Right: girls' athletics and (top) polo.

The standard of personal and collective achievement has never been higher.

A small but dedicated band of golfers continues to stride down the fairways and negotiate the greens of courses far and wide. Firmly established by E.A. Beulah during a lengthy stint of service to the School (1952–88), the Felsted **golf** team continues to thrive, under the tutelage of R.L. Feldman and I.W. Gwyther. Schools matches and national competitions, such as the HMC foursomes, are included on the fixture card, alongside well-established (friendly) rivalries with Uppingham, Oundle and Bedford. An especially pleasing recent season was enjoyed in 2010, when the School's team reached the national finals of the Independent Schools Golf Association match play competition, having been crowned champions of Area 4 in the regional rounds. The long-standing in-house triangular match with the Common Room and parents remains a firm favourite with all participants.

For many years, Felsted's **shooting** was the preserve of the CCF, and overseen by R.C. Down. Open range competitions at Bisley were regularly attended, and the *Country Life* postal matches against other schools were the chief employment for the indoor .22 marksmen. The arrival of C.R.S. Lee in 1993 would prove a step change in this area of sporting endeavour. Lee was involved already in the management of the British Schools Shooting team, and brought with him many useful contacts in the shooting world, as well as considerable expertise in coaching and developing the necessary skills and tactics for success at the sport.

Since the mid-1990s, many of the School's best shots have graced the lists of prize-winners at British and overseas competitions, and a score or so have been selected for the national schools team. Although the feats of Felsted's best acknowledged shooters, Herbert Perry (fa 1906–12), Olympic Gold medallist in 1924, and Andrew Tucker (a 1951–5), England and Great Britain team member 1962–76, are now a distant memory, it may with some confidence be predicted that one or more of Felsted's recent shooting stars will soon be lighting up the international scene.

Even a cursory perusal of the foregoing will have drawn to the reader's attention the considerable and sustained successes achieved by Felsted School's sportsmen and sportswomen in a wide range of athletic fields. Over a good many years,

the School's sporting reputation has been maintained and enhanced at local, regional and national levels, and foreign tours have bruited abroad the sportsmanship and competitive edge of Felsted's teams. Such success can only be sustained and developed by the concerted efforts and professional expertise of a dedicated army of coaching staff and Masters and Mistresses in Charge, whose efforts have nurtured keenness and promoted excellence at all levels of ability. To these unsung heroes this chapter is dedicated.

Shooting: (below) inter-House Shield winners Gepp's, 1909, with Herbert Perry second from right and (bottom) Felstedians competing internationally in Denmark, 1999.

OLD FELSTEDIANS OF DISTINCTION

It must surely come as little surprise to readers that a school such as Felsted, whose history spans four and a half centuries, will count a stellar array of luminaries among its former students. The following listings are intended to give a snapshot of the wealth of talent and enterprise nurtured at Felsted over the past hundred years or so; there is no suggestion that the names appearing here represent either a comprehensive or an exhaustive catalogue of the worthiest of Old Felstedians. A fair number of distinguished alumni of more recent times may not find themselves included, either through lack of space or, much the likelier, because their records at the School Archives have yet to receive the crucial updating, requested in time for the 450th anniversary edition of the *Alumni Felstediensis*. To those who may feel aggrieved by their omission, we extend sincere apologies; please rest assured that no personal offence was ever intended. Equally, notable Old Felstedians who are mentioned individually elsewhere in the book may have been omitted from the following pages, which are a digest of the much more detailed listing of distinguished Old Felstedians, compiled by A.D.G. Widdowson (Master 1982–2012) and posted on the School Archives website (www.archives.felsted.org).

CLERGY

The nineteenth century saw the rapid expansion of the British Empire throughout the globe, and hand in hand with that expanding hegemony went the spread of the Church of England. Felstedian bishops served in sees at home and overseas as diverse as Lincoln, North China, Zanzibar and East Africa. Among those alumni who gained clerical distinction during the twentieth century, the following are of particular interest: **Revd E.F. Edge-Partington, MC and Bar** (b 1900–4), Canon Emeritus, Chaplain to TRH the King and Queen (1941–56), Hockey for England (1909);

Very Revd C.K. Waller (b 1905–10), Provost and Rector of Chelmsford Cathedral (1949–51); **Rt Revd G.E. Ingle** (b 1910–15), Felsted Housemaster and later Suffragan Bishop of Willesden; **Rt Revd T.G.S. Smith** (b 1914–20), Asst Bishop of Leicester (1966–73), Canon Emeritus (1977), Preacher Select University of Cambridge (1957); **Revd Dr L.A. Garrard** (d 1918–23), Professor of Philosophy and Religion, Emerson College, Boston, US, Principal Manchester College, Oxford University; **Rt Revd G.E. Reindorp** (fb 1921–31), Bishop of Salisbury; **Dom W.K.I. Trethowan, OSB** (c 1921–5), Philosopher, Sub-Prior of Downside Abbey; **Rt Revd R.S. Cutts** (fa 1930–7), Bishop of Argentina and Eastern South

Revd. G. E. Ingle (caricature by E.H. Lockwood).

G.E.I.

America; **Rt Revd J.R.G. Neale** (d 1940–4), Bishop of Ramsbury (1974–88); **Rt Revd G.D.J. Walsh** (b 1943–8), former Suffragan Bishop of Tewkesbury.

Members of Parliament

The School produced a significant number of MPs throughout the seventeenth and eighteenth centuries, and in the 1800s and 1900s the following saw service in the House of Commons: **John Bullock** (1744–8), MP for Steyning (1754–68), Maldon (1768–84), Essex (1784–1809), MP for 55 years, Father of the House; **William Mills** (1763–7), MP for Coventry (1805–12); **J.H. Strutt** (1769–73), MP for Maldon (1790–1826), Okehampton (1826–30); **Isaac Gascoyne** (1776–81), MP for Liverpool (1802–31), anti-slavery campaigner; **W.L. Hughes** (1780–4), Baron Dinorben of Kenmel Park, Denbigh, MP for Wallingford (1802–31), ADC to the Queen; **C.C. Western** (1780–4), Baron Western of Rivenhall, MP for Maldon (1790–1812), MP for Essex (1812–32); **T.G. Bramston** (1782–6), MP for Essex (1830–1); **J.A. Houblon** (1787–91), High Sheriff of Essex (1801), MP for Essex (1810–20); **J.T. Tyrell** (1808–12), MP for Essex (1830–1), MP for North Essex (1832–57); **T.W. Bramston** (1809–13), MP for South Essex (1835–65); **C.G. Round** (1810–14), MP for North Essex (1837–47); **Col. J.D. Palmer** (1865–7), MP for Gravesend (1892–8), businessman and philanthropist; **Sir Ivor Philipps, KCB, DSO** (r 1873–6), Liberal MP for Southampton (1906–22); **The Rt Hon. J.W. Philipps (1st Viscount St Davids), GBE, PC** (r 1873–8), financier and politician, MP for Mid Lanarkshire (1888–94), MP for Pembrokeshire (1898–1904); **R.A. Brabner, DSO, DSC** (a 1925–30), Fleet Air Arm Second World War pilot ace, MP for Hythe (1939–45), Under Secretary of State for Forces; **Rt Hon. Lord Chelmer of Margaretting (E.C.B. Edwards), KB, MC, TD, DL** (a 1928–33), Conservative Party joint Treasurer and Deputy Chairman; **D.E.T. Luard** (c 1940–5), Labour MP for Oxford (1966–70 and 1974–9), Parliamentary Under Secretary of State (Foreign Office), Fellow of St Antony's College, Oxford, Labour and subsequently SDP politician; **H.P. Thompson** (fe 1946–53), MP (Con.) for Norwich North (1983–97); **A.G. Tyrie** (g 1970–5), MP (Con.) for Chichester (Chairman of the Treasury Select Committee); **B.C.A. Elphicke** (fa 1979–87), MP (Con.) for Dover.

Military and colonial service

During the lengthy period of British colonial and military dominance up to the Second World War, the School provided a steady stream of combatants and administrators; a representative sample would include: **Sir Alfred Gaselee, GCB, GCIE** (1853–61). Aide-de-camp to Queen Victoria, action Afghan Wars, Boxer Uprising, China and India; **Brig. J.M. Rymer-Jones, CBE, MC** (b 1911–15), Assistant Commissioner, Metropolitan Police (1950–9); **Maj. Gen. J.M. Benoy, CBE** (d 1913–14), GS03 Supreme Council, Versailles (1918–20), , Chief Administrator, Eritrea (1945–6); **Maj. Gen. G.P. Walsh, CB, CBE, DSO** (a 1913–17), Director of Weapons at the War Office (1949–52); **Gen. Sir Campbell Hardy, KCB, CBE, DSO** (d 1920–4), Commandant Gen., Royal Marines (1955–9), Director of the Coal Utilisation Council (1960–70); **Maj. Gen. G.F. Upjohn, CB, CBE** (e 1926–9), Colonial Service Malaya and West Africa; **Air Vice Marshal E.D. Crew, CB, DSO (and Bar), DFC** (b 1931–6), Second World War Mosquito flying ace **Air Vice Marshall J.N.C. Cooke, OBE, CB** (a 1935–40), Consultant Physician to the Civil Aviation Authority; **Lt Col. A.M. Brooks, DSO, MC** (g 1937–9), intelligence officer, undercover agent in France, Second World War Croix de Guerre, Legion d'Honneur (France); **Air Chief Marshal Sir David Harcourt-Smith, GBE, KCB, DFC** (g 1945–9), Controller of Aircraft for United Kingdom Ministry of Defence, MoD Procurement Executive; **Lt Gen. Sir Peter Beale, KBE** (b 1948–52), RAMC, formerly Queen's Honorary Physician, Chief Medical Officer for the Red Cross (1994–2000), Surgeon General to UK Armed Forces 1991–4; **General the Lord Dannatt (F.R. Dannatt), GCB, CBE, MC, DL** (f 1960–4), Chief of the General Staff (2006–9); **Maj. Gen. A.D. Macklin** (c 1973–5), Leader Armoured Fighting Vehicles Group.

Public servants and philanthropists

Among the elite corps of Old Felstedians to make their mark in the service of King (or Queen) and Country, at home and abroad, are to be numbered: **A.W. Hodson, CMG, KCMG** (a 1895–8), Governor of Falkland Isles (1926–30), of Sierra Leone (1930–4) and of Gold Coast (1934–41), Knight of St John, African explorer, author; **Sir Maurice Holmes** (fd

Top: The Rt Hon. J.W. Philipps GBE, PC and (above) General Sir Alfred Gaselee GCB, GCIE.

Above: M.I. Spacie MBE and (bottom right) Col. D.C. Phillott.

1924–9), Barrister, Chairman of London Transport Executive (1965–9); **Sir Roger Jackling, GCMG** (c 1927–9), HM Diplomatic Service, Permanent UK Representative to UN (1963–7), former HM Ambassador to the Federal Republic of Germany; **Sir Terence Garvey, KCMG** (a 1929–34), HM Ambassador to USSR (1973–5); **P.R. Oliver, CMG** (a 1930–5), HM Ambassador to Uruguay (1972–7); **B.N.A. Weatherill, CBE** (c 1952–6), Chairman of Guide Dogs for the Blind Association; **Sir Robert Finch, KB, JP, DL, FRICS (Hon.), FCEM(Hon.)** (fa 1953–62), Lord Mayor of London (2003); **O.W. Everett, CVO** (b 1956–61), Librarian Emeritus Windsor Castle, former Private Secretary to the Princess of Wales (1981–3); **Brigadier J.E.B. Smedley, LVO** (d 1960–5), Private Secretary to The Earl and Countess of Wessex; **R.H. Grimshaw, LVO, MBE** (fh 1961–70), Irish Guards, Equerry to HM Queen Elizabeth, The Queen Mother; **B.F. Houlder, QC, DL** (b 1961–5), Government Director of Service Prosecutions; **Revd R.E.L. ter Haar, QC** (g 1965–9), Deputy High Court Judge (2003–); **H.B. Dean III** (g 1966–7), Governor of Vermont (1991–2002), Democratic candidate United States presidential election (2004); **M.E. Keene, MVO** (g 1971–6), royal photographer; **M.J.L. Kirk** (g 1974–8), HM Ambassador to Finland (2002–6), Director, Group External Affairs Vodafone Group plc, since 2009; **F.J. Cochrane-Dyet** (a 1978–83), diplomat, British High Commissioner: the Seychelles (2006–9) and Malawi (2009–11), HM Ambassador, Republic of Liberia (2013–); **M.E. Cutts** (a 1978–80), Senior Coordinator, Humanitarian Coordination Support Section, United Nations Office for Co-ordination of Humanitarian Affairs, formerly with Save the Children and UNHCR (Bosnian War); **M.I. Spacie, MBE** (d 1983–5), founder and Director of Magic Bus charity (India).

ACADEMICS AND WRITERS

The worlds of literature and academic writing are represented by this selection of noteworthy individuals: **A.W. a'Beckett** (1858–9), humorist and journalist, Editor of *Punch*; **G.G. Coulton** (r 1872–7), historian, schoolmaster and university lecturer; **Col. D.C. Phillott** (r 1874–8), Persian Fellow of Calcutta University, University of Cambridge lecturer; **Hugh Chisholm** (1877–84), journalist, Editor of *Encyclopaedia Britannica* (editions 11 and 12); **Thomas Seccombe** (1880–5),

writer, Deputy Editor ODNB, Professor English Literature, Queen's University, Canada; **A.F. Pollard** (1884–7), Professor of Constitutional History, London University, founder of the Historical Association (1906); **J.R.H. Weaver** (d 1895–9), President of Trinity College, Oxford (1938–54), Editor ODNB; **Douglas Goldring** (d 1900–4), writer and journalist; **Prof. W.J.H. Sprott** (b 1910–13), sociologist, philosopher, psychologist, Bloomsbury group member; **Prof. A.L.F. Rivet** (b 1929–34), Emeritus Professor Roman Provincial Studies, Keele University (1974–93), archaeologist and cartographer; **Prof. Sir Colin Wilson, KB, RA** (g 1935–40), architect of the British Library, Professor of Architecture, University of Cambridge (1975–89); **Prof. C.J. Herington** (c 1938–43), Talcott Professor of Greek and Chairman Classics Department, Yale University; **Prof. R.H. Freeborn** (b 1941–4), Professor of Russian Literature, London University, translator, author; **Prof. J.K.G. Shearman** (d 1945–9), art historian, Professor of Fine Art at Princeton and Harvard (1994–2002), specialist in Italian Renaissance; **Robin Briggs** (fg 1950–60), Senior Research Fellow, All Souls College, Oxford (1978–2009), writer on European affairs; **P.L. Goldie** (g 1960–4), Samuel Hall

Professor of Philosophy, Manchester University (2005–); **Prof. J.C.N. Horder** (h 1975–80), Professor Criminal Law, Oxford University (2006–10), Fellow of Worcester College, Edmund Davies Professor of Criminal Law, King's College, London (2010–); **P.W.M. Redmond** (fa 1975–81), playwright, novelist, writer of psychological thrillers including *The Wishing Game*.

SCIENCE AND MEDICINE

Perhaps the most influential of all divisions of Old Felstedian luminaries is the following constellation of leading scientists and medical practitioners and academics: **P.C. Gilchrist** (1862–7), Fellow of the Royal Society, inventor of steel-making from phosphorus-rich iron; **Charles Hose** (r 1876–81), zoologist and ethnologist; **C.V. Durell** (fc 1895–1900), mathematician, prolific writer of school textbooks; **R.K. Pierson, OBE, CBE** (a 1905–8), Chief Aircraft Designer (latterly Chief Engineer) with Vickers-Armstrong (1917–47),responsible for designing the Vickers Vimy, Wellessley and Wellington bombers, and the Viking commercial airliner; **F.B. Halford** (e 1907–10), aircraft designer, motor-racing pioneer, Technical Director and Chairman de Havilland, designer of DH Ghost engine fitted to DH Comet, the world's first jet airliner; **Prof. J.F. Kirkaldy** (b 1922–6), Emeritus Professor of Geology, London University (1974–90); **Prof. R.D. Emslie** (c 1929–31), Professor and Dean of Dental Studies, Guy's Hospital (1968–80), Professor of Periodontology and Preventive Dentistry, London University (1970–80),(Emeritus 1980–2002); **Dr David Stafford-Clark** (e 1930–3), psychiatrist, BBC and ITV psychiatry programme-maker, Consultant Emeritus Guy's Hospital and United Hospitals, London University, Consultant Bethlem Royal Hospital and Maudsley Hospital (1954–73); **Prof. M.L.V. Pitteway** (g 1947–53), Professor of Computer Science, Brunel University; **Dr L.R.M. Cocks, OBE, TD** (b 1952–7), Keeper of Palaeontology, Natural History Museum, London (1986–98); **Prof. R.W. Lacey** (a 1954–8), Professor of Medical Microbiology, Leeds University (1983–98); **Dr A.M. Roberts, RD** (d 1955–60), Consultant Physician, MO British Nuclear Fuels, Advisor Atomic Weapons Research, Aldermaston; **Prof. A.R. Hunter, FRS** (e 1956–61), Professor of Molecular and Cell Biology, Salk Institute, California; **Prof. R.J. Nicholls** (a 1956–61), Emeritus Professor of Colorectal Surgery and Clinical Director, St Mark's Hospital, London,

Visiting Professor Imperial College, London University; **M.E. Setchell, CVO** (c 1957–61), Surgeon-Gynaecologist to HM Queen Elizabeth II; **Prof. Sir Patrick Sissons, CB** (c 1958–63), Professor of Medicine (1988–2005), Regius Professor of Physics (2005–12), University of Cambridge; **Prof. N.P. Manning** (fd 1959–67), Professor of Social Policy and Sociology, Nottingham University; **Prof. M.D. Kopelman** (c 1963–7), Professor of Neuropsychiatry, St Thomas' Hospital, University of London (1998–); **Prof. P.G. Kopelman** (c 1964–9), Principal of St George's, University of London, Professor of Clinical Medicine, London Hospital (2008–); **Prof. R.D. Pringle** (c 1965–9), Professor of History and Archaeology, Cardiff University; **Dr J.D. Shiers** (fd 1966–74), physicist at CERN, LHC Computing Grid project; **Prof. Lucilla Poston** (m 1970–2), Professor of Foetal Health, Guy's Hospital, King's and St Thomas' Hospital, University of London; **Prof. A.G. Galione** (fh 1975–81), Professor of Pharmacology (2006–), Fellow of Lady Margaret Hall, Oxford University; **Prof. S.A. Haslam** (d 1976–80), Professor of Social Psychology, Exeter University; **Prof A. T. Prevost** (e 1981–6) Professorof Medical Statistics, King's College, University of London (2012–), Senior Visiting Research Fellow, University of Cambridge (2009–).

THE ARTS, THEATRE AND BROADCASTING

The names of successful Old Felstedians are also found to grace the modern fields of creative and performance arts: **Captain R.C. Lyle, MC and Bar** (fd 1897–1906), Sports Editor and Racing Correspondent for *The Times*; **W.C.M. Palmer** (e 1904–5), Hollywood film actor (1929–50), 74 films including starring role in Oscar-winning *Bulldog Drummond* (1929); **S.M.H. Burge, CBE** (b 1931–4), film director, producer, actor; **Kenneth.G.F. Kendall** (fa 1935–42), British broadcaster; **C.Philip. Latham** (fe 1939–47), West End

Right: Max Stafford-Clark and (below) Sir Robert Finch.

theatre, film and TV actor; **Richard.K. Johnson** (g 1941–3), West-End theatre and film actor, writer and producer; **J.D. Moynihan** (fc 1943–9), sports journalist for *The Sun*, *Sunday Times*, *The Observer*, author; **J.T. Alldis** (a 1944–7), Chorus Master of the London Philharmonic Choir and Guildhall School of Music Choir, Grammy award winner; **Dr J.D. Sanders, OBE** (fa 1944–50), composer, organist Gloucester Cathedral; **A.J.C. Marriott, JP** (g 1945–9), playwright, *No Sex Please, We're British* and TV plays; **J.N. Allen** (b 1946–51), sports journalist for *The Times*, covered 14 Olympic Games, Chairman International Athletics Writers Association; **J.B. Wright** (d 1946–51), golf writer and TV commentator, BBC, CBS (US), sports writer *Sunday Times*, *The Observer*, author; **P.M. Bonner, OBE** (c 1947–52), formerly Head of BBC Science Documentaries and Community Broadcasts; **S.R. Walters, MBE** (fe 1948–58), London theatre director, founder of the Orange Tree Theatre, Richmond; **M.R.G.S. Stafford-Clark** (fe 1950–9), London theatre director; **T.R. Foster** (fe 1958–67), theatre architect (Tricycle Theatre, Norwich Theatre Royal, Trafalgar Studios, Parabola Arts Centre, Cheltenham); **C.M. Clarke, CBE**

(c 1965–70), Director of the National Galleries of Scotland, author; **H.D. Keelan** (d 1971–6), Conductor and Musical Director, North Eastern Pennsylvania Philharmonic, extensive guest conducting; **D.R. Pringle** (e 1974–7), former England Test cricketer, University of Cambridge and Essex, journalist for *The Independent* and *Daily Telegraph*; **N.V. Knight** (fb 1978–88), former England Test cricketer, Warwickshire (Capt.), Sky TV cricket commentator and broadcaster; **P.G. Dyson** (fd 1977–86), Musical Director, Belmont Ensemble, St Martin-in-the-Fields and the South Bank Centre; **R.K. Marson** (d 1979–82), British TV writer and producer, formerly Chief Editor, *Blue Peter* children's TV programme; **D.C. Stainer** (a 1981–5), Managing Director, Universal Classics and Jazz (part of EMI); **J.A.P. Simpson** (fa 1982–1990), TV and radio playwright, film director; **S.T. Fletcher** (b 1987–92), sports broadcaster with BBC television, journalist.

BUSINESS AND COMMERCE

The world of business and finance includes the following notable high-flyers: **Sir Montague Prichard, CBE, MC** (c 1930–3), Chairman, Belgrave Holdings plc; **G.W. Dunkerley, MC** (a 1933–8), Chairman, Oil and Pipelines Agency, Director, STC; **J.T. Edwards, CBE** (a 1934–7), Chairman, Halcrow (1986–92); **J.P. Roed** (g 1945–50), entrepreneur, Norwegian shipowner, multinational sustainable energy entrepreneur, Commodore of the Order of the North Star, Norway, Order of Falcon Iceland; **W.J.A. Dacombe** (b 1948–52), Chairman, Postern Ltd; **M.C.J. Jackaman** (d 1949–53), Chairman, Allied Lyons (1991–6); **Sir Martyn Arbib** (g 1953–6), financier, philanthropist, founder, Invesco Perpetual Investment company (1973–2000); **O.H.J. Stocken** (e 1954–60), banker, formerly Finance Director, Barclays plc, Chairman, Home Retail Group (2006–12), MCC Club Chairman (2009–) and Trustee; **G.R. Suggett** (fa 1954–62), Managing Director, Alliance (Investment) Trust and Second Alliance Trust (Dundee); **C.J.S. Woodwark** (g 1960–4), Chairman, Rolls-Royce Motors, Managing Director, Land Rover; **C.J. Lendrum, CBE** (d 1960–5), Executive Director (1998–2004), Group Vice Chairman (2004–), Barclays Bank plc; **A.M. Stewart** (fe 1960–7), financier; **N.R. Gold** (b 1965–9), Managing Director, ING Bank (1986–2008).

Lt Col. J.W.H.T. Douglas.

OLYMPIANS AND INTERNATIONAL SPORTS HONOURS

Since the revival of the Olympic Games of the modern era, Felsted has seen a fair number of its former pupils selected as Olympians: **J.K. Matthews** (fe 1895–1903), England (pre-GB) Olympic hockey squad (1912),; **Captain I.F. Fairbairn-Crawford** (b 1896–8), GB Olympic athlete (1908), 800m and 1500m (finalist), engineer, pilot, Executive Foreign Armament Department for Vickers Armstrong, International Half-Mile Champion (1906–7), One-Mile International Champion (1909), skiing for GB, International Roller-Skate Champion at Olympia, London (1914–19); **Lt Col. J.W.H.T. Douglas** (a 1897–1901), English Test cricket (Capt.) and GB Olympic boxer (Gold Medal, 1908), football for England (amateur); **N.F. Hallows** (fc 1899–1904), GB Olympic athlete, 1500m (Bronze Medal, 1908); **W.C. Moore** (a 1903–9), GB Olympic athlete (1912), 1500m; **Lieut. D. Macmillan** (e 1904–9), GB Olympic athlete (1912), 400m; **H.S. Perry** (fa 1906–12), GB Olympic shooter (Gold Medal, 1924; team running deer double shots); **D.F.C. Scott** (e 1915–18), GB Olympic pentathlete (1924); **W.G.T. Burne** (d 1916–19), GB Olympic high-diver (1928); **D.D. Macklin, CBE, DL** (e 1942–7), GB Olympic rower (1952; Eights); **F.H.V. Davis, CBE** (e 1946–50), GB Olympic hockey player (1956, 1960, 1964 (Capt.); **Dr M.T. Lucking** (fd 1947–56), GB Olympic athlete, shot put (1960, 1964), Commonwealth Gold Medal (1962); **Dr P.R. Decker** (b 1952–3), US Olympic skier (winter 1960); **R.M. Oliver** (fa 1953–63), GB Olympic hockey player (1968, 1972); **D.H. Jones** (g 1954–7), GB Olympic athlete, 4x100m (Bronze Medal, 1960), Commonwealth Gold Medal, and Commonwealth Silver Medal, 200m (1962); **T.M. Lawson** (fd 1954–61), GB Olympic hockey player (1968); **A.H. Ekins** (d 1957–61), GB Olympic hockey player (1968); **R.L. Cattrall** (fh 1966–75), GB Olympic hockey captain (Bronze Medal, 1984); **C.W. Hunnable** (fc 1973–82), GB Olympic three-day eventer (1996); **Dr Fiona R. Pyke (née Jacklin)** (m 1984–6), GB Olympic sailing squad (1986–7).

In addition to those listed elsewhere in the book who have found success at international level in the various individual sports are added the following: **Revd Canon R.S. King** (1873–80), clergyman and football for England (amateur); **Clement Mitchell** (1874–9), football for England (amateur); **H.E. Wood** (d 1899–1902), football for England (amateur); **Brigadier A.H. Williams, MC, CIE** (f 1900–1), polo for England (1925, 1927); **F.E.B. Guise** (c 1907–10), Winner GB Hundred Roll Rifle competition (1934, 1936), Winner Spencer Cup (Bisley, 1910); **J.W. Watts** (fb 1951–9), Classic-winning racehorse trainer; **J.M.Q. Polturak** (b 1975–80), British America's Cup squad (1983), Winning 12M Yacht World Championship for Great Britain (1982; bowman); **J.P. Stephenson** (fa 1974–83), England Test cricketer (Essex CCC and Hampshire CCC (Capt.)), MCC Director of Cricket; **C.R.B. Pitcher** (b 1977–8), transatlantic single-handed oarsman (record-holder), British America's Cup squad organiser (1986/7); **T.M. Lerwill** (fa 1985–95), Junior international athlete, 800m (Silver Medal, IAAF World Junior Games 1996); **T.J. Bridgman** (fc 1993–2003), motor-racing driver, Formula BMW UK winner (2004), Formula Palmer Audi series winner (2007).

Schoolmasters and Headmasters of Felsted School: 1564 to 2014

1. Revd John Daubeney (1564–6)
2. Revd John Berryman (1566–76) St John's College, Cambridge
3. Revd Henry Greenwood (1576–96) St John's College, Cambridge
4. Revd George Manning (1597–1627) Corpus Christi College, Cambridge
5. Revd Martin Holbeach (1627–49) Queens' College, Cambridge
6. Revd Christopher Glascock (1650–90) St Catharine's College, Cambridge
7. Revd Simon Lydiatt (1690–1712) Christ Church, Oxford
8. Revd Hugh Hutchin (1713–25) Christ Church, Oxford
9. Revd John Wyatt (1725–50) Christ Church, Oxford
10. Revd William Drake (1750–78) Christ Church, Oxford
11. Revd William Trivett (1778–94) Christ Church, Oxford
12. Revd William Carless (1794–1813) Merton College, Oxford
13. Revd Edmund Squire (1813–35) Christ's College, Cambridge
14. Revd Thomas Surridge (1835–50) Trinity College, Dublin
15. Revd Albert Wratislaw (1850–55) Christ's College, Cambridge
16. Revd William Grignon (1856–75) Trinity College, Cambridge
17. Revd Delaval Ingram (1876–90) St John's College, Cambridge
18. Revd Herbert Dalton (1890–1906) Corpus Christi College, Oxford
19. Revd Frank Stephenson (1906–33) Christ's College, Cambridge
20. Revd Julian Bickersteth (1933–43) Christ Church, Oxford
21. Alistair H. Andrew, MA (1943–7) Trinity College, Cambridge
22. Cecil M. Harrison, MA (1947–51) Trinity College, Cambridge
23. Henry E. Reekie, MA (1951–68) Clare College, Cambridge
24. Anthony F. Eggleston, MA (1968–82) St John's College, Oxford
25. Edward J.H. Gould, MA (1983–93) St Edmund Hall, Oxford
26. Stephen C. Roberts, MA (1993–2008) University College, Oxford
27. Dr Michael J. Walker (2008) Corpus Christi College, Cambridge

LIST OF SUBSCRIBERS

This book was supported by the generosity of the subscribers listed below.

Sophy Aitken — *Staff* 2004–
Jeremy Allgrove — *e* 1962–7
Christopher Amory — *g* 1956–61
Jack C. Anderson — *a* 1948–53
Graham Appleyard — *b* 1982–7
Oliver Richard Appleyard — *b* 1986–91
Robert Appleyard — *b* 1952–5
Brian Ashley — *b* 1955–8
Annabel Atkinson — *m* 1979–81
F.S.J. Austin — *fa* 1936–40
Alexandra Louise Back — *mb* 2009–
Georgina Elizabeth Back — *fb* 2007–
Nick Backhouse — *fa* 1973–81
Lucy Bailes — *f* 2008–
Max Bailes — *fh* 2006–13
Jonathan Charles Noel Baker — *fa* 1987–98
Julie Balchin — *Staff* 2001–
Philip Ball — *b* 1982–7
John Charles Banner — *fd* 1953–9
Ros Barclay — *n* 1991–3
John Barford — *b* 1946–50
Nicholas Barker — *e* 1980–5
Caroline Barkham — *m* 1977–9
Peter Barlow MBE TD — *a* 1958–62
Matthew Barrell — *Staff* 2010–
Francis Barrett — *Staff* 2009–
Lucy Barrett — *Staff* 2007–
John M. Beatty — *d* 1949–54
Carol Bell
Natasha Bell — *m* 2011–
George Bellingham-Smith — *b* 1948–52
Wilfred Bennison — *f* 1964–7
J.R.S. Benson — *g* 1964–8
P.C.S. Benson — *g* 1969–74
Stuart C.S. Beresford — *a* 1953–8
Christopher Berry Green — *b* 1947–51

Joe Bichard — *a* 1997–9
Peter Bing — *d* 1940–3
Chester Birch — *hc* 2008–13
Flavia Birch — *b* 2000–5
Pascia Birch — *bn* 2003–8
Spencer Birch — *h* 2006–11
Zegnia Birch — *b* 2001–6
George Lovewell Blake — *g* 1949–51
Mandy Bonnett — *Staff* 2010–
Matthew Paul Booker — *fd* 1982–91
Euan Alfred Bookless — *f* 2012–
Jake Boulton — *fd* 2002–
Jodie Boulton — *fgm* 1999–2013
Dr Tim Boyle — *d* 1949–54
Robert Brooker — *h* 1978–83
David A. Brooks — *d* 1947–52
Oliver Brooks-Ward — *ec* 2008–13
Alexander Brown — 1993–8
Paul Burgess — *Staff* 2005–
Rory Burns — *ac* 2008–13
Jenny Burrett — *Headmistress (FPS) Staff* 1983–5 and 1992–
Tommy Burslem — *d* 2012–
Barny Bury — *Staff* 2010–
Christina Bury — *Staff* 2004–
Elise Bury — *f* 2004–
Luke Bury — *fh* 2010–
Nicola Bush — *Staff* 2012–
Stephanie Byrne — *fbm* 2006–11
Nigel R. Cairns — *fc* 1980–7
Edward Caley — *fa* 1982–9
Tim Callan — *d* 1956–61
Charlie Campbell — *f* 2009–
Isabel Campbell — *f* 2011–
Ian Caplin — *fc* 1983–91
Joel Caplin — *fc* 1991–9
Pat Caplin

Michael S. Carey — *a* 1956–60
Simon Cavalier — *dh* 1962–7
David Cavill — *c* 1959–61
Alan Chamberlain — *Staff* 1992–
Colin Chamberlain — *fh* 1960–9
Hugo Chaplin — *ec* 2006–13
Olly Chaplin — *fec* 2007–
Toby Chaplin — *fec* 2004–11
A. Charles Chapman — *c* 1950–5
Geoffrey W. Chapman — *e* 1956–60
Nigel Chapman — *c* 1958–64
T.G.A. Chappell — *fe* 1947–55
Gunnar Chrestin — *a* 2000–1
Martin G. Christy — *d* 1956–61
Robert B. Church — *fh* 1971–8
David Churcher — *fb* 1975–84
Frances D. Clark — *Staff* 1984–96
Pelham Clark — *c* 1952–6
The Revd Bob and Mrs Kate Clarke — *Staff* 1981–92
Rachel Clarke — *Staff* 2003–
Robert Aston Clegg — *fb* 1951–60
Claire Clements — *Staff* 2007–
Diane Clift — *Staff* 2009–
Max Clover — *fb* 1952–60
John A. Cockett — *Staff* 1951–89
John Basset Collins — *a* 1954–9
Ben Cooper — *h* 1982–6
Gyles Cooper — *fc* 1952–60
Tom Cooper — *a* 1984–9
Will Cooper — *a* 1987–92
C.R. Copeman — *fb* 1948–56
Michael Craven — *Staff* 1955–95
Kevin Cresswell — *Staff* 1979–
Alistair J.W. Crowle — *g* 1980–5
Caroline Croydon — *Staff* 2008–
H.D.G. Cruickshank — *d* 1939–43

Michael S. Cubitt — *fb* 1945–54
Norman Cuddeford — *g* 1947–52
Roger Cull — *Staff* 1979–87
W.S.C. Cullum — *b* 1964–7
Douglas Dashwood-Howard — *fd* 1948–57
Charlotte Dauman (née Brown) — 1992–4
J.H. Davies OBE — *Chairman of Governors* 1990–3, 1998–
Philip Edward Hamilton Davies — *fb* 1984–92
Simon Lewis Hamilton Davies — *fe* 1990–2001
William Miles Hamilton Davies — *fba* 1985–95
F. Howard V. Davis — *e* 1946–50
M. William L. Davis — *e* 1943–7
Guy Dixon Davison — *fbh* 1984–94
Nigel A. Dawes — *c* 1974–9
Nick Day — *Staff* 1975–
Richard de Berry — *fc* 1947–54
Oliver Deacon — *fed* 2001–10
Dr Peter R. Decker — *b* 1952–3
Robert Delahunty — *c* 1985–90
Jonathan Dennis — *fdec* 2005–12
Robert Dennis — *fe* 2005–12
Tim Dossor — *e* 1984–9
C.B. Doubleday — *c* 1950–5
Jack Dougherty — *Staff* 2010–
J.C.R. Downing DL — *e* 1945–9
Ben Downs — *fe* 1942–52
Andrew Dudley-Smith — *fdh* 1956–65
Anthony John Beaumont Dunstan — *fe* 1961–9
Anthony Eallett — *fd* 1944–9
James Eastaway — *fc* 1991–2001
John E. Eastwood — *g* 1952–7
Martin E. Eastwood — *fg* 1957–65

Tony Eggleston	*Headmaster*	1968–82
Bethany Elms	g	2009–11
Guy Elms	a	1982–4
Ian Elms		
Kimberley Elms	n	2012–
Mia Ely	*Staff*	2009–
Suzanne and James Emson	d	1952–6
Dr Dan M. Etherington	b	1950–4
A. Guy Evans	c	1944–8
Bruce Evans	*Staff*	2007–
Hugh David Charles Evans	c	2010–
Chris Ewbank	a	1974–9
Anthony Facey	*Staff*	2012–
James Falkener	fc	1964–73
Robin Fanshawe	b	1959–62
for the Fanshawe Family		1726–1995
Anthony H. Fasey	fb	1933–42
Joelle Feldberg	g	2011–
Lisa Feldman	*Staff*	1994–
Richard Feldman	*Staff*	1981–
Chloe Fennell	f	2012–
Bryan Fletcher	fb	1951–60
Bernhard Fohrmann	ec	2007–9
K.M.R. Foster	d	1958–63
Dr John V. Fowles OC	g	1949–54
Simon J. Frankel	d	1981–2
Andrew (Jack) Frost	g	1986–91
Imogen May Gander	fm	2011–
Robert Gardiner	fe	1945–52
Tim Gardner	c	1959–63
N. Garton	g	1944–7
Christopher Gibb	f	1971–6
John Gilbert	g	1963–7
Simon A.D. Gill	h	1969–72
Paul Gover	g	1987–92
Gowing Family		1947–86
Langley Granbery	d	1972–3
		(ESU Scholar)
Rebecca Grant	*Staff*	2007–
P.J. Grantham	fb	1941–8
Charlie Grave	fh	1975–84
Daniel Grave	fh	1978–87
Chloe Green	f	2008–
Emily Green	f	2008–
Spencer Green	fa	1978–86
Tim Grierson Rickford	fa	1987–97
Simon Griggs	h	1973–8
Nina M.R. Guenter	g	1997–9
Charlotte Guild	f	2013–
Toby Guild	fe	2011–
Trevor Hadley	fa	1943–51
Charles Hall	fg	1969–78
Wiz Hampson-Smith	*Staff*	2001–
Richard Hancock	fb	1970–9
Katarina Hargasova Bendikova	n	1999–2000
Tony Harries	*Staff*	2005–
Jonathan Hartnell-Beavis	a	1975–9
Martin Hasler	*Staff*	2011–
Philip Hawkes	fd	1956–66
Antony Haynes	fb	1975–83
Leslie Head	a	1943–7
Anthony Heathcote	e	1945–8
Michael Ryley Heathcote	e	1948–51
David R. Heller	fd	1962–9
Jeremy Henshaw	d	1954–8
Tony F. Herbert	e	1931–5
H.A. Hickling	g	1951–6
Cyril Paul Hickson	h	1972–6
David Hiett	fc	2000–7
Victoria Hiett	fgn	2002–9
William Hiett	fhc	2006–13
Richard Hill	*Staff*	2011–
Michael Eugen Hiller	ac	2011–13
Nicholas Hinde	*Staff*	1967–2004
Neil R. Hitchcock	g	1985–90
Richard G. Hodgson	*Staff*	1966–93
Alan C. Holden	a	1966–71
Florence Holmes	f	2014–
Peter Holmes	a	1947–51
Phoebe Holmes	f	2011–
John Hopkins	b	1967–72
Sara-Jane Horne	gn	2008–13
A.J.E. Hudson	fg	1976–80
D.L.T. Hudson	g	1949–53
M.E.C. Hudson	g	1976–80
Bethan Hudson-Lund	fg	2011–
Matthew Hudson-Lund	f	2012–
Mark Hughes	a	1977–83
John A. Humby	fd	1938–44
John Colin Hunt	c	1944–8
Philip Hunt	fb	1949–56
W.W. Hunt	c	1936–40
Roderick Hunter	d	1947–52
Reece Hussain	h	2012–
Travis Hussain	hd	2003–9
Philip Hutley	fd	1960–9
Fergus Hynd	fh	1986–97
Polly Hynd	fb	1992–2003
Daniel Imison	fh	1984–94
Edward Ives	fhc	1997–2010
William Ives	fh	1986–96
Olivia Jackson	bn	2008–13
Thomas Jackson	e	2011–
William Jackson	e	2010–
His Honour Christopher James	a	1947–52
W.D. Jeans	c	1941–6
Amelia Grace Jenkins	f	2011–
David H. Jones	g	1954–7
Luke B.P. Jones	d	2002–7
Anushka Kangesu	fn	2000–8
Prashan Kangesu	fed	2000–9
Graham Keene	g	1978–82
Roger Keys	fe	1969–73
Brian Stuart King	c	1957–61
David Stuart King	c	1959–63
Jasper Stuart King (In Memoriam)	c	1923–8
Joseph King	fh	2008–
Andrew Kinloch	fb	1965–74
Rupert Kirby	a	1984–9
Andrew Latham	e	1978–83
Cameron Laudrum	f	2008–12
Freya Laudrum	f	2008–
Kristian Laudrum		
Rachel Laudrum	m	2008–10
Nicholas Lawes	fb	1975–8
Tim Lawrence	*Staff*	1970–2000
Howard Leaman	c	1947–52
Dr C.R. and Mrs C.A. Lee	*Staff*	1993–
Jonathan C. Lee	fa	1974–84
Béatrice Lemoine-Chicoine	*Staff*	1993–
Chris Lendrum CBE	d	1960–5
Jonathan Leung	h	1995–7
Katie Lewis	fb	2004–
Rebecca Lewis	fb	1995–2007
Sarah Lewis	fb	2001–
Thomas Lewis	c	2000–5
Derek Lidstone	b	1955–9
Revd and Mrs N.J. Little	*Chaplain*	2012–
Simon Little	*Staff*	2005–
R.J. (Dick) Lloyd	b	1947–52
Nick Lockhart	*Staff*	1996–
Tony Lofts	fh	1963–72
Thorsten D. Lonishen	e	1990–2
Robin Lowndes	g	1949–54
Alex Lu	d	1995–7
April Lu	g	2002–4
Sam Luckin	a	1951–5
Mark J. Lyall	fa	1986–97
Mark R. Macfee	fc	1967–75
Uma MacGeoch	f	2008–
Richard Mackley	fg	1962–70
D.D. Macklin	e	1942–7
Paul Mager	fh	1964–74
Canon Brian Maguire	d	1947–51
C.J. Maitland	f	1982–7
H.K. Maitland	*Staff*	1961–94
J.A. Maitland	m	1988–90
Michael Malone	c	1945–50
Alexander Manson	fa	2008–
N.D. Mant (In Memoriam)	a	1914–19
Peter Mapley	fe	1969–78
Paul C.J. Markey	d	1968–72
Mike Marriage	fe	1994–2001
Peter Marsden	g	1946–50
Mrs Frances Marshall	*Staff*	1972–7 and 1984–
Dr Michael Marston	d	1946–50
Adrian Martin	a	1985–90
Alastair Martin	fe	1981–91
Julian Martin	fe	1982–93
Nichola Martin	*Staff*	2011–
Jan-Philipp Matzen	c	2006–8
Anne Jennings Mayne	n	1999–2001
Sam McArdle	fd	1999–2013
Craig McCarthy	c	1968–72
Oliver McCrudden	fba	1985–95
George J.B. McKelvey	f	2005–
Christopher James McLeod	fc	2000–8
Ewen McLeod	h	1994–9
Priya McNamara	fm	2006–11
Sean McNamara	fb	2010–
Christopher Megahey	*Staff*	1981–
Karen Megahey	*Staff*	1994–
Kay Milford	*Staff*	2004–13
G.P. Millett	c	1946–9
Peter Milner	c	1952–7
Tim Moore-Coulson	fe	1984–93
Brian Purser Morgan	fd	1942–7
Hugh Morgan	b	1982–7
Alastair Morley-Brown	fc	1944–52
Andrew Morrison	fcec	2002–9
Lena Muenzel	n	2012–

Andrew and Gabrielle Murphy	*Staff* 2007–9	Jeremy Rees	*h* 1968–73	The Stuchfield Family	1997–	Peter Webb	*fd* 1962–71
Major Jeston Na Nakhorn	*fe* 1985–90	A.L.G. Rice	*g* 1950–5	Captain Garry Studd	*a* 1967–72	James West	*fa* 1986–96
John Alister Neil	*d* 1954–8	Murray Roberts	*d* 1955–60	Brian Stutchbury	*b* 1937–41	Kristian West	*fa* 1985–94
P. Ian A. Neil	*g* 1964–8	Dr Tim Roberts	*b* 1987–92	Geoffrey W. Sudbury	*f* 1935–38	Matthew West	*fa* 1982–91
P.H. Nevell	*e* 1962–6	Nick Robinson	*e* 1979–85	Anthony Swing	*g* 1960–64	Samuel Weston	*h* 2003–7
Lucy Nicholls	*n* 1987–9	D.H. Robson	*b* 1967–72	Benjamin J. Tabor	*fd* 1987–97	David Whatham	*fd* 1975–81
P.A. Nicholls	*d* 1980–5	James Roome	*e* 1987–92	Dr Bill Tasker	*fg* 1970–80	Charles Wheeldon	*g* 1959–63
Tom Nicholls	*fd* 1980–9	Richard Rothwell	*a* 1977–81	Colin and Sylvia Taylor		P.E.G. Wheeler	*fb* 1952–61
Chris Nicholson	*d* 1972–6	Sarah Rowledge	*m* 1985–7	Dr Jonathan B. Taylor	*Staff* 2001–	E.J. White	*fg* 1945–51
Jack Oakshatt	*fe* 2000–7	Harriet Rowntree-Taylor	*fbn* 2007–12	Michael Taylor	*a* 1970–5	Charles Eduardo Whitehead	*c* 1964–5
John Oakshatt	*Staff* 1986–2007	Lauren Rowntree-Taylor	*n* 2004–6	The Thomas Family	2007–	A.D.G. Widdowson	*Staff* 1982–2012
Charles Peter George Osborne	*fd* 1998–2003	William Rowntree-Taylor	*fe* 2010–	H. Patrick Thompson	*fe* 1946–53	Ian Widdowson	*a* 1969–73
Ruby E. Osborne	*bm* 2009–13	John R. Rudd	*c* 1960–5	Michael Thompson	*g* 1945–50	Alexandra Wieland	*n* 2005–7
Ehren Painter	*d* 2012–	John A. Rymer-Jones	*g* 1946–50	Jasper Thorogood	*Staff* 1993–2003	Georgia Wieland	*n* 2004–8
Stephen Park	*c* 1986–90	Anna Salmon	*Staff* 2002–	Matthew James Thorpe-Apps	*fd* 2004–12	David Wildey	*fa* 1960–8
Callum Parradine	*d* 2012–	Peter S. Saunderson	*g* 1965–8	James Tibbitts	*fg* 1960–70	C.J.V. Williams	*f* 1977–9
Tim Pearce Higgins	*c* 1952–7	Olivia M.M. Schwier	*fg* 2005–	Chris Tongue	*Staff* 1968–84	D.B. Williams	*fg* 1943–8
Maurice Peel	*b* 1944–8	Julian Scofield	*d* 1988–93	C.J. Townsend	*Staff* 2010–	James Williams	*f* 2010–
Dr Chris Penn	*g* 1953–7	Patrick Seal	*fe* 1995–2004	Adam J.M. Tuke	*b* 1966–71	Canon A.M.S. Wilson	*e* 1946–50
John G. Pennant-Jones	*b* 1953–6	The Searle Family	1985–	Brian Turner	*Staff* 1998–	Tim Winter	*d* 1981–5
Chris R.J. Perks FCA	*g* 1955–60	Thomas Seccombe	*c* 1947–52	David Turner	*g* 1973–8	Hannah Louise Wise (née Booker)	*n* 1992–4
Christopher Perry	*fg* 1986–94	Dr J.M. Shaw	*Staff* 1990–2011	Edgar C. Turner	*fh* 1987–97	Stephen Wong	*c* 1967–9
Jim Perry	*c* 1945–50	Andrew Garcia Shores	*c* 1977–82	Graham Turner	*b* 1961–6	James H. Wood	*g* 1979–84
Carolyn Phillips	*Staff* 1993–	Simon Simmonds	*g* 1974–9	Robert Beaumont Turrall-Clarke	*a* 1951–5	Lt Col Mark Wood	*h* 1988–93
Bruce Pinkerton	*c* 1978–82	Alexandra Simpson	*Staff* 1995–	Amy Tydeman	*fb* 2009–	Robert A. Wood	*b* 1956–61
Roger Pipe	*g* 1948–51	D.M. Simpson	*b* 1957–60	Emily Tydeman	*fb* 2009–	John Woodington	*b* 1955–8
Stevie Platts (née Menhinick)	*b* 1996–9	Mark Sissons	*c* 1962–7	Poppy Tydeman	*f* 2009–	Elizabeth Woods	*fnbn* 2002–10
Timothy Platts	*fe* 1991–9	Thomas Slator	*fh* 1962–70	Edward Vernon	*c* 2012–	Gareth Woods	*d* 1998–2003
Grant Polkinghorne	*hc* 2008–13	Brigadier John Smedley	*d* 1960–5	Giles Walker	*c* 1984–9	Ruth Wyganowski	*Staff* 2000–
Jeremy Polturak	*b* 1975–80	Elliott Smith	*f* 2007–	Michael Walker		Angus Yeatts	*fe* 2001–10
Andrew Prebble	*d* 1968–72	Esme Smith	*f* 2003–		*Staff* 1964–70, 1972–89	Edward Yeatts	*fe* 2004–
Professor A.T. Prevost	*e* 1981–6	Elliot Snooks	*f* 2012–	Dr Mike Walker	*Headmaster* 2008–	Marcus Yeatts	*fe* 2001–7
James C. Prichard	*fc* 1953–61	Oliva Snooks	*f* 2012–	Tony Walker	*a* 1952–56	Megan Yeatts	*fgn* 2001–9
Fiona Priest (née Main)	*m* 1991–3	Anthony Charles Southgate	*fd* 1941–5	Jeremy Waller	*fd* 1980–90	Michael Yeatts	*e* 1976–81
James Priest	*fbc* 1984–93	Allan Spooner	*Staff* 1991–2013	Rowan Waller	*fd* 1978–87	Garo Yerevanian	*d* 1960–5
Arabella Prior	*fb* 2004–	Nicholas Spring	*Staff* 1980–	Brian Ward Lilley	*fe* 1946–54	Krios Yeung	*ge* 1993–8
Esme Prior	*fm* 2001–	James Squier	*fe* 1962–71	Alex Wareham	*fd* 1993–2007	Benjamin Young	*f* 2012–
Anna Pugh	*m* 1982–4	Max Stafford-Clark	*fe* 1950–9	John K. Waring	*b* 1959–64		
P.M. Raffan	*b* 1955–60	Robert E. Stamp	*e* 1944–8	Ben Warner	*fhc* 2007–	Felsted School Library	
Mike Ranson	*fg* 1957–65	Suzanne Stanier (née Eastaway)	*g* 1996–8	Stefan Warner	*fh* 2008–	Felsted Preparatory School Library	
Sam Rawlinson	*a* 1970–5	Oliver Stocken	*e* 1954–60	Claudia Watts	*m* 1978–80	Felsted School Combined Cadet Force	1857–
J.L. Rees	*g* 1941–6	Barnaby Stoner	*f* 2005–	Zoë Watts (née Armitstead)			
		Sebastian Stoner	*fe* 2003–	Barry Weatherill CBE	*c* 1952–6		
		Fritz Streng	*h* 2011–				

INDEX

Principal locations are denoted in **bold.** Illustrations are denoted in *italics.* Additional illustrations will often be found within **bold** page spans. Chapter 18 (pp 172–7) provides additional information on many distinguished Old Felstedians. Each individual is denoted there in **bold** for ease of reading. These entries are not included in this index.